# Reading by Doing
## An Introduction to Effective Reading

An Introduction to Effective Reading

# Reading by Doing

**Third Edition**

**John S. Simmons**
**Barbara C. Palmer**
Florida State University

National Textbook Company
a division of *NTC Publishing Group* • Lincolnwood, Illinois USA

The authors are grateful to the following for their assistance in the development
of *Reading by Doing,* 3rd edition: Paul Haigh, De Funiak Springs, Florida;
Harold L. Herber, retired Director of Reading at Syracuse University,
Syracuse, New York; and Barbara Neal, Reading Specialist,
Dallas, Texas, Independent School District.

Book design by Linda Snow Shum.
Interior photos: Art Shay
Illustrations by Marcia Lamoureux.
Cover photos: Jeff Ellis, bottom left, center
                    Jill Salyards, top left, bottom right

**1995 Printing**

Published by National Textbook Company, a division of NTC Publishing Group.
© 1994, 1988, 1980 by NTC Publishing Group, 4255 West Touhy Avenue, Lincolnwood
(Chicago), Illinois 60646–1975 U.S.A.
Manufactured in the United States of America.
Library of Congress Catalog Card Number: 93–85065

5 6 7 8 9 ML 9 8 7 6 5 4 3 2

# Acknowledgments

1992 Presidential Returns. Reprinted by permission of the Associated Press, New York.

U.S. Territory Map. Copyright John Bradley, *World Geography,* 4th edition, Ginn & Company, 1971

Weather Forecast from *The Washington Post* © 1992. Reprinted with permission.

Checking Accounts Information Sheet. Copyright, *Florida Federal Bulletin,* Tallahassee Office.

Time Zone Map. Copyright John Bradley, *World Geography,* 4th edition, Ginn & Company, 1971.

"Mystery of the Bermuda Triangle" by Barbara C. Palmer. Reprinted by permission of the Department of Education, State of Florida. Originally prepared in *Shifting Gears with Short Stories,* edited by C. Glennon Rowell, Department of Education, Tallahassee, Florida, 1979.

"Growing Up Overnight" by Barbara C. Palmer. Reprinted by permission of the Department of Education, State of Florida. Originally prepared in *Shifting Gears with Short Stories,* edited by C. Glennon Rowell, Department of Education, Tallahassee, Florida.

"Time Enough to Win" by Stan M. Tullos. Reprinted by permission of the author. Originally prepared in *Shifting Gears with Short Stories,* edited by C. Glennon Rowell, Department of Education, Tallahassee, Florida.

"Naming of Parts" by Henry Reed from *Map of Verona.* Reprinted by permission of Jonathan Cape LTD, London.

"As I Walked Out One Evening" by W. H. Auden, Copyright 1940 and renewed 1968 by W. H. Auden. Reprinted from *Collected Poems* by W. H. Auden. Edited by Edward Mendelson, by permission of Random House, Inc.

"When I Was One-and-Twenty" by A. E. Housman. Reprinted by permission of the Society of Authors as the literary representative for the estate of A. E. Housman and Jonathan Cape LTD, publishers of A. E. Housman's *Collected Poems.*

"The Cub" by L. D. Kleihauer, Lenninger Literary Agency. From *Collier's,* copyright 1958 by the Crowell Collier Publishing Company.

"Auto Wreck" by Karl Shapiro, © 1987 by Karl Shapiro. Reprinted by arrangement with Wieser & Wieser, New York.

# Contents

# Introduction

Reading is more than rapidly running your eyes over the words printed on a page. It is more than practicing vocabulary skills. To *really* read a passage, you must understand how all the words together say what the writer intends. If you understand what you've read, you'll be able to put the writer's ideas and information into your own words. We've written this book to help you understand better what you read.

All reading is done for a purpose. When you read a comic strip in the newspaper because you enjoy it, your purpose is entertainment. When you read the sports section to see which teams won, or the classified ads to see if there's a used ten-speed bicycle for sale, you are reading with a purpose. You are reading for information. In these examples, *you* set the purpose for reading.

Other people also may give you a purpose for reading. A teacher will say something like, "I want you to read Section Two and then…" The words that follow "and then" set the purpose for that reading task. If you pay attention to those words, you can establish a clear focus for your reading. Such a focus, or purpose, helps make your task easier. Knowing the purpose of your assignments also will help you get better grades. Whether you or another person decides that it's time for you to read, knowing your purpose will make the reading easier and worth your time and effort.

Reading, whether for a school assignment or for your own enjoyment, is one of the best ways for you to discover and understand yourself and your world. Do you want to know how to put together a stereo? Do you want to find the best route from one town to another? Do you want to find out what your favorite singer is doing? Do you want to get along better with other people? Do you want to decide on a career? Do you want to protect the environment? For the rest of your life, reading will help you to answer questions and to be what you want to be.

In this book, you will practice *establishing purposes* for reading specific passages. You also will practice *understanding the meanings* of passages. The selections you'll read are based on three kinds of topics. One kind concerns what is going on in the world. These passages are about the events, concerns, and people that we all think about. The second kind— "survival issues"—centers on things people must learn as they take charge of their own lives—as consumers, as employees, as citizens. The third kind of topic may seem familiar. These passages are about science, social studies, home economics, literature, and the humanities. They are based on school courses.

Follow the steps shown below as you work on the activities in this book.

1. Read carefully the purposes, or reasons, given for each reading selection.
2. Read the selection with the purpose in mind. (The assigned passages become longer and the tasks more challenging as you go along.)
3. Check back to discover whether you have remembered the information for which you were asked.

By the time you've finished the five sections of *Reading by Doing,* you should read more easily and with more understanding than when you started.

# Finding Details

# Part 1
# Finding Details in Special Formats

## About This Part...

There are many different kinds of information included in the reading passages that have been selected for this book. Some of the different types of information are facts, details, items, events, elements, incidents, steps, units, places, and names. In *Reading by Doing*, the word *details* means the specific items or types of information you will be asked to find in the passages you read. Identifying these details is a purpose for reading that can be very important, particularly when reading your assignments.

In this Part, you will read passages that contain a few or many details. Sometimes, details do not appear in sentence or paragraph form, but in formats such as maps, charts, and tables. Details that appear in these *special formats* can be easier to find because you don't have to search through as many words. Practice finding details in special formats. It is a useful skill! The activities in this Part will prepare you for finding details in regular or paragraph formats.

# Here's How to Do It

Whenever you read a selection, follow these steps.

1. *Look over* the passage carefully. Notice what kind of format or appearance it has.

2. *Observe* the special way the information is organized.

3. *Read* only the information you need.

4. *Check* yourself when you finish reading the details. Close the book. *Repeat* the details quietly to yourself or write them down to make certain that you understand and remember them.

5. *Wait* for about ten or fifteen minutes; then try to recall the details you read in the passage.

## Sample Activity:  Presidential Returns

*Look* at the table on page 4. It gives the voting returns from the 1992 presidential election in the United States. *Observe* the special way in which the information is organized. Note that the states are listed alphabetically in a column and the information headings go across the top of the table.

To complete this activity, first, study the table. Then, *read* to find only the information you need to help you answer the following questions. Use a separate sheet of paper for your answers. *Repeat* the details to yourself. Wait a few minutes then try to *recall* them. Check your replies with the answers provided below.

a. How many votes did George Bush receive in New Jersey (N.J.)?

b. What percentage of Hawaii's vote did Bill Clinton receive?

c. Which candidate won Texas?

d. What percentage of Iowa's vote did Ross Perot receive?

e. What percentage of Pennsylvania's (Pa.) vote is found in the table?

f. Who won in California (Calif.)?

g. How many votes did Clinton receive in Wisconsin (Wis.)?

h. What percentage of the total vote did Perot receive?

**Answers:** a) 1,309,724   b) 49%   c) Bush   d) 19%   e) 99%   f) Clinton   g) 1,035,943   h) 19%

# 1992 Presidential Returns

| STATES | % REPORTING | CLINTON | % | BUSH | % | PEROT | % |
|---|---|---|---|---|---|---|---|
| Alabama | 99 | 686,571 | 41 | 798,439 | 48 | 180,514 | 11 |
| Alaska | 99 | 63,498 | 32 | 81,875 | 41 | 55,085 | 27 |
| Arizona | 99 | 525,031 | 37 | 548,148 | 39 | 341,148 | 24 |
| Arkansas | 99 | 498,548 | 54 | 333,909 | 36 | 98,215 | 11 |
| California | 100 | 4,815,039 | 47 | 3,341,726 | 32 | 2,147,409 | 21 |
| Colorado | 99 | 626,207 | 40 | 557,706 | 36 | 362,813 | 23 |
| Connecticut | 100 | 680,276 | 42 | 575,778 | 36 | 346,638 | 22 |
| Delaware | 100 | 125,997 | 44 | 102,436 | 36 | 59,061 | 21 |
| D.C., Washington | 100 | 186,301 | 86 | 19,813 | 09 | 9,284 | 04 |
| Florida | 100 | 2,051,845 | 39 | 2,137,752 | 41 | 1,041,607 | 20 |
| Georgia | 99 | 1,005,889 | 44 | 989,804 | 43 | 307,857 | 13 |
| Hawaii | 100 | 178,893 | 49 | 136,430 | 37 | 52,863 | 14 |
| Idaho | 99 | 136,249 | 29 | 201,787 | 43 | 129,897 | 28 |
| Illinois | 98 | 2,379,510 | 48 | 1,718,190 | 35 | 832,484 | 17 |
| Indiana | 99 | 829,176 | 37 | 970,457 | 43 | 448,431 | 20 |
| Iowa | 100 | 583,669 | 44 | 503,077 | 38 | 251,795 | 19 |
| Kansas | 100 | 386,832 | 34 | 444,599 | 39 | 310,458 | 27 |
| Kentucky | 100 | 664,246 | 45 | 616,517 | 42 | 203,682 | 14 |
| Louisiana | 100 | 815,305 | 46 | 729,880 | 42 | 210,604 | 12 |
| Maine | 100 | 261,859 | 39 | 207,122 | 31 | 205,076 | 30 |
| Maryland | 100 | 941,979 | 50 | 671,609 | 36 | 271,198 | 14 |
| Massachusetts | 100 | 1,315,016 | 48 | 804,534 | 29 | 630,440 | 23 |
| Michigan | 99 | 1,858,275 | 44 | 1,587,105 | 37 | 820,855 | 19 |
| Minnesota | 97 | 998,552 | 44 | 737,649 | 32 | 552,705 | 24 |
| Mississippi | 99 | 392,929 | 41 | 481,583 | 50 | 84,496 | 09 |
| Missouri | 100 | 1,053,040 | 44 | 811,057 | 34 | 518,250 | 22 |
| Montana | 100 | 153,899 | 38 | 143,702 | 36 | 106,869 | 26 |
| Nebraska | 100 | 214,064 | 30 | 339,108 | 47 | 172,043 | 24 |
| Nevada | 99 | 185,401 | 38 | 171,378 | 35 | 129,532 | 26 |
| New Hampshire | 100 | 207,264 | 39 | 199,623 | 38 | 120,029 | 23 |
| New Jersey | 99 | 1,366,609 | 43 | 1,309,724 | 41 | 505,698 | 16 |
| New Mexico | 99 | 259,500 | 46 | 212,393 | 38 | 91,539 | 16 |
| New York | 99 | 3,246,787 | 50 | 2,241,283 | 34 | 1,029,038 | 16 |
| North Carolina | 99 | 1,103,716 | 43 | 1,122,608 | 44 | 353,845 | 14 |
| North Dakota | 100 | 98,927 | 32 | 135,498 | 44 | 70,806 | 23 |
| Ohio | 100 | 1,965,204 | 40 | 1,876,45 | 39 | 1,024,598 | 21 |
| Oklahoma | 100 | 473,066 | 34 | 592,929 | 43 | 319,978 | 23 |
| Oregon | 98 | 525,123 | 43 | 394,356 | 32 | 307,860 | 25 |
| Pennsylvania | 99 | 2,224,897 | 45 | 1,778,221 | 36 | 896,177 | 18 |
| Rhode Island | 99 | 198,924 | 48 | 121,916 | 29 | 94,757 | 23 |
| South Carolina | 99 | 476,626 | 40 | 573,231 | 48 | 138,140 | 12 |
| South Dakota | 100 | 124,861 | 37 | 136,671 | 41 | 73,297 | 22 |
| Tennessee | 100 | 933,620 | 47 | 840,899 | 43 | 199,787 | 10 |
| Texas | 99 | 2,279,269 | 37 | 2,460,334 | 40 | 1,349,947 | 22 |
| Utah | 100 | 182,850 | 26 | 320,559 | 45 | 202,605 | 29 |
| Vermont | 99 | 125,803 | 46 | 85,512 | 31 | 61,510 | 23 |
| Virginia | 99 | 1,034,78 | 41 | 1,147,226 | 45 | 344,852 | 14 |
| Washington | 99 | 855,710 | 44 | 609,912 | 32 | 470,239 | 24 |
| West Virginia | 100 | 326,936 | 49 | 239,103 | 36 | 106,367 | 16 |
| Wisconsin | 100 | 1,035,943 | 41 | 926,245 | 37 | 542,660 | 22 |
| Wyoming | 100 | 67,863 | 34 | 79,558 | 40 | 51,209 | 26 |
| **Totals** | | **43,728,375** | **43** | **38,167,416** | **38** | **19,237,247** | **19** |

*Source: Associated Press*

## How Did You Do?

Did you notice as you found your answers that you skipped many details? Looking only for what you are asked to find saves you time when you are reading. This process of looking for specific details is called *scanning*.

# Activities

The following activities offer you more practice in scanning for details. Use the five steps listed in "Here's How to Do It" to complete them.

## Activity 1-1:  Football Roster

On page 6 is a roster or list of names for a state university football team. Find the details that will help you answer the following questions.

**a.** What class is Guido Colón in?

**b.** Who wears number 82?

**c.** How much does Chuck Hunter weigh?

**d.** How tall is Tony Stamos?

**e.** What position does Ed Connor play?

**f.** What number does Floyd Lincoln wear?

## FOOTBALL ROSTER

| Number | Name | Position | Class | Height | Weight |
|--------|------|----------|-------|--------|--------|
| 11 | Bill Hammond | QB | Jr. | 6-1 | 185 |
| 14 | Yoshi Hirota | QB | Soph. | 5-11 | 176 |
| 15 | Ed Connor | QB | Sr. | 6-3 | 204 |
| 20 | Jake Gray | RB | Jr. | 5-10 | 174 |
| 22 | Cesar Lopez | DB | Soph. | 5-11 | 187 |
| 23 | Frank Geordano | RB | Sr. | 6-0 | 195 |
| 26 | Kevin Campbell | DB | Jr. | 6-2 | 188 |
| 31 | Chuck Hunter | RB | Sr. | 5-11 | 190 |
| 33 | Butch Ridner | RB | Soph. | 6-1 | 200 |
| 35 | John Hoskins | PK | Fr. | 5-9 | 170 |
| 40 | Mick Blattner | LB | Sr. | 6-1 | 212 |
| 44 | Floyd Lincoln | RB | Fr. | 6-3 | 225 |
| 47 | Pang Lee | LB | Soph. | 6-2 | 220 |
| 50 | Barry Jaynes | C | Fr. | 6-0 | 210 |
| 51 | Fred Richards | C | Jr. | 6-1 | 217 |
| 55 | Guido Colón | LB | Sr. | 5-11 | 205 |
| 61 | Eli Eliot | OG | Fr. | 6-3 | 227 |
| 62 | Dave Douglas | DG | Soph. | 6-0 | 196 |
| 64 | Tony Stamos | DG | Jr. | 6-2 | 209 |
| 66 | Ken Hartz | OG | Sr. | 6-4 | 231 |
| 70 | Ossie Robinson | DT | Sr. | 6-3 | 240 |
| 73 | Tomas Molina | DT | Fr. | 6-2 | 232 |
| 74 | Jamie O'Toole | OT | Soph. | 6-0 | 221 |
| 75 | Frank Vollmer | OT | Jr. | 6-3 | 224 |
| 77 | Jeff Mendenez | DT | Sr. | 6-1 | 227 |
| 80 | Doug Furness | OE | Fr. | 5-10 | 196 |
| 82 | Mike Bernstein | OE | Jr. | 6-3 | 205 |
| 84 | Paul Taylor | DE | Sr. | 6-2 | 219 |
| 85 | Andrew Pendleton | DE | Soph. | 6-0 | 214 |

# Activity 1-2: Properties of Selected Woods

The table below shows the different properties or characteristics of certain woods. Use it to answer the following questions. Write your answers on a separate sheet of paper. Remember to follow the five steps listed on page 3.

a. What is the degree of hardness for hemlock?

b. Which of the woods listed has poor holding power when glued?

c. How many are listed as hard woods?

d. Which class of workability indicates woods that are best to use on a lathe (a machine used for shaping pieces of wood)?

e. What is beech's workability rating?

f. What is the color of poplar wood?

| | | | | | | HOLDING POWER | |
| Name of Wood | Color | Grain | Weight | Hardness | Workability | Nails & Screws | Glue |
|---|---|---|---|---|---|---|---|
| ASH | pale brown | open | heavy | hard | difficult | average | average |
| BALSA | pale brown | open | very light | soft | easy | poor | good |
| BASSWOOD | creamy white | close | light | soft | easy | good | good |
| BEECH | white and reddish brown | close | heavy | hard | difficult | high | poor |
| BIRCH | brown | close | heavy | tough | difficult | good | good |
| CEDAR | red | straight, even, close | light | soft | easy | medium | good |
| CHERRY | light to dark red | close | medium | hard | good | high | good |
| CYPRESS | reddish | close | medium | soft | good | good | poor |
| FIR | white to reddish | close | medium | medium | good | reasonably good | average |
| GUMWOOD | reddish brown | close | medium heavy | hard | medium | average | average |

(continued on page 8)

## PROPERTIES OF SELECTED WOODS

| Name of Wood | Color | Grain | Weight | Hardness | Workability | HOLDING POWER | |
| | | | | | | Nails & Screws | Glue |
|---|---|---|---|---|---|---|---|
| HEMLOCK | buff | close | light | medium | easy | good | good |
| HICKORY | reddish brown | open | heavy | hard | difficult | low | poor |
| MAHOGANY | red to dark brown | open | medium | medium | easy | good | good |
| MAHOGANY, PHILIPPINE | pink to dark red | open | medium | medium | medium | good | good |
| MAPLE | light brown and tan | close | heavy | hard | medium to difficult | average | good |
| OAK | tan to reddish | open | heavy | hard | difficult | good | average |
| PINE, EASTERN | light brown | close | light | soft | easy | good | good |
| PINE, PONDEROSA | yellowish | close | light | soft | easy | good | good |
| PINE, YELLOW | yellowish and reddish brown | close | heavy | medium | medium | good | good |
| POPLAR | greenish yellow to brown | close | moderately light | soft | good | good | good |
| REDWOOD | reddish brown | close | moderately light | soft | good | good | good |
| SPRUCE | yellowish to pale brown | close | light | soft | good | good | good |
| WALNUT | chocolate brown | open | heavy | hard | good | good | good |
| WILLOW | purplish brown | close | light | soft | good | good | high |

# Activity 1-3:  President's Physical Fitness Test

The table on page 9 shows the skills and desired goals for the President's Physical Fitness Test. Find the details that will help you answer the following questions. Use a separate sheet of paper for your answers.

**a.**  What events are required in this fitness test?

**b.**  How many events are there?

**c.** What type is used to indicate the girls' score?

**d.** What type is used to indicate the boys' score?

**e.** A boy who is twelve years old achieved 7.1 in an event. What was that event?

**f.** If you are fourteen years old and a girl, how many sit-ups will you be required to do?

**g.** The time was 2:21 in the 600 yard walk/run. Whose time was this?

## PRESIDENT'S PHYSICAL FITNESS TEST

**Boys' scores are in bold type.**
*Girls' scores are in italic type.*

| Event | 10 | 11 | 12 | 13 | 14 | 15 | 16 | 17 |
|---|---|---|---|---|---|---|---|---|
| | | | | (Age in years) | | | | |
| Pull-ups (boys only) | **5** | **5** | **6** | **7** | **9** | **11** | **11** | **12** |
| Flexed Arm Hang (girls only) | *24 sec.* | *24* | *23* | *21* | *26* | *25* | *20* | *22* |
| Sit-ups (performed in 60 sec.) | **42** *38* | **43** *38* | **45** *38* | **48** *40* | **50** *41* | **50** *40* | **50** *38* | **49** *40* |
| Shuttle Run (test scores in seconds and tenths) | **10.4** *10.9* | **10.1** *10.5* | **10.0** *10.5* | **9.7** *10.2* | **9.3** *10.1* | **9.2** *10.2* | **9.1** *10.4* | **9.0** *10.1* |
| Standing Long Jump (test scores in inches and feet) | **5'8"** *5'5"* | **5'10"** *5'7"* | **6'1"** *5'9"* | **6'8"** *6'0"* | **6'11"** *6'3"* | **7'5"** *6'1"* | **7'9"** *6'0"* | **8'0"** *6'3"* |
| 50 yd. Dash (test scores in seconds and tenths) | **7.7** *7.8* | **7.4** *7.5* | **7.1** *7.4* | **6.9** *7.2* | **6.5** *7.1* | **6.3** *7.1* | **6.3** *7.3* | **6.1** *7.1* |
| 600 yd. Run (walking is permitted; test scores in minutes and seconds) | **2:11** *2:30* | **2:9** *2:25* | **2:0** *2:21* | **1:54** *2:16* | **1:47** *2:11* | **1:42** *2:14* | **1:4** *2:19* | **1:38** *2:14* |

## Activity 1-4:  Table of Contents

A table of contents from a high school short story collection appears with this activity. Use it to answer the following questions on a separate piece of paper.

**a.** What is the title of the section that begins on page 47?

**b.** On what page does the story, "To Build a Fire," begin?

**c.** What is the theme of Part Five?

# Contents

**d.** Who wrote the story, "The New Kid"?

**e.** What is the title of the story which beings on page 63?

**f.** What story comes first in this book, "D.P." or "A & P"?

# Activity 1-5: Checking Accounts

It is likely that you will want to open a checking account some day. On page 13, you will find an Information Sheet to guide customers when choosing a checking or other account at a bank. Use it to answer the following on a separate sheet of paper.

**a.**    How much money must you have to open a Checking + Interest account?

**b.**    Name one disadvantage of a Money Market account.

**c.**    What type of interest does a TRANSACT Investment Checking account pay?

**d.**    Name one advantage of a Checking + Interest account.

**e.**    What determines the rate of interest on a Money Market account?

**f.**    What terms are placed on all three accounts?

# Information Sheet: Checking and Transactional Accounts

| Type of Account | Term | Minimum to Open | Type Interest | Rate Determination |
|---|---|---|---|---|
| **CHECKING + INTEREST** | None | $100 | Interest is compounded daily. | Government regulation. Rate is fixed. |
| **TRANSACT Investment Checking** | None | $2,500 | Simple interest, floating rate. | Management decision. Rate normally changes weekly. |
| **MONEY MARKET** | None | $2,500 | Floating rate. Interest is compounded monthly. | Management decision. Rate normally changes weekly. |

| Type of Account | Advantages | Disadvantages |
|---|---|---|
| **CHECKING + INTEREST** | ☐ Traditional checking account with added benefit of interest earnings<br>☐ No per check service charge<br>☐ Totally liquid<br>☐ Free of monthly service charges for:<br> • $500 balance or more<br> • senior citizens 62 or older<br> • direct deposit of payroll, retirement or disability checks<br>☐ Monthly statement of account activity<br>☐ FSLIC insured | ☐ $5 monthly fee if balance falls below $500 (except for senior citizens and direct deposit customers) |
| **TRANSACT Investment Checking** | ☐ Pays premium interest on checking accounts<br>☐ Unlimited checking<br>☐ Brokerage services<br>☐ VISA Gold card availability<br>☐ Travelers check delivery service<br>☐ Foreign currency exchange<br>☐ FSLIC insured | ☐ High minimum required<br>☐ Floating rate; rate is not guaranteed for any term<br>☐ No interest earned during statement cycle if balance falls below $2,500 during the statement cycle<br>☐ Interest earned is usually lower than that on money market account |
| **MONEY MARKET** | ☐ Pays market interest rate<br>☐ Up to 3 checks per month<br>☐ Unlimited in-person withdrawals<br>☐ Unlimited number of additions<br>☐ Unlike money market funds offered by brokerage houses, this account is FSLIC insured | ☐ Limited checkwriting<br>☐ Floating rate; rate is not guaranteed for specific term<br>☐ Additions only in $100 or more<br>☐ 5¼% interest paid if balance falls below $2,500 during the statement cycle<br>☐ Checks or withdrawals of less than $500 have a $10 service charge |

# Activity 1-6: Weather Forecast

Below, you will find a weather map that includes the temperatures forecast for various cities in the eastern United States. You will also find specific information about the weather in Washington, D.C. Look over these data carefully and use them to answer the questions below on a separate sheet of paper.

**a.** What will be the high temperature in Pittsburgh today?

**b.** How cold will it get in Virginia Beach today?

**c.** Will people in Washington, D.C., need umbrellas today or not?

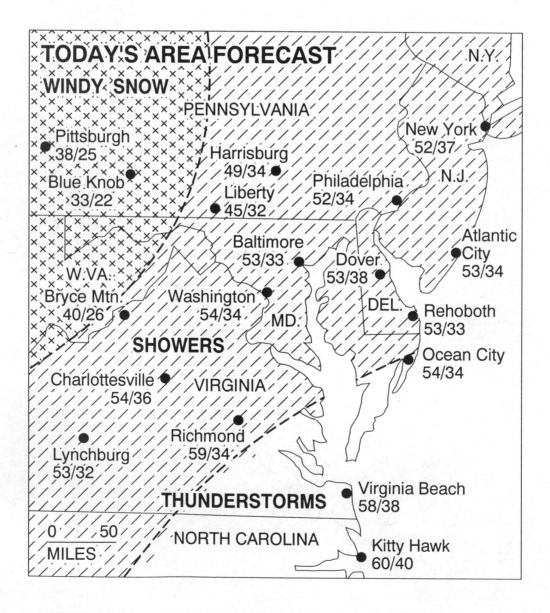

**d.** Which city is found in the northeast corner on the map?

**e.** Where will it be snowing?

**f.** What will be the highest barometric pressure today?

**g.** When will it be low tide in Norfolk?

---

## WASHINGTON WEATHER DATA
### THROUGH 9 P.M. YESTERDAY

**National Airport**

**Temperature:**

High, 50° at 4:00 p.m.
Low, 44° at 2:27 a.m.
Normal: 59°/40°
Record*
High, 87° in 1921
Low, 23° in 1955

**Precipitation:**

Past 24 hours: 1.66"
Total this month: 2.53"
Normal month to date: 2.91"
Total this year: 8.54"
Normal year to date: 8.29"

**Wind chill:**

38° (comfort index
combines temp./wind)

AQI: Good 24 carbon monoxide

**Barometric pressure:**

High, 30.18"
Low, 29.63"

**Relative humidity:**

Max. 100% at 4:00 a.m.
Min. 93% at 1:00 a.m.

---

**Dulles Airport**

High, 49° at 2:00 p.m.
Low, 42° at 2:30 a.m.

**BWI Airport**

High, 49° at 3:00 p.m.
Low, 41° at 3:00 a.m.

---

**Today's Tides**

| Location | High | Low | High | Low |
|---|---|---|---|---|
| Washington | 2:49 a.m. | 9:03 a.m. | 2:54 p.m. | 9:59 p.m. |
| Annapolis | 12:42 p.m. | 5:41 a.m. | ---------- | 6:51 p.m. |
| Ocean City | 1:46 a.m. | 8:22 a.m. | 2:21 p.m. | 8:44 p.m. |
| Norfolk | 4:05 a.m. | 10:29 a.m. | 4:27 p.m. | 10:34 p.m. |
| Point Lookout | 8:54 a.m. | 1:54 a.m. | 8:59 p.m. | 3:04 p.m. |
| Solomons I. | 9:35 a.m. | 2:38 a.m. | 9:40 p.m. | 3:48 p.m. |

---

**Heating Degree Days:***

Thursday: 18; this month: 542; this season: 3636; normal to yesterday: 3724; last season: 3061

*An index of fuel consumption indicating how many degrees the mean temperature fell below 65 for the day. If a day's mean temperature were 45, there would be 20 "degree days" for the date.

# *Activity 1-7:  Classified Ads*

On page 17 is a portion of the classified ad section from a newspaper. Such advertising contains want ads for various kinds of products and services. All ads for a particular kind of product or service are grouped under one heading. Look at the classified ad carefully. Then, on a separate sheet of paper, answer these questions.

**a.**   Which one would you call if you want to sell your Bears football tickets?

**b.**   How much would you pay for a Canon 35mm camera?

**c.**   What kind of boat can you take for fishing?

**d.**   What number would you call to get two tickets to Lake Tahoe?

**e.**   Who would you call to buy drums?

**f.**   List three different types of jobs in Help Wanted.

**g.**   What phone number would you call to buy a nine-week-old cocker spaniel?

**h.**   What is the price of a queen size hide-bed?

## Pets

### Dogs

**ADOPT!**

Get the best pets at The Anti-Cruelty Society. OPEN NOON-5 EVERY DAY. Dogs/pups, $45; Cats/kittens, $30. Includes spay/neuter, rabies & other shots, collar, ID tag, dog leash/cat carrier. Cash, Visa, Master Charge 510 N. LaSalle      644-8338 Free Parking—Bring the Kids.

★ Aftens★Beagles★Cockers ★
**PUPPY SALE**
★ WE SELL ALL BREEDS ★
★ Over 100 Pups-$45/up ★
★ Call us 1st-SAVE $$$ ★
★Archer Puppies 594-2240★
★ 5436 S. HARLEM AVE ★

AIRDALE TERRIER PUPPIES Champ lines, shots, paper trnd. From $200. 599-2015

Basset Pups-m/f, champ blood lines, exc temperment      $350 Call      414-857-7634

COCKAPOO BLOND PUPS Home Raised 1-815-469-2648

COCKER PUPS, AKC, males & females, 6 wks old, blks & buff. $200-$250. call 795-0635

COCKER SPANIEL-AKC pups, 2 buff males, 9 wks, $175. 1st shots. 815-468-8873 or 815-468-8746.

COCKER SPANIEL PUPS AKC M/F buff-blk/tan-blk 9½ wks. Ch. bld-lns, shots, home raised, ppr. train. 627-1221

DALMATION-AKC, 2 yrs old, exc w/children. Blk and wht $200/bo. (219) 836-1067

DALMATIONS, AKC, 6 wks old, wkdays 8-11am, wkends anytime. 6 Males, 5 Females. 616/538-0471

ENGLISH POINTERS-reg, exc w/kids, hunt, male/female. 6wks. $250      (815) 478-4347

GERMAN SHEPHERD PUPS King sz, lrg boned, reg, shots, paper trained. From $250. Also trained adults. 599-2015

IRISH SETTER PUPS 6 WEEKS OLD, AKC $150 879-0396 892-1811

LHASA APSOS Champ sired. AKC. $250 & up. Call 464-4150

MALTESE - AKC Tiny. Shots. $250 & up 325-9871

POODLES, 6 weeks, white & cream, 3 Male, 2 Female, AKC, $250-$275.      671-7524

SHELTIE pups, AKC, sable, healthy, shots, M $250, F $325 NW sub. (815) 675-2890

Sheltie Pups- AKC, sables, shots, wormed, hlth guarntd. $225 & up. 815-943-7295.

YORKSHIRE TERRIER PUPS, AKC, 8 wks, $300-$350. 354-1775

### Other Pets

DOMESTIC Hand-Fed Super-Tame & Talking Medium Sulfur-Crested Cockatoo. 2 years old. Loves people.      $1200 232-6040 or 584-0939

Siamese Kittens, pure breed, $120; Adorable blk/wht Siamese/tabby, $35. Raised w/lots of hugs & kisses. 971-2689

Blue & Gold MACCAWS-3 domestic babies born 7/15, 7/18 & 7/22/87. Still spoon feeding. $1450/ea. FLA (305) 969-2582

. . . kittens, give away . . . sensible & lov- . . . 2250

. . . 8wks.

AND FEATHERS BIRD Studio 1015 W. Webster. 549-6944 HAND-MIXED BULK SEED

Himalayan kittens M/F, flame & cream pt. CFA reg, home raised, $250 & up. 524-1938

PERSIAN KITTENS-Reds, blacks, tortis, all shots, home raised. $200 & up      888-1265

KITTENS Beautiful 7wks old to good home only. Please call 924-2732

## Household Goods/ Equipment

### Furniture & Furnishings For Sale

Moving-Nice chrome & glass din rm set, gray sectional sleeper sofa, like new. Exc quality furniture. Other misc. items. 653-5920, 858-3397 /ev

Country French solid wood pedestal table w/leaf, hutch cab w/5 drawers, 4 ladder back chrs w/cushion. Good cond. $600/bo 367-1671

INTERIOR DESIGNER Save 40% to 50% off retail prices finest furniture lines. Cptg, drapes-acces.    467-6360

ALL Wood Cntry style bdrm set, 2 night stands dresser w/mirror box, Man's bureau, Queen size 4 poster head & foot board, $1000; 963-7920

MOVING: 10 pc pit, never used, $3000 value/sacrifice $875, free delivery. 5 pc Bdrm set, $799 value/sacrifice $295. Will separate. 676-0711

Estate Sale-7/25,26,27,28 Pastel mink jacket, Classic din. rm. set. Other choice furn. 4101 Clausen, Western Springs 246-4106

Hide-bed makes into queen size, good cond. $125 or best offer. Complete Encyclopedia (Brittanica) $75 or best offer. 432-8398

King sz bed, brass hdbrd, night stands, 2 triple dressers wth mirror, 2 desks & chair. Make offer, 729-6747

### Musical Instruments Miscellaneous

♪♪♪♪♪♪♪♪♪♪♪ DON'T MISS BIASCO'S ROCK 'N' ROLL MILLION DOLLAR LIQUIDATION!!!
Ludwig 5pc. Prof.      Only $295
Pearl 9pc. Power Shells      $749
Fender Stratocaster Only $239
Peavey 50 Watt      Only $139
Roland Synth.      Only $259
CASH • CREDIT • VISA/M.C. Save in our BIG USED Dept.
**BIASCO MUSIC—Chgo's #1** ROCK 'N' ROLL SUPERSTORE 5535 W. Belmont, CHICAGO Call our HOTLINE 286-5900
♪♪♪♪♪♪♪♪♪♪♪
GUITAR & AMP-Ibanez Destroyer $350 Ampeg amp w/200 watts & 2 hvy duty 12" spkrs, $450 Both for $650. 390-4405 day 943-3347 eves

For Sale: Fender Tele, pink paisley, $400. Fender Strat Elite, emerald green, $400. Mesa Boogie w/case & effects. $600. Call: 968-3702

RHODES 73 STAGE elec. piano w/prac. amp. Exc cond, $350/ Bst Ofr.      963-4878

DRUMS! DRUMS! DRUMS! Ludwig 5pc $259. See 200 Sets! BIASCO - Call Paul      286-5900

WANTED Guitar Amps Drums Keybds, Band Inst. Top Cash. Call BIASCO Now      286-5900

5 piece Tama w/3 Roto Toms, symbols and hardware incld. $900. 478-3389

JUNO-10 . . . . . . . MSQ-700 . . .

## Cameras & Optical Goods

### Cameras & Optical Goods

CANNON A1 35MM, flash attachment, power winder, data back, 2 lens 35x105mm, 28x200 Vivator lens. Asking Price $450      568-8562

Celestron 800 Telescope: Complete pkg. w/trunk case & 35mm camera mount. Many other extras. $900   Jeannette, days 666-8866 eves 664-3539

Nikon F3; Nikkor 35-105 zoom lens, exc cond, $550. 227-2074 after 5pm

### Tickets

★BUYING & SELLING★ ALL MAJOR AIRLINES TOP$$$ Immediate Cash/Local People Dis/Fares      312-325-1032 ★BEST PRICED TRAVEL★

2 Airline Tickets Orig $500, best ofr to Albuquerque Mexico leaving Fri. Aug. 7, returning Wed. Aug 12. 462-1768

4 AA 1st class rt tkts to Hawaii w/car & hotel. Good for 1 yr. No restrictions. $895 ea. 800-527-4659 anytime

BEARS TICKETS PLEASE! PRICE IS NO OBJECT!! PLEASE CALL 260-0101

CUBS VS. METS Ticks available. Aug. 15 & 16. CALL 317-897-7777

Two round trip tickets to Lake Tahoe. Only $500. 8/30-9/2. Call Lisa at 338-1712.

For Madonna tickets. Alpine valley. Excellent reserve seats. Call 250-8829 after 4 p.m.

BEARS TICKETS WANTED Only good seats. Any or all games. (412) 344-9900 9 to 5.

1 WAY UNITED TICKET: Chgo to Long Beach, Calif. July 30. $125. 835-4160 aft 6pm

MADONNA TICKETS Grt seats. 26th row center. Call 577-5948 lv msg

WANTED: Bears Season tickets & Bulls box seats. 803-8874 ask for Bob, 8am-4pm, M-F.

Pan Am Games 2 season tickets for all equestrian events. $400. (818) 445-9733

Madonna, Whitney Houston, Pink Floyd, Cubs, Sox, all Popular Creek Events 803-9977

### Wanted Miscellaneous

BUYING TRAVEL AWARDS ALL MAJOR AIRLINES Best prices for bump tickets Coupon Broker 312-284-2400

SLOT MACHINES OLD WURLITZER JUKEBOX OR PARTS. CA$H. 312/985-2742

BUYING Baseball Card Collections Call 369-8029

TOY SOLDIERS Trains, cars & trucks Farm toys ANY OLD TOYS! 296-5465

### Hobbies/Arts & Crafts

★ ELECTRIC TRAINS ★ CASH PAID By Private Party No one can top my price 349-0550      North 447-3881

I PAY THE HIGHEST PRICES FOR OLD TRAINS AND TOYS Cash. Private Party: 699-0268. CALL ME BEFORE YOU SELL

### Country Corner

Horses, Tack, Equip.

★★ TB chest. yrlg, filly (Vencedor-Gr. II SW) out of proven 17.1 hunt/jump mare; TB Bay geld, 4, 16H-sound, sane, willing, started ovr fences; TB brown hunter geld., 8, 16.1-broke, safe, attract; QH dap. gray geld., 5, 16.3-quiet, sensible, shown hunter div. w/success. (815) 338-8842 ★★

### Boats, Mtrs. & Equip.

**SUPER BOAT SALE**
OVER 300 BOATS MOTORS TRAILERS "EVERTHING" GOES "ANYTHING" GOES '88 MODELS COMING MUST MAKE ROOM CLOSING OUT NEW '87'S 17' BOWRIDER
Was $12,640      NOW $9488*
19' BOWRIDER
Was $13,320      NOW $9988*
19' CUDDY CABIN
Was $15,400      NOW $10,988*
*Plus Freight & Prep
OPEN 7 DAYS
Slips Available 16 – 46'
**SEQUOIT HARBOR**
ANTIOCH, IL      312-395-6101 Take 94 or 294 No. to Rte 173, go West 7 miles to marina.

All you need is your toothbrush. 1986 42' twin Diesel Motor Yacht, ONAN, air, full electronics, canvas, professionally decorated, too much to list, must see. $179,500. May take trade. Call 398-1115 days; 564-1014 eves/wknds.

★★★FISHING MACHINE★★★ '86 Harborcraft. Dlx Lk MI fishing boat. 26', 260 hp Merc, custom top, dlx trlr. Huge open back fishing area w/ or w/o fishing eqpt. Lo hrs, lk new. Must see. Must sell. $25,500. 485-7841

'76 21 ft Tahiti Jet boat, like new, 460 Ford gale banks twin turbos, motor & Berkley pump, both blueprinted, many extras, $10,500 or offer. 941-0346 or 530-2114

**NEW 40' TOLLYCRAFT**
AFT CABIN AIR, GENERATOR, ARCH, DUAL STATIONS, LOADED! Retail 219,000 NOW $159,000
**SEQUOIT HARBOR**
312-395-6101

### Help Wanted

AUTOMOTIVE Exp. Installer of mufflers, shocks & springs. 599-4158

Aviation
**FLIGHT INSTRUCTOR**
Looking for a dedicated flight/ground instructor for a college flight program. CFII required. Preference given to college grads with FAR Part 141 experience. Send resume by 7/31/87 to:
University of Dubuque Chief Flight Instructor 2000 University Ave Dubuque, IA 52001

BAKER, EXPERIENCED, bread & mixing. Days. Good benefits, no Sundays. Call for appt., 421-5016 .      120 N. Green.

Baker, exp. Bread & mixing. Start 2am. Good benefits. No Sundays. 281-7300 for appt.

BANK TELLER      #4929 Refer to Emply. Svce 427-1848 Fee $75 Access 1 Job Ref Svc

BANK TELLERS The Job Store      384-0700 Refer to employment svc. ad.

BANKING

General Office
**ADMINISTRATIVE CLERK**
Busy Park Ridge office needs reliable individual to fill permanent full-time position (9 to 5:30). Will perform varied office duties and be trained in small business computer operations. Must type at least 40 wpm, adjusted for errors. Please send cover letter and resume with salary history to: Contract Courier Services, Inc. 1550 N. Northwest Hwy, #117 Park Ridge, IL 60068 Attn: TR-AD

General
★★DESIGNING★★ ★★WOMEN/MEN★★
22 openings in Mgmt training. Ground flr. oppty. If you're career oriented, fashion conscious & money motivated. Mgmt, asst. Mgmt., bkkpg, sales, Sal. benefits, bonuses, & comm. 953-0999 ext. 14.

General
★ JOBS IMMEDIATELY ★
Booming response to our company has caused need for 10 enthusiastic people to fill all management training positions. Excellent earnings while you learn. No experience necessary. Call 635-8830 ext. 15

GENERAL OFFICE $16-$18,000
Expanding firm needs individual with team attitude, good typing and stable office experience Will handle 8 line phone system, greet visitors as receptionist, help with office variety. Client firm. 966-0700

Painter
Full-time position. Min. 5 yrs. exp. Must have own transportation. Call 7-4 pm 439-9820

Painters-Hangers, PERSONNEL HDQTS. 386-0400 See our ad under Employment Services

PAINTERS-EXP. Job Store      384-0700 Refer to employment svc. ad.

PARALEGAL **DALLAS**
As an experienced paralegal, have you considered expanding your career horizons to the Dallas, Texas area? Our client law firms are aggressively expanding their paralegal staff. Areas of specialization are:
• LITIGATION Primarily large complex cases
• CORPORATE
• REAL ESTATE
• BANKING

Requirements for consideration are an undergraduate degree, paralegal certification and a minimum 1 year experience with a law firm or major corporate legal department. If your qualifications meet that of those listed above and relocation is a possibility you will explore, please submit your resume in strictest confidence to:
Colby & Associates 700 N. Pearl LB 406 Dallas, TX 75201

PARALEGAL Expanding pl, P.I. . . . paralegal with b . . . ground. Co . . .

## Activity 1-8: U.S. Territory

Below, you see a map of the continental United States showing the dates and the means by which land was acquired. Use it to answer the following questions on a separate sheet of paper.

**a.** What area was ceded by Great Britain? When?

**b.** When was the Oregon Cession made?

**c.** What took place in 1853?

**d.** What country ceded land to the U.S. in 1845?

**e.** In 1783, what area constituted the original United States?

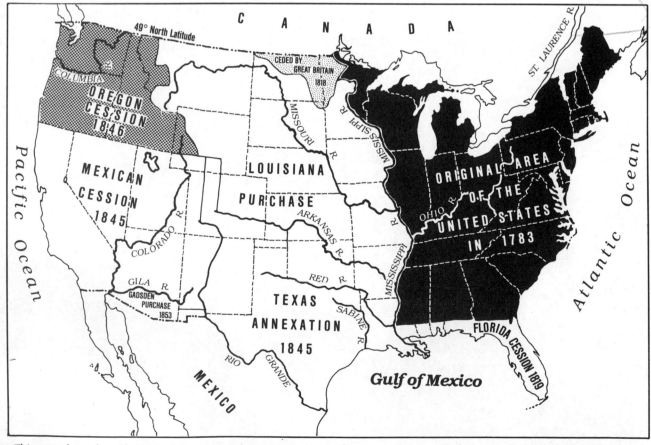

This map shows how the United States grew from east to west.

# Activity 1-9:  Television Listings

Television guides in your newspaper provide information to help you make decisions about which programs to watch. Programs are listed according to the time of day they are being broadcast. Channel numbers are listed from the lowest to the highest (Channel 2, Channel 5, etc.) within each time category.

Scan the television listing that appears below. Then answer the questions below. Use a separate sheet of paper for your answers.

**a.**  What program is on Channel 7 at 7:00 A.M.?

**b.**  On what channel can you find "Geraldo"? At what time?

**c.**  Which channel features Instructional Programming?

**d.**  Which channels offer "20/20"?  At what time?

**e.**  Which channels broadcast CBS programs?

**f.**  Which channel is showing the movie *Dreams Don't Die?* When?

## BROADCAST

**Channels: 4 NBC/WRC; 5 WTTG; 7 ABC/WJLA; 9 CBS/WUSA; 20 WDCA; 50 WFTY; 22 & 67 WMPT; 26 PBS/WETA; 32 PBS/WHMM; 2 NBC/WMAR; 11 CBS/WBAL; 13 ABC/WJZ**

| | 4 | 5 | 7 | 9 | 20 | 50 | 22 | 26 | 32 | 2 | 11 | 13 |
|---|---|---|---|---|---|---|---|---|---|---|---|---|
| 6:00 | News | News | ABC News | News | K. Copeland | Movie (cont'd) | West Tradition | | | News (cont'd) | News | NewsMatch |
| 6:30 | | News | News | | Widget | Raring to Read | A.M. Weather | Zoobilee Zoo | | | News | |
| 7:00 | Today | Fox Morning News | Good Morning America | This Morning | G.I. Joe | New He-Man | West Tradition | Sesame Street | | Today | This Morning | Good Morning, America |
| 7:30 | | | | | Bond Jr. | Jetsons | Lamb Chop | | | | | |
| 8:00 | | | | | Melodies | Robert Tilton | Sesame Street | Station | Mister Rogers | | | |
| 8:30 | | | | | Flintstones | | | Mister Rogers | Sesame Street | | | |
| 9:00 | Jenny Jones | I Love Lucy | Live-Regis & Kathie Lee | Donahue | Robert Tilton | James Robison | Reading Rainbow | Sesame Street | | Donahue | Live-Regis & Kathie Lee | Highway to Heaven |
| 9:30 | | I Love Lucy | | | | Victory | Instructional Programming | | Where Is Carmen Sandiego | | | |
| 10:00 | Candid Camera | Andy Griffith | Geraldo | Sally Jessy Raphael | 700 Club | Self Enhancement | | Sesame Street | Homestretch | Sally Jessy Raphael | Jenny Jones | Joan Rivers |
| 10:30 | Classic Concentration | Andy Griffith | | | | Inspector Gadget | Musical Encounter | | Body Electric | | | |
| 11:00 | Closer Look | Beverly Hillbillies | Home | Price Is Right | Jeffersons | Voyage to the Bottom of the Sea | Instructional Programming | Shining Time Station | For the People | Geraldo | Price Is Right | People's Court |
| 11:30 | One on One | Beverly Hillbillies | | | Love Connection | | Spanish TV Magazine | Lamb Chop's Play-Along | Write Course "Definition" | | | Candid Camera |
| 12:00 | Santa Barbara | Matlock | Jeopardy! | News | People's Court | Ruta Lee | | Body Electric | Business and The Law | News | News | News |
| 12:30 | | | Loving | Young and Restless | Benson | Movie: "Dreams Don't Die" | Instructional Programming | All About TV | Growing Years | Closer Look | Young and Restless | Loving |
| 1:00 | Days of Our Lives | Perry Mason | All My Children | | Mama's Family | | | Nature | Evening Exchange | Days of Our Lives | | All My Children |
| 1:30 | | | Bold & the Beautiful | | Odd Couple | | Sewing With Nancy | | | | Bold & the Beautiful | |
| 2:00 | Another World | Peter Pan & The Pirates | One Life To Live | As the World Turns | Head of the Class | | We're Cooking Now | QED | Focus on Society | Another World | As the World Turns | One Life To Live |
| 2:30 | | Woody Woodpecker | | | ALF | McCloud | Nathalie Dupree | Family Album | Government By Consent | | | |
| 3:00 | Maury Povich | Dennis the Menace | General Hospital | Guiding Light | Duck Tales | | Nature | Sesame Street | Welcome to My Studio | Montel Williams | Guiding Light | General Hospital |
| 3:30 | | Alvin & the Chipmunks | | | Chip 'n' Dale | | | | Today's Gourmet | | | |
| 4:00 | Inside Edition | Beetlejuice | Oprah Winfrey | News | Tale Spin | Self Enhancement | Sesame Street | Shining Time Station | Where is Carmen Sandiego | Oprah Winfrey | Maury Povich | Head of the Class |
| 4:30 | Hard Copy | Tiny Toon Adventures | | | Darkwing Duck | Raring to Read | | Reading Rainbow | Reading Rainbow | | | Growing Pains |
| 5:00 | News | Mr. Belvedere | News | News | Teenage Ninja Turtles | Highway to Heaven | Square One Television | Square One Television | Lamb Chop's Play-Along | News | Golden Girls | Cosby Show |
| 5:30 | | Full House | | | Saved by the Bell | | Where is Carmen Sandiego | Where is Carmen Sandiego | Square One Television | | Who's the Boss? | Night Court |

# Activity 1-10:  Road Map

Road maps often are used by people who drive long distances through unfamiliar territory. Look at this road map on the facing page. It includes sections of Missouri, Arkansas, Tennessee, Mississippi, and portions of Illinois, Kansas, Oklahoma, and Texas. While examining the map, locate the following details. Use a separate sheet of paper for your answers.

**a.** What city is about halfway between Kansas City and St. Louis?

**b.** What is the best route from Memphis to St. Louis?

**c.** What is the only route from Little Rock to Springfield?

**d.** The Ozark Mountain region is found in what two states?

**e.** How would you travel from Ft. Smith to Hot Springs?

**f.** How would you travel from Cape Girardeau, Missouri, to Jonesboro, Arkansas?

# Part 2

# Finding Details in Regular Formats

## About This Part...

Now that you have practiced finding details in special formats, you are ready to tackle finding details in *regular formats*. Details in regular formats can be difficult to locate because there are many words to look through. Read carefully when you search for details in paragraphs, essays, or stories.

In the following activities, you will be asked to find only a *few* details, even though there might be more in the passages. You will be told ahead of time how many details to find. You will have a chance in the next part of this book to find *more* details.

# Here's How to Do It

Follow this set of steps for finding details in regular formats.

1. *Know* how many and what kind of details you are asked to find before reading the passage.

2. *Read* the passage carefully.

3. *Look* for the information you need.

4. *Check* yourself when you finish finding the details. Repeat the details to yourself or write them down to make certain that you remember them.

5. *Wait* for about ten or fifteen minutes. Then try to *recall* the details you read in the passage.

## Sample Activity:  Catcher's Equipment

Read the selection below to learn about equipment worn by a catcher in baseball. Choose three items of equipment a catcher wears. Then list these details on a separate sheet of paper.

### Catcher's Equipment

To some people, a catcher on a baseball team may look like a monster from outer space. He wears a mask over his face. His face mask has a heavy wire front and padding around its edges. His large vest protects his chest and stomach. He wears hard, plastic guards that go from his knees down to his shins. The catcher catches the ball with a big mitt. If his pitcher throws quite hard, he may wear a small sponge inside the mitt. To be extra careful, the catcher also may use a metal cup to protect himself. When he puts all this equipment on, it is hard to think of him as a person.

**Answer:** Select from these—face mask, vest, plastic guards, mitt, metal cup.

# How Did You Do?

Did you notice these details were harder to find than the details in the previous activities? In this passage and the passages you read in Part 2, you will notice there are more details than are asked for. Choose only those that seem most important in describing the subject.

# Activities

Because finding details in a regular format sometimes can be difficult, be sure to read the selections carefully. Also remember to follow the four steps outlined in the "Here's How to Do It." This will help make your task easier.

## Activity 2-1: Popular Writers

After reading the passages on today's writers of popular novels, list three of the authors. List them on a separate sheet of paper.

### Popular Writers

Although there are those who claim that Americans don't read anymore, the popularity of today's "hot" writers of novels is great indeed. Stephen King has written a number of books on the strange and mysterious. Several have been best sellers. Danielle Steele's novels on romance have been almost as popular. The adventure and intrigue of global spy stories have made Tom Clancy famous. Another popular writer, Pat Conroy, appeals to millions of American readers with his novels. Robert Ludlow is yet another writer of blood-and-thunder thrillers who has gained fame across the nation. The works of Alice Walker are often found at the top of the "bestseller" list; her novel, *The Color Purple,* was made into a hit movie a few years ago. Thus reading, especially of exciting books, is alive and well in the U.S.A. today.

## Activity 2-2:  Book Reports

Book reports can be an effective way to assess student ability in reading. But as the following selection reveals, some students have found ways to avoid preparing their reports. On a separate sheet of paper, list three ways students do their reports.

### Book Reports

Students have found many ways to avoid doing their book reports. They don't know that they are cheating themselves. They also don't know that teachers are aware of every little trick. Some students skim through a book the night before the report is due. Then they write the report on the bus to school or in the homeroom. Others try to avoid reading the book at all. They may look at the *Classic Comics* version of the book. They may also find book reviews and restate those reviews in their own words. Some students even copy the statements on the book jacket for the report. One old-fashioned way to avoid reading the book is to use *Cliff's Notes*. These little booklets provide outlines and explain the meanings of many books. However, teachers read *Cliff's Notes*, too!

# Activity 2-3:  *Fiction and Fact in Shakespeare*

The following paragraph gives information about Shakespeare's plays. Some plays are based on mythology and some are based on historical fact. After reading the paragraph, use a separate sheet of paper to name a play that is based on mythology. Label it with an M. Then, name a play that is based on historical fact and label it with an H.

## Fiction and Fact in Shakespeare

Many of Shakespeare's plays have to do with events from the ancient world. They are based more often on mythology than on history. *Troilus and Cressida* is about people who fought in the Trojan War. *A Midsummer Night's Dream* is a comedy, also from ancient Greek myths. So is *Timon of Athens*, although its tone is tragic rather than comic. *Julius Caesar* has to do with the violent death of Rome's best-known leader, and *Antony and Cleopatra* with the time just after the murder of that famous ruler. That Shakespeare was interested in both fiction and fact can be seen in most of his plays.

# Activity 2-4:  *Romantic Poetry*

The following paragraph is a brief description of romantic poetry—the literary movement that emerged in England during the nineteenth century. As you carefully read the paragraph, locate the names of three romantic poets. Then indicate the usual theme or subject about which each of these poets wrote. Use a separate sheet of paper for your answer.

## Romantic Poetry

Romantic poetry was written by poets who lived during the nineteenth century. William Wordsworth wrote poems about love for nature, mostly the English countryside. Samuel Taylor Coleridge, who was a friend of Wordsworth, wrote about strange events. George Gordon Noel Byron, known as Lord Byron, wrote about action and love. Freedom and hatred of slavery were the themes of a great Romantic writer, Percy Bysshe Shelley. His friend, John Keats, wrote about beauty in art. Even though each poet wrote on a different topic, each was a part of the larger than-life movement of the times. Their writing was loved by the English. Even the common people read their poems.

## Activity 2-5:  States and Their Products

Each state in the U.S. gains recognition for its history, culture, or products. The following passage discusses states and their products. Read the passage. Then, select details about four states and the products they produce. Use a separate sheet of paper for your answer.

### States and Their Products

Most states in the U.S. are known for their products. Michigan has long been known for its auto industry. When people think of Detroit, they think of cars. Idaho is the country's leading producer of potatoes. Television ads tell of the quality of Idaho potatoes. Georgia calls itself the "Peach State" because of its many peach orchards. In fact, each year the Peach Bowl, a post-season college football game, is held in Atlanta. Florida, of course, is known for its citrus products—mainly oranges and grapefruit. Other states are also known for their products. Texas is known for oil, Iowa is known for corn. Vermont is famous for maple syrup and Wisconsin, for dairy products. California is known for its Silicon Valley, where many companies that design and manufacture computers are located.

## Activity 2-6:  Promissory Note

It's a good idea to understand the details of a written promise. Read the following promissory note carefully. On a separate sheet of paper, list three things that a person signing this note agrees to do.

### Promissory Note

For the goods and services described above, I agree to pay _____. My payments will begin on the _____ day of _____, 19_____. The title to the goods shall be retained by the seller until the entire balance is paid. I agree not to dispose of the goods without the seller's written consent. In addition, I will protect the seller against any loss or damage to the goods until the date of full payment. If I fail to comply with this contract, the seller may declare the unpaid balance to be due and payable.

## Activity 2-7:  Who's Who in Jury Trials

Read the statement about people in the courtroom during a trial. Then list four of them on a separate sheet of paper.

### Who's Who in Jury Trials

In our country, crimes are often dealt with by having an accused person tried by a jury. Many people are involved in such trials. The judge presides over the case. He or she directs the progress of the trial. The jury hears the evidence. The members of the jury decide the verdict. Usually there are 12 citizens on a jury. There are at least two lawyers present at a trial. One represents the accuser; the other defends the person accused of breaking the law. Witnesses make statements of what they know about the cases. There may be a few or many witnesses. They must all swear that they are telling the truth. There is an accuser, who may be one person or a government, such as the "United States" or the "State of Wyoming." There is also an accused person who must be proved guilty. A courtroom deputy clerk swears witnesses in, marks exhibits, and generally keeps the trial moving along. Finally, a court reporter takes down, on a special machine, all that is said during the trial. That person's work provides the record of the trial.

## Activity 2-8:  New England

The following passage relates information about New England. As you carefully read the selection, locate the names of three New England states and two capitals. Use a separate sheet of paper for your answer.

### New England

The section of our country that was settled first is a six-state region called "New England." This region was settled early in the 1600s, and its people were leaders in the American Revolution. The northernmost New England state is Maine with its capital, Augusta. Maine is a state that has large tourist and lumber industries. South of Maine are New Hampshire and Vermont. Their capitals are Concord and Montpelier. Some of the oldest colleges in the land can be found in these two states. The American Revolution began in Massachusetts, the state located in the middle of New England. Its capital, Boston, is one of the true historical centers in the United States. The two southernmost states, Rhode Island and Connecticut, with capitals in Providence and Hartford respectively, have their share of history, too. For people interested in learning about America's roots, this six-state region offers a wealth of material.

## Activity 2-9:  Prince Ludwig's Castles

Read the following passage about some of the most elaborate castles built. On a separate sheet of paper, write the names of two castles built by Prince Ludwig.

### Prince Ludwig's Castles

In the nineteenth century, the southern German province of Bavaria was ruled by a young prince named Ludwig. He loved beautiful things and spent most of his time planning to build expensive castles. During his rule, he built three of the most beautiful castles in the world. The best known is Neuschwanstein in southern Bavaria. This castle has served as the model for the magic castle in Disney World in Orlando, Florida. Near Neuschwanstein, Ludwig built a smaller but very elaborate castle named Hohenschwangau. This is near a lake for which the symphony *Swan Lake* was written. Prince Ludwig's smallest, most elaborate castle, is named Linderhof. It is near the Bavarian town of Garmisch-Partenkirchen. Thousands of tourists visit these castles every year.

## Activity 2-10:  Endangered Species

As the following selection reveals, animals of the world are being destroyed. Read the passage. Then select five examples of endangered species. Use a separate sheet of paper for your answers.

### Endangered Species

Throughout the world, as people settle in certain areas, build places to live, and hunt wild prey, some animals may no longer survive. In Africa, traders looking for ivory may soon wipe out all elephants. Big-game hunters who seek adventure are killing off the rhinoceros population. Off the coasts in many warmer climates, sea turtles are being caught and destroyed. Earlier in this century, sportsmen placed the American buffalo in danger of being wiped out. More recently, loggers in the West have put the spotted owl at risk, while in Florida, gentle manatees are being cut to pieces by boat propellers. In the same state, hunters stalk the reduced number of alligators and have done the same to the Florida panther. Without laws and people to enforce them, the number of wild animals still around in the 21st century may be small indeed.

# Activity 2-11:  Sun Belt States

Read the following passage about the Sun Belt. Then, on a separate sheet of paper, list the names of three states that have grown in population.

### Sun Belt States

During the past four decades, we have been using the term *Sun Belt* to refer to some states in the South and Southwest. Because these states offer a temperate climate, many people have begun to migrate there. Florida, for example, has attracted people who are fascinated by sun, beaches, and palm trees. Texas, with its wide open spaces, has enticed many northerners to live there. The Mississippi Gulf Coast has also become the home for many others. Two neighboring states, Arizona and New Mexico, both have seen their populations increase. Phoenix, Arizona, with its hot, dry weather and lovely desert surroundings, has been called the Valley of the Sun. But the Sun Belt state that claims the most population growth is California.

# Activity 2-12:  Income Tax Recordkeeping

Carefully read the following selection concerning income tax recordkeeping. On a separate sheet of paper, list four details you should remember when keeping records for income tax purposes.

### Income Tax Recordkeeping

You must keep your income tax records for a certain length of time. Their contents may be needed by the Internal Revenue Service. Any records that support items of income, deduction, or credit mentioned on your tax return should be saved until the statute of limitations expires. Usually, this is three years from the date the tax was paid. Some records need to be kept for an indefinite period. Records of transactions relating to the basis of property, including your personal residence, should be stored carefully. They are used to determine the basis of the original or replacement property.

# Part 3
# Finding More Details

## About This Part...

In previous activities, you have practiced finding a specific number
of details both in special and regular formats. In this Part, your goal
in reading is to find *as many details as you can.* There are times
when finding more details can help you, both in and out of school.
For example, when you work on a research paper, you look for as
many details as you can about a subject. You may look through
newspapers, encyclopedias, or other reference materials. This type
of reading for details is different from the reading activities you
have just practiced.

## Here's How to Do It

When reading a selection for more details, follow these suggested steps.

1.  *Look* at the assignment. You need to know what kind of details to look for.

2.  *Read* the passage carefully. Remember that you are trying to find all the details you can.

3.  *Look* for key words that indicate details: *another, further evidence, the next step, a different case,* etc.

4.  *Write* down each detail as you see it. Use a separate sheet of paper.

5.  *Look* up unfamiliar words in a dictionary. It isn't enough to find details; you must know what the words mean.

6.  *Reread* the passage carefully. Be sure you have not missed anything important.

## Sample Activity:  Female Firsts

The following passage cites many women who were "firsts" in their fields. On a separate sheet of paper, write the names of these women. Use the steps listed in "Here's How to Do It."

### Female Firsts

What would it be like to be the first person to do something? Many women have been firsts. In 1849, Elizabeth Blackwell became our country's first female doctor. She also founded and raised funds for a hospital. It was The New York Infirmary for Women and Children. Another first was Victoria Claflin Woodhull. She ran for president in 1872. In this century, many women have been firsts. In 1924, Nellie T. Ross was elected the first female governor in Wyoming and Miriam Ferguson in Texas. Frances Perkins was the first woman to be named to a cabinet post. She was Secretary of Labor from 1933 to 1945.

Not all firsts happened long ago. Some are more recent. In 1981 Sandra Day O'Connor became the first female U.S. Supreme Court Justice. Dr. Mae C. Jemison became the first African American woman in space. She was one of seven astronauts aboard the space shuttle *Endeavor,* which took off in September, 1992. So even today, it is still possible to be a "first."

**Answer:** *Elizabeth Blackwell,* first female doctor in U.S.; *Victoria Claflin Woodhull,* first woman to run for U.S. president; *Nellie T. Ross,* first female governor elected in Wyoming; *Miriam Ferguson,* first female governor elected in Texas; *Frances Perkins,* first woman named to a cabinet post; *Sandra Day O'Connor,* first woman who became a U.S. Supreme Court Justice; *Dr. Mae C. Jemison,* first African American woman in space.

## *How Did You Do?*

How many firsts did you find? Go back and read the passage again. Note where each fact is located. Every sentence does not contain a person's name. That means you must check all of the sentences, all of the way through. Don't stop in the middle of a sentence. Don't skip parts of sentences just because you have found one detail you were looking for. What key words do you find in the passage? What words did you look up?

# Activities

In the following activities, you will notice that the first few are easy to read. But they become longer and more challenging. Find as many details as you can. Continue to look up unfamiliar words in your dictionary. Don't forget to follow the steps listed in "Here's How to Do It."

## *Activity 3-1: New York City*

The following passage contains many details about New York City. Find as many details as you can. List them on a separate sheet of paper.

### New York City

Do you think New York is one huge city? In fact, New York City is made up of five sections. These sections are called *boroughs*. Boroughs are really mini-cities within the larger one. Manhattan, an island, is the best known of the boroughs. It contains many famous places. Broadway, Wall Street, Harlem, Times Square, and Greenwich Village are there. Besides Manhattan, there are four other boroughs. The Bronx is located northeast of Manhattan. It is on the mainland and covers a large area. East of Manhattan is Queens, on Long Island. Many people who work in Manhattan live in Queens. Brooklyn is also on Long Island. The Brooklyn Dodgers, a baseball team, began there. The team moved to Los Angeles in 1958. To the southwest of Manhattan is Staten Island. Many people who live there work in Manhattan. They take a ferry boat to and from work. On that ferry, they pass the Statue of Liberty. This statue became a national monument in 1924. You might say that the largest city in the U.S. is really five cities in one.

# Activity 3-2:  Women's Jobs

Women have made great strides in the employment market. After reading the following selection, list the types of jobs women are now holding. Write the details you find on a separate sheet of paper.

### Women's Jobs

Women used to have only certain jobs, such as teaching and nursing. Many people said "A woman's place is in the home." That has changed. Today, women hold many kinds of jobs and positions of leadership. Many women are lawyers and doctors. They have also entered politics. Women are running for public offices. Some women have been elected mayors and governors. Others have been appointed as judges or to cabinet posts. In business, women are officers of many large corporations. In some congregations, women are rabbis, ministers, priests, or bishops.

Military services are now open to women. Women are graduating from West Point, Annapolis, and the Air Force Academy. The ranks of lieutenant, captain, major, colonel, and general are no longer limited to men.

# Activity 3-3:  Advertising Approaches

The following passage contains details about various advertising approaches. Identify as many approaches as you can. Then write them on another sheet of paper.

### Advertising Approaches

Advertisers want to persuade people to buy their products or services. They use many approaches to do this. One approach is to show people how their lives will improve. For example, some trade schools say that if you take their courses, you will get high-paying jobs.

Another approach makes you think everyone will like you if you use a certain product. You will be popular if you use Brand X toothpaste. Advertisers often use this approach to sell their products.

A different approach is to have a celebrity praise the product. Actors and athletes appear on commercials. For instance, advertisers say that you can be a winner like the famous athlete. Just eat their cereal! As consumers, we should all be aware of the approaches advertisers use in their commercials.

# Activity 3-4: Spring

Of all the seasons, spring is the great favorite. Read the following selection to find the different reasons why people like spring. List all the reasons on a separate sheet of paper.

### Spring

Spring is the season that stirs people's hearts, minds, and bodies. Poets say spring is a season of love. Athletes, both professional and amateur, like spring because they can exercise outdoors. Spring also brings the start of baseball season. Astronomers like spring because the sky lights up with stars and planets. In April, stargazers can see Venus, Mercury, Mars, and Saturn.

In spring, gardeners keep their sights closer to the ground. To them, spring means crocuses, tulips, lilacs, and hyacinths. It also means getting the garden ready for planting vegetables. When spring comes, homeowners get out the hammers, saws, paintbrushes, and cleaning supplies for the yearly ritual of spring cleaning. People who live in places where the seasons do not change very much don't know what they're missing.

# Activity 3-5: Henrik Ibsen and Women

Read the following on the writings of Henrik Ibsen. Find the titles of as many of his plays as you can. Write them on a separate sheet of paper.

### Henrik Ibsen and Women

More than 100 years before the feminist movement became widespread in the world, a Norwegian playwright was placing liberated women in his dramas. Henrik Ibsen wrote most of his plays between 1860 and 1890. Many of them featured women who had the courage to assert themselves. Hedda Gabler, the main character in the play of the same name, goes to great lengths to escape her role as an overlooked housewife. Nora, in *A Doll's House,* goes so far as to leave her boring, demanding husband. That just wasn't done a century ago! Mrs. Alving, the heroine of *Ghosts,* shows great courage. She protects and defends a son who has venereal disease. Ibsen also portrayed strong women in two other plays, *Peer Gynt* and *The Pillars of Society.* In doing so, he was far ahead of his time.

# Activity 3-6: Writers' Other Occupations

Read about the occupations of some famous writers. Then write down as many writers, along with their occupations, as you can find. Use a separate sheet of paper.

### Writers' Other Occupations

It is commonly believed that famous literary figures aren't "normal" people. Most of them are believed to be hermit-like, living in small lodgings apart from everyday life. This certainly isn't true of several great American writers of the twentieth century. William Faulkner did many odd jobs for a living, including being a janitor in a boiler factory. The poet Wallace Stevens was a lawyer for an insurance company most of his adult life. Jack London went around the world as a deck hand on a tramp steamer and prospected for gold in Alaska. William Carlos Williams, who wrote both poems and stories, was a medical doctor. Another poet, Merrill Moore, practiced psychiatry in Boston, Massachusetts. A famous philosopher, Eric Hoffer, worked from childhood into his 70s as a longshoreman and had little formal education. For many years, the novelist Toni Morrison worked as a textbook editor for a prominent New York publishing firm. None of these were what some call "ivory tower" types.

# Activity 3-7: Carnivals

As you read the following selection about carnivals, find all the features that make them so popular. List these features on a separate sheet of paper.

### Carnivals

Thousands of people love to go to carnivals. In small and medium-sized communities all over the country, the traveling carnival comes to town every summer. The variety of events and attractions appeals to people of all ages.

Most traveling carnivals have rides set up for those who enjoy thrills and spills. Bumper cars, roller coasters, and tilt-a-whirls are the most common types of rides. Games of chance are also in abundance. You might win a prize by throwing balls, shooting at moving targets, or tossing beanbags. Prizes range from key chains to large stuffed animals.

There are also plenty of things to purchase at carnivals. Aside from souvenirs, people can purchase candy, ice cream, soft drinks, and other snack foods. Cotton candy and taffy apples are carnival favorites.

# Activity 3-8:  *Studying a Foreign Language*

In this selection, you will find many reasons why one should study a foreign language. Find the reasons and write them on a separate sheet of paper.

### Studying a Foreign Language

For quite a while, students did not study foreign languages in school. Recently, that trend has changed. Some states have even made the study of at least one language a high school graduation requirement. People are realizing that foreign languages are important.

The U.S. deals with people in all countries. Government agencies and private companies need people who can speak a foreign language and understand other cultures. If a business student takes a foreign language, he or she may find a better job.

Several foreign countries employ large numbers of Americans and Canadians. Learning the language of these countries is important. In addition, men and women in the U.S. armed services find that knowing another language is very helpful. It helps them make friends and get along better in their tours of duty in other countries.

Also, more people are traveling to countries in Europe, Asia, and South America. Learning to speak and read a foreign language helps them in their travels and increases their enjoyment of the countries. As more people visit and travel around the globe, knowing another language becomes a valuable asset.

# Activity 3-9:  *Shopping Malls*

Many consumers find it more convenient to shop at malls than at city stores. You'll understand why as you read the following passage. Try to find all the details given and write them on a separate sheet of paper.

### Shopping Malls

People used to shop on Main Street. As more people moved to the suburbs, more people began shopping at malls.

Now, millions of people shop in malls all over the country. These malls contain supermarkets and large department stores. Smaller clothing stores cater to almost every possible taste. Gift shops sell a wide variety of merchandise, ranging from inexpensive items to costly ones. Art and music buffs are not forgotten. Art and photography shops are found in great numbers. Record shops are around every corner.

Shopping malls provide other services, too. Health spas offer people a way to tone their bodies. Eating places, ranging from hot dog stands to chic French restaurants, also can be found. No mall is complete without a large cinema complex that features current box office favorites. It is difficult to think of a product or service not found in malls.

# Activity 3-10: Joint Accounts

Many couples have joint bank accounts. Read the next selection and find all the details you can about joint accounts. Write the details you find on a separate sheet of paper.

### Joint Accounts

A husband and wife, or any two or more persons, may have, in addition to their individual insured accounts, a joint account in the same bank. Each account is separately insured to $100,000.

An individual may be co-owner of several insured accounts. Each may be held jointly with a *different* individual, but all joint accounts held by the same combination of individuals are insured only to a maximum of $100,000.

Each depositor's funds are insured to $100,000. That limitation applies to the *total* of the depositor's funds in checking deposits, savings deposits, time certificates of deposit, and all other funds for which an insured bank is liable. There is no way to increase insurance by putting $100,000 into a savings account and $100,000 into a checking account in the same bank. Only $100,000 is insured, not $200,000.

Actual title to each insured account is in the name of the account holder named. So if a depositor sets up a number of accounts under different names, the funds will be insured only as the funds of the true owner.

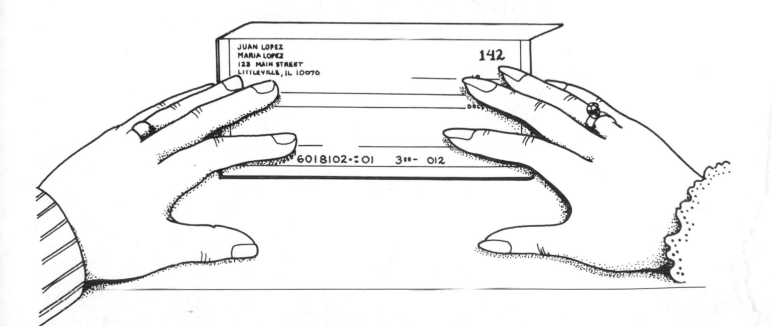

## Activity 3-11:   T-Shirts

As the following selection reveals, T-shirts are more than just a piece of apparel. They also make statements. Find as many details as you can about the different things expressed on T-shirts. Use a separate sheet of paper for your answer.

### T-Shirts

The T-shirt used to be worn only as an undershirt, but today, many people wear T-shirts as separate apparel. T-shirts are now available in different colors and often make a statement. T-shirts express a wearer's likes, beliefs, or commitments. For example, some T-shirts express the wearer's love for a spouse, friend, children, and even cars. One of the common statements found on T-shirts is "I Love _____."

There are also colorful T-shirts that express enthusiastic support for teams in various sports, such as "Go Cubs," "_____ We're Number 1," and "Superbowl Shuffle." Still others make political statements about candidates or issues, such as "Schmaltz for President" or "Stop Nuclear Testing."

T-shirts have also become a major advertising device, extolling the merits of some beverages ("Gotta Have It," for Pepsi), footwear ("Reebok"), and fast foods ("Your Way Right Away," for Burger King). A common subject of T-shirt advertising is the name of a city or state or well-known landmark. These T-shirts are usually purchased by tourists.

Heroes of all kinds—athletes, rock stars, actors and actresses, even criminals—find themselves portrayed on T-shirts. Jokes also have become a popular T-shirt topic, many of which are take-offs on popular causes. "Love an Animal, Hug a Skunk" is an example of such satire.

# *Activity 3-12: Ecology*

The following passage tells about many aspects of the study of ecology. After you have read the selection, identify as many details as you can. List your findings on a separate sheet of paper.

## Ecology

Ecology is the study of the interrelationship of living things to their environment. This includes the study of nonliving things. In recent years, ecology has become a source of considerable interest to many people who live in the United States and Canada. The interest has been increasing because some experts feel that we are destroying the land on which we live. They also feel that we can stop this destruction by being more careful.

Some of the environmental problems are caused by industry. Wastes pollute the waters. Gases and fumes poison the air. When air and water are polluted, then fish, birds, and other living creatures die. Human life is also affected by industrial neglect. People become poisoned in many ways while working in and around unsafe plants and factories. Nuclear power plants have caused great controversy.

People also cause some of the problems. Cars that people drive pour fumes into the air we breathe. Garbage is sometimes dumped into streams that supply drinking water. Forest fires often are caused by careless campers. Beaches and city streets are littered with debris.

Several action groups are now working hard to inform Americans and Canadians about the serious nature of this problem.

# Part 4

# Finding Certain Details

## About This Part...

Up to now you have had choices in the details that you found. First you were asked to find a specific number of details. There were many more in each passage, but you did not have to find all of them. Later, you were asked to find as many details as you could. If you followed the suggestions, you reread the passages carefully to spot the details you missed.

There is another approach for finding details. It is often used in tests given in school. In this task, you are asked to find only certain details. Choosing just any detail won't work. You *must* locate only certain ones, and some of these may not have been of your choosing.

In working on this skill, remember one basic difference between what you do in this book and what you may have done before in other school subjects. For the activities in this book, you will always be told which specific details to look for before you read the passage that contains them. Knowing what you are looking for *beforehand* directs your search for details of importance.

# Here's How to Do It

You will be given a set of details to look for. Then you will be given a short passage to read. Whenever you read a passage, follow these steps.

1. *Read* the assignment very carefully. Know in advance which details you must find.

2. *Read* the passage quickly. Slow down *only* when you spot a detail you need. Disregard sentences that don't contain the details you need.

3. *Continue* to look for key words and phrases. They help you pick the right details and save you time.

4. *Cross-reference* when you have to. This means if you're not sure that a certain detail in the passage is one you're looking for, look elsewhere in the passage.

5. *Write* down each detail as you see it.

6. *Use* a dictionary when you stumble over an unfamiliar word.

7. *Reread* only if you need to.

## *Sample Activity:  Ernest Hemingway*

Look at the following questions carefully. Read the short passage below. Then, pick out only the details you need. Follow the steps listed in "Here's How to Do It." Check your replies with the answers provided.

**a.**  What country was Hemingway from?

**b.**  *A Farewell to Arms* was set in what country?

**c.**  What was the name of the character in *The Old Man and the Sea?*

### Ernest Hemingway

Ernest Hemingway was an American Nobel Prize winner. He described many places and kinds of people in his writing. "The Killers" is set in a small Midwestern town. *A Farewell to Arms* describes Americans fighting in Italy during WWI. *For Whom the Bell Tolls* describes the Spanish Civil War. Big-game hunting in Africa was one of Hemingway's favorite hobbies. This is the topic of "The Short Happy Life of Francis Macomber." Often, Cuba and the Florida Keys are described in his work. Perhaps his best-known work about this area is *The Old Man and the Sea.* It is a novel about a man named Santiago. It tells of his adventures with a big fish in the waters off Cuba. The geographical settings of Hemingway's writing are worldwide.

**Answers:** a) America; b) Italy; c) Santiago

## *How Did You Do?*

In addition to the answers, did you find other details about Hemingway and his writing? However, you *needed* only those three, as you knew when you started. Knowing what to look for in advance can make you a more efficient reader.

The above assignment should have been quite easy for you. Your goal is to be able to pick out and remember many details in much longer passages. Try out this skill on the following passages.

# Activities

Complete as many of the activities as you feel you need in order to become skillful in finding certain details. The activities proceed from easier readings to more difficult ones. Concentrate on the more difficult readings. They offer the toughest challenge. Use the steps outlined in "Here's How to Do It" to complete the activities.

# Activity 4-1:  School Nicknames

Look at the following carefully. Answer them *only* after you have read the passage about school nicknames. Use a separate sheet of paper for your answers.

**a.**  List two nicknames that are named after natural disasters.

**b.**  Name two southern schools that are nicknamed Tigers.

**c.**  Which midwestern teams are called the Tigers?

**d.**  Which school team is called the Golden Bears?

**e.**  What animal name did the Mississippi State sports team select as its nickname?

**f.**  What school team is called the Gators?

**g.**  What school team is known as the Blue Hens?

## School Nicknames

Almost all colleges and universities have nicknames. Usually these nicknames are linked to sports teams. Some of the names are of colors. Two of these are Big Red and the Green Wave. Other nicknames are of natural disasters. Examples are the Hurricanes and the Cyclones. The animal kingdom, however, has provided the most nicknames.

In many parts of the United States, the Tigers are on the loose! In the South, Auburn (Alabama), Clemson (South Carolina), Memphis State (Tennessee), and Louisiana State are all Tigers. In the East, Princeton (New Jersey) and Towson State (Maryland) and in the Midwest, the University of Missouri and Wittenberg (Ohio) also have one thing in common. Their sports teams are also Tigers. Of course, other big cats roam the campuses. The Wildcats, Lions, Cougars, Leopards, and Panthers also are found.

Bears are the source of many popular nicknames, too. There are the Black Bears of the University of Maine, the Polar Bears of Bowdoin College in Maine and of Ohio Northern University. The Bruins are from UCLA, and the Golden Bears are from California. The Bears of Baylor University in Texas, though, are just plain bears.

Smaller animals also find fame. The Bulldogs is the nickname for the sports teams at Yale University, at the University of Georgia, and at Mississippi State University. The University of Michigan sports teams are nicknamed the Wolverines. The University of Florida teams are called the Gators.

The names of birds are not overlooked, either. There are the Blue Hens of the University of Delaware and the Redbirds of Illinois State. Then there are the Eagles of North Texas State. With all the Lions, Tigers, and Bears, could a team called the Ducks stand a fighting chance?

# Activity 4-2: African American Writers

Before you read the selection on these writers, study the following questions. Then try to answer them *only* after you've read the passage. Use a separate sheet of paper for your answers.

**a.** Who was one of the earliest novelists?

**b.** What was done with *The Color Purple*?

**c.** Whose poetry often dealt with young people?

**d.** What common theme did these writers develop?

**e.** Who wrote *Invisible Man*?

## African American Writers

During this century, a growing number of African American writers have gained worldwide fame. Both male and female writers have earned this acclaim for their poems, short stories, and novels about the Black Experience in America. Richard Wright's *Black Boy* and *Native Son* were two of the earliest novels about the poverty and suppression of his people. Ralph Ellison's *Invisible Man* has become a classic story of the second-class status of African Americans of modern times. So has James Baldwin's *Go Tell It on the Mountain*. Gwendolyn Brooks' poetry often describes the plight of blacks, especially those who are young or poor. Two contemporary novelists, Toni Morrison and Alice Walker, have portrayed similar situations in their fiction. Ms. Morrison's novel, *Beloved,* has won a national award, and Ms. Walker's *The Color Purple,* has been made into a famous motion picture. Possibly the best known of this entire group, Langston Hughes, wrote poems, novels, and short stories on the hard times of African Americans. Many black American writers concentrate on the theme of despair and hope that Hughes called "the dream deferred."

# Activity 4-3:  Popular Books of the Past

Before reading the passage about popular books of the past, look at the following first. Answer them *only* after you have read the selection. Use a separate sheet of paper for your answers.

**a.**  Where do today's young people find their books?

**b.**  Who was Edgar Rice Burroughs' great hero?

**c.**  Where was Burroughs' hero found other than in books?

**d.**  Name two of Zane Grey's topics.

**e.**  What kind of heroes were found in most of Grey's war novels?

**f.**  Who was an early writer of books for young women?

**g.**  Name two kinds of adventures Sue Barton had.

## Popular Books of the Past

Books for teenagers have been popular for a long time. Today, paperback editions are produced by the hundreds every month. Young people spend a lot of money on these books. They buy them through school book clubs, bookstores, supermarkets, and other outlets.

Many writers specialize in books for teenagers. They write about sports, adventure, and foreign travel. They also write about mystery, romance, fortune hunting, and other topics that readers enjoy. Three of the first popular authors of these books wrote more than fifty years ago. One was Edgar Rice Burroughs. He was the author of the famous Tarzan series that featured jungle adventures. Burroughs frequently wrote stories in which people from the U.S. and Europe went into the jungle and faced its dangers. Through these books and, later, through early movies, Tarzan, his wife, Jane, and his chimp, Cheetah, became well-known heroes.

Zane Grey was another adventure writer. He wrote many western frontier stories. They involved struggles with nature, Indians, and out-laws. Grey also wrote books about heroes of World War I. His heroes were usually combat pilots fighting in air battles with the enemy over France. Grey's third major topic was sports. He described the exploits of football and baseball players. Most of these characters started out as unknowns but soon rose to stardom. Their teams never lost the big game.

One of the early writers of books mostly for girls was Emily Loring. She wrote a series of novels on the life and adventures of Sue Barton. These books describe the training, achievements, and life of a young nurse. She was a bright and hard-working nurse. In these adventures, Sue saved lives, solved mysteries, and fell in love. Her boyfriends were mostly young, handsome, brilliant doctors. To the end, Sue remained dedicated to her job. Like the main characters in the books by Bur-roughs and Grey, she was a true superstar.

# Activity 4-4: Elected Officials

Study the following carefully. Answer them *only* after you have read the passage about various jobs of elected officials. Use a separate sheet of paper for your answers.

**a.** List three jobs for which people are elected at the local level.

**b.** There are three jobs for which people are elected at the state level. What are they?

**c.** To be elected at the national level, what three jobs can politicians run for?

**d.** What is the title given to the chief law officer at the county level?

**e.** What is the title given to the chief law officer at the state level?

**f.** What is the highest office for most cities or counties called?

**g.** What is the highest state office?

**h.** Name the title of the highest office in the U.S.

**i.** What are lawmakers at local levels called?

## Elected Officials

The kinds of elected jobs people seek depend on the level of government they choose. At *local* levels—city, county, or district—the highest elected office is usually mayor. Another high office is county sheriff. The sheriff is the chief law officer of the county. Most cities and counties also elect a group of lawmakers called commissioners. At least three commissioners are usually elected. Another group elected in most places is the school board. The board rules over funding and operation of all public schools.

Each of the fifty states has its own elections. The governor is the highest state office people vote for. The chief law officer at the state level is the attorney general. Also elected state-wide in many places is the commissioner for state education. He or she enforces state laws and policies affecting public schools. Some states elect their Supreme Court judges or justices. Other states appoint theirs. There are two groups of elected lawmaking bodies in states. These are the Senate and the House of Representatives. Together they are called the Legislature.

At the national level, the American people vote for a president and a vice-president. They are elected every four years. The people of each state vote for the presidential and vice-presidential candidates. The ones who get the most votes receive all of the state's electoral votes. The two persons who receive the most electoral votes are named president and vice-president. Each state also elects two U.S. senators and several representatives to the two federal lawmaking groups. Each state gets two senators. The number of representatives elected depends on each state's population.

# Activity 4-5: *Read This Warranty*

Look at the following limited warranty statement carefully. Answer the questions only after you've read the entire warranty statement. Use a separate sheet of paper for your answers.

a. For how long is this warranty good?

b. If you send the product by mail to be repaired, what must you do?

c. What must you have with you when you bring the product in?

d. Where can you take the product for repairs?

e. Who finally makes the decision as to whether the product should be repaired or replaced without charge?

### Read This Warranty

This Moonburst product is warranted for exactly one year from the date of its purchase. In addition, it is warranted that the original motor of this product will be free from defects in workmanship or materials under normal use for five years. If during this period of normal use the product shows defective operation in materials or workmanship, the purchaser can take the product to the nearest Moonburst Appliance Service Company or authorized independent service station. The purchaser can also send it, postage prepaid. It is recommended that the purchaser retain a copy of the dated sales receipt as verification for in-warranty service. The product will be repaired or replaced without charge at the option of Moonburst Appliance Co.

## Activity 4-6:  *American Writers of the 1920s*

First, look at the following questions listed here. Keep them in mind as you read the selection on the next page about American writers of the 1920s. Then answer the questions on a separate sheet of paper.

a.   What part of the U.S. did Faulkner write about?

b.   About what kind of people did Fitzgerald write?

c.   What was the title of Lewis's novel about a small town?

d.   What city was sometimes the focus of Sandburg's poetry?

e.   Which poet wrote about the South?

f.   Which poet went to Harvard but moved to England?

g.   Can you name one play written by Eugene O'Neill?

h.   Which author and play caused anger among some Americans?

## American Writers of the 1920s

The 1920s was an era of great change in American society. World War I was over. Americans began to learn more about the rest of the world. They started seeing themselves as world leaders. And they set about creating a happier and more comfortable way of life at home.

Many American writers became well-known in the 1920s. Ernest Hemingway was one. William Faulkner, another novelist, described the South in many of his novels. *The Sound and the Fury, As I Lay Dying,* and *Intruder in the Dust* became classics. F. Scott Fitzgerald wrote about the rich in America. His book *The Great Gatsby* has become world famous. Sinclair Lewis wrote about life in the Midwest. His novel *Main Street* was about life in a small Minnesota town, and *Babbitt* told of living in a big and growing midwestern city. The entire world became aware of these writers.

The world also started to take notice of American poets. Robert Frost's poems about New England began to appear in literature. Carl Sandburg wrote poems about the Midwest and Chicago, in particular. Allen Tate, John Crowe Ransom, and Robert Penn Warren wrote about the South. T. S. Eliot, who was born in St. Louis and went to Harvard, wrote some of his early poems in the U.S. before moving to England. In New York, a number of African American poets joined with other authors and artists in a movement called "the Harlem Renaissance." Prominent among the poets were Claude McKay and Countee Cullen.

American playwrights were not ignored. One writer of musicals, George Gershwin, produced works for such shows as *Lady, Be Good!* and *Strike Up the Band.* Eugene O'Neill wrote serious plays on the problems of life in New England. *The Hairy Ape, Desire Under the Elms,* and *Mourning Becomes Electra* are the best known of these. Maxwell Anderson wrote plays on political themes. One of these, *Winterset,* caused a great deal of anger among many Americans. Elmer Rice wrote some unusual plays about his times, among them *Street Scene* and *The Adding Machine.*

Life in America began to change in the 1920s. Writers who described these changes became widely known. Today they are read by students of literature all over the world.

# Activity 4-7:  Natural Foods

The following refer to the natural foods passage. Read them carefully. Answer the questions *only* after you have read the selection. Use a separate sheet of paper for your answers.

**a.**   What popular grain is sold in many natural-food stores and restaurants?

**b.**   What do health-food restaurants add in many of their dishes?

**c.**   What type of butter is sold in many natural-food stores?

**d.**   Some health-food restaurants offer a natural sweetener. Can you name the sweetener?

**e.**   What type of beverages are found in many health-food stores and restaurants?

## Natural Foods

In recent years, many Americans have become food conscious. They choose to eat foods that are good for their health. One result of this concern is the growth of stores and cafés that feature natural foods. Granola has become a very popular grain. It is sold in many forms. Guacamole salads are featured in most health-food restaurants. Some of these restaurants add alfalfa sprouts to many dishes they serve. They also offer brown rice, tofu dishes, and low-fat cottage cheese as a side dish. Salt-free butter is provided in many natural-food restaurants and also can be bought in health-food stores. Pure honey is another popular item found in both natural-food restaurants or stores. It often replaces sugar as a recommended sweetener. Drinks are an important feature of these stores and cafés. But in place of hard liquor or sugar-rich carbonated soft drinks, one finds herbal tea and natural juices such as apple, orange, grape, and grapefruit. Today, millions of people swear by such diets.

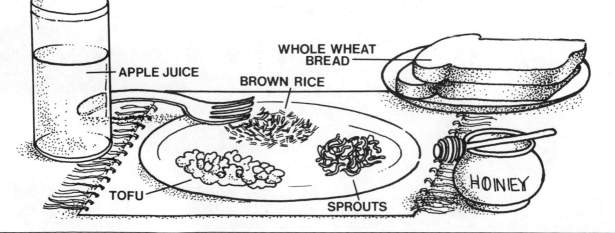

APPLE JUICE  
WHOLE WHEAT BREAD  
BROWN RICE  
TOFU  
SPROUTS  
HONEY

# Activity 4-8:  Brass Rubbings

Study the following questions. Read the passage about brass rubbings. Then, answer the questions on a separate sheet of paper.

a.   In what area of the world is the hobby of brass rubbing practiced by many visitors?

b.   When did laying down brasses come to the East of England?

c.   In which century did brass rubbing become available to common people?

d.   What did some brasses show about the shaving habits of men?

e.   In the Middle Ages, what happened to many wives soon after childbirth?

## Brass Rubbings

Brass rubbing has recently become a hobby that has captured the imaginations of thousands of visitors to the British Isles. It provides a surprisingly easy means of making beautiful wall-hangings, which can look extraordinarily impressive. Brass rubbing also provides visitors with a link with medieval ancestors. It, therefore, brings history to life in a very personal and tangible way.

It was the medieval fashion to lay down brasses to commemorate knights and their ladies. This fashion spread to the East of England from the Continent during the thirteenth century. These engraved plates provided alternative types of memorials. Stone effigies were popular in churches at the time.

At first, only wealthy knights and bishops could afford brasses. However, during the fourteenth century, there was a rise in power of the middle classes. An increasing number of merchants (as well as members of the aristocracy) could afford to commission brasses.

The brass rubbings provide a revealing contemporary record. They reflect the overall appearance of the person commemorated. They show how he or she preferred to dress. They reveal whether it was fashionable to have long hair or short, and even whether it was appropriate to be clean-shaven. Some brasses include very well-defined "five o'clock shadows."

Sometimes inscriptions are carved beneath the brass. These inscriptions provide fascinating information on the typical family histories of the period. Often one finds that a knight had several wives (in succession) and surprisingly large numbers of children. Not all of these children survived childhood. Since midwifery was very crude, many wives died in childbirth.

# Activity 4-9:  France

First, study the following. Then, read the passage about France. Next, use a separate sheet of paper to answer the questions.

**a.**   What is the name of the principal river system of France?

**b.**   What river connects Lake Geneva and the Mediterranean?

**c.**   What major crop is grown in southwest France?

**d.**   Name the mountains that separate France from Italy and Switzerland.

**e.**   What covers nearly one-fourth of France?

**f.**   Why is the country around Paris famous?

**g.**   What English historian described the beauties of France?

## France

Geography favors France in many ways. The country's principal navigable river system, the Seine, is connected by a canal with other rivers. It flows through Paris, one of the greatest inland ports of Europe. Other great rivers have other assets. The Rhone dashes out of Lake Geneva. It rushes to the Mediterranean with too great a drop to be naturally navigable. That same drop, however, makes it ideal for the generation of hydroelectric power. The Dordogne and the Garonne rivers, which join to make the Gironde estuary in southwest France, are also important because some of the most famous vineyards in the world are situated on their banks. The Rhine, to the east, is a French frontier river. Joint exploitation of its resources for navigation and power by France and West Germany is a notable sign of the times.

Two other frontiers are guarded by magnificent mountains. The Alps separate France from Switzerland and Italy. The Pyrenees mark the border with Spain. Mont Blanc, which is the highest mountain in western Europe, is located in France. The dramatic heights of the Alps and the Pyrenees are not typical of French landscape. Instead, the sunny,

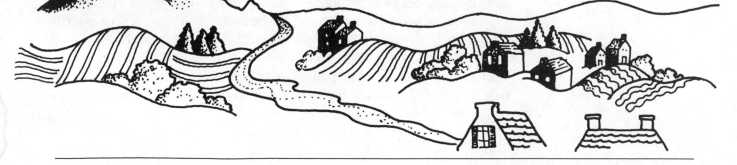

vine-clad hills or the great plains, which are usually framed with forests, are more typical of the French landscape. Nearly a quarter of France is forest. Paris is surrounded by the great forests that were the hunting parks of the French kings: Fontainebleau, Compiégne, Chantilly, Bamvouillet. Each has its great castle in the center of the woods.

The country around Paris is familiar. It probably has been the subject of more great paintings than any other area in the world. Its villages, meadows, groves, and streams have been painted by renowned artists for more than a hundred years. No wonder Macaulay, the English historian, wrote, "...thy cornfields green, and sunny vines, oh pleasant land of France!"

# Activity 4-10:  Propaganda Devices

Before reading the passage about propaganda devices, look at the following . Answer them *only* after you have read the selection. Use a separate sheet of paper for your answers.

a.  If a speaker uses only one side of an argument, what is he or she known as?

b.  What is another name for the "God, mother, and apple pie" approach?

c.  Name the propagandistic technique that uses the "our way of life" approach.

d.  What label is a speaker using if he or she says a local hero would support an idea or cause?

e.  If a speaker labels a person as a "war monger," what technique is he or she using?

f.  Propaganda techniques do not appeal to reason. What do they appeal to?

## Propaganda Devices

A speaker or writer often wishes to convince his or her audience of something. He or she might therefore use propaganda devices. Propaganda devices are techniques or methods used to influence people to think or act in a certain way. One of the most effective techniques is called *card stacking.* It is generally true that there are two sides to any argument, but a card stacker uses only those pieces of evidence that support one side. The propagandist piles them up and uses anything to support his or her argument. He or she totally ignores any evidence that would support the other side.

Another device commonly used is called *glittering generalities.* Glittering generalities are used when a person wishes to appeal to the sentiments of the audience, especially their love of home and country. Some critics call this the "God, mother, and apple pie" approach. Such phrases as "our way of life," "the common man," "the democratic spirit," "freedom-loving Americans," "the spirit of rugged individualism," and many other expressions, are frequently used. There is no appeal to the thinking processes.

Then there is the *testimonial* technique. The speaker chooses a person who is much admired by his or her audience. Sometimes the person is local but more often he or she is a national figure. Names such as Abraham Lincoln, Susan B. Anthony, Dwight Eisenhower, and Martin Luther King, Jr., inspire good feelings in the audience. The speaker then implies that if one of these heroic people were here, that person would do something this way or that way. There is seldom any evidence that these people ever spoke about the particular issue, but the speaker claims he or she knows how these famous people would feel.

Another device commonly used is *name calling*. This device is obvious. The speaker finds out what kinds of people or attitudes the audience doesn't like. Then the speaker calls his or her opponents by those names. The names may be "liberal" or "conservative," "intellectual," "atheist," or "war monger." The idea is to saddle the opponent with one or more of these negative labels. The audience is led to believe that the opponent *is* that kind of person.

There are many other devices that the user of propaganda has at his or her command. Those mentioned above are frequently called upon because they are the most effective. The careful thinker in the audience must be on guard to avoid being influenced by them.

# Activity 4-11:  Prelude to War

First, look at the following carefully. Next, read the passage, Prelude to War. Finally, answer the questions on a separate sheet of paper.

**a.**  Who spoke early about the coming war?

**b.**  What country did Italy attack in 1935?

**c.**  What country did Japan occupy? What name did they give this country?

**d.**  What was the name of the American ship sunk by the Japanese before the war began?

**e.**  Who did the Nazis throw into jail?

**f.**  What country did Germany take over after occupying the Sudetenland?

**g.**  On what date did World War II begin?

## Prelude to War

Long before the outbreak of World War II, a thoughtful person could have figured out that trouble was brewing. The odd thing is, few people spoke openly about the rising, worldwide danger. Winston Churchill was one person who did. But few listened, and no one did anything about it.

The actions of the Italians were a good example. Led by their dictator, Benito Mussolini, they attacked the small, weak country of Ethiopia in 1935. The Ethiopians fought bravely but were no match for the modernized Italian army. Ethiopia was soon conquered. During the thirties, the Italians were also stamping out all opposition in their own country. They enslaved and killed those who opposed them. Then, in 1939, Mussolini sent his armed forces into neighboring Albania, another weak country. The Albanians soon surrendered. Italy was ready for more blood as the big war began.

In the Far East, Japan was showing its desire for power. During the thirties, the Japanese occupied Manchuria. They changed its name to Manchukuo and enslaved its people. They also began a long, bloody war with the Chinese. By 1939, Japan had taken over much of the Chinese mainland. In the Pacific, they had shown hostility on several occasions toward American naval forces. They even sank an American vessel, the *Panay*.

During the entire pre-war period, Germany was the country most watched and feared. Under Adolph Hitler, the Nazis built a mighty war machine. They threw millions of innocent Jews and political opponents into prison camps. Then Germany took over Austria with hardly a shot fired. Soon afterwards, they occupied the Sudetenland—an area that at this time belonged to Czechoslovakia. Then, while the rest of Europe looked on fearfully, they seized the rest of Czechoslovakia. There, they deposed its government. No one tried to stop them. On September 1, 1939, they attacked Poland. World War II began. People finally realized that there were countries determined to conquer the world.

# Activity 4-12:  City Road Signs

Look at the following. Keep them in mind as you read the passage on city road signs. Answer them *only* after you have read the selection. Use a separate sheet of paper for your answers.

**a.**   What road sign advises a driver to change lanes?

**b.**   In some cities, what sign tells drivers *not* to turn after their vehicles stop?

**c.**   Name the road sign that helps drivers get through intersections.

**d.**   What road sign must a driver strictly observe?

**e.**   Who is at fault if an accident involves a pedestrian?

**f.**   What road sign should a driver be alert for when the roads are wet?

## City Road Signs

As young people learn to drive and prepare to take tests to obtain their driver's licenses, they need to anticipate seriously the several demands of driving. One of these is the frequent appearance on city streets of road signs that must be scrupulously observed and obeyed. For example, "Merge" instructs a driver that a particular lane is ending and he or she must move into the specified lane. "No Turn on Red" indicates just what it says: while most cities allow motorists to turn right after they stop, there are some streets on which it would be unsafe to turn. Drivers must observe "Don't Block Intersection" signs that are posted to ensure that turning lanes are free of autos. Displayed in certain park and residential areas are "No Commercial Vehicles" signs, which facilitate passenger cars to move more quickly and safely through such zones. "Pedestrian Crossing" is a sign that must be strictly observed. Accidents involving pedestrians are usually judged as the fault of the driver inasmuch as the driver must keep his or her vehicle under control at all times. Citations are always given to drivers who violate the "No Parking Fire Lane" sign. These parking areas belong exclusively to the Fire Department, twenty-four hours a day. Although the message "Slippery When Wet" is pretty obvious, it needs to be carefully noted, particularly since many accidents occur when drivers ignore the rain, snow, or ice covering certain streets.

# Establishing Sequence

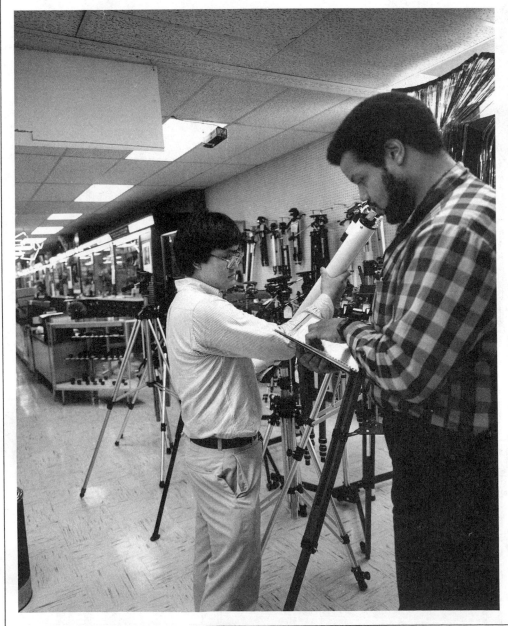

# Part 5

# The Importance of Sequence

## About This Part...

In Section One, you practiced finding details in special and regular formats. Now you will work on establishing the order, or sequence, of details in the materials you read.

As a reader, you must follow a certain sequence to understand main ideas. You must be able to 1) identify the details; 2) place these details in their *proper order* so you can understand the main ideas.

Like other things you read, comic strips have a main idea. Comics communicate this main idea through a *sequence of ideas* or events that are arranged in a certain order. The humor of the comic often depends on our perceiving this order and understanding these relationships.

In this series of exercises with comic strips, you will get practice in placing elements in logical order. As you'll see, the frames of a comic strip, like the ideas in a paragraph, must be in proper logical order if their main idea is to be conveyed.

**Here's How to Do It**

1. *Study* the content of each comic frame. *Find* the details in each.

2. *Think* about the relationships of ideas in the comic strip as a whole.

3. *Decide* on the logical order of details to convey the main idea.

4. *Renumber* the frames of the comic in the new, logical order.

## Sample Activity: The Laundry Basket

The comic strip below is in mixed-up order. Its frame numbers are incorrect.
Use the steps listed in "Here's How to Do It" to place the frames in logical order.

### The Laundry Basket

**Answer:** The correct order of frames is 4, 1, 3, and 2.

## How Did You Do?

Did you see that when the frames of the comic strip are out of order, they don't make much sense? When the frames are in the correct sequence, the dog tells us that the basket is a perfect place to sleep—provided that he checks once in a while to see whether anyone misses him.

# Activities

In the following activities, you will work with more comics in mixed-up order. Find the correct sequence of frames for each comic. Use the steps listed in "Here's How to Do It."

## Activity 5-1:  Perfect Spot

Study the mixed-up comic strip shown below. Find the correct sequence of frames. Write your answer on a separate sheet of paper.

**Perfect Spot**

Frame 1        Frame 2        Frame 3

## Activity 5-2:  The Sale

Study the mixed-up comic strip shown below. Find the correct sequence of frames. Write your answer on a separate sheet of paper.

**The Sale**

Frame 1        Frame 2

Frame 3        Frame 4

# *Activity 5-3: Stranded*

Study the mixed-up comic strip shown below. Find the correct sequence of frames. Write your answer on a separate sheet of paper.

**Stranded**

**Frame 1**

**Frame 2**

**Frame 3**

**Frame 4**

**Frame 5**

# Part 6
# Following Directions

## About This Part...

Following directions is one area of everyday living in which sequence is very important. This Part will help you to understand the importance of following directions properly.

Directions may be given orally, such as when someone tells you how to get to a certain location. Directions also are frequently found in print, such as in an instruction sheet on how to build a bookcase.

Usually, directions in print appear in two forms. Directions can be given step by step in a list. This form usually is easier to follow. Directions also can appear in paragraph form. This type of directions can be harder to read because you have to search to find the details. Whatever form directions take, they are given in a certain order, or sequence. You will work with both forms of directions.

Consider the following when reading a set of directions.

1. The details in a set of directions are important.

2. The proper order of the steps is also important.

**Here's How to Do It**

The following steps will help you understand written directions.

1.  *Read* each step in the directions. Pay close attention to each detail.
2.  *Place* the directions in proper order. Pay close attention to sequence words such as first, last, before, after, then, etc.
3.  *Follow* each direction in detail and in order. Do not skip any step.
4.  *Review* your work to make sure the directions are in the right order.

## Sample Activity: Making Soup

The following directions for making soup are out of order. Place them in the correct sequence.

a.  Open can and empty contents into saucepan.

b.  Heat until soup simmers.

c.  Place over low heat, stirring occasionally.

d.  Mix in one can of water.

**Answer:** The correct order is a, d, c, and b.

## How Did You Do?

Did you notice that when the directions are out of order, the recipe does not make sense? When placing directions in proper order, ask yourself which detail should come first and which should follow.

# Activities

The following activities deal with different types of following directions. You will be told what to do for each activity. Use the general guidelines above in "Here's How to Do It."

## Activity 6-1: Tuna Salad

The list of steps below is from a recipe for tuna salad. The directions are listed in incorrect order. Read all the directions; then place them in correct order. Write your answers on a separate sheet of paper.

a.  Place the drained tuna in a small mixing bowl and break into pieces with a fork.
b.  Finally, season with salt and pepper to taste.

**c.** First, open one 6½-ounce can of light tuna.

**d.** Chill the tuna salad before serving.

**e.** Drain the liquid (water or oil) from the opened can of tuna.

**f.** Mix ¼ cup of mayonnaise, ½ tablespoon of lemon juice, and 1 tablespoon of sweet relish before adding to the tuna.

**Answer:** The correct order is c, e, a, f, b, and d.

# Activity 6-2:  The Right Road

Look at the illustrations below. Then, read the directions in the paragraph.  Decide which illustration shows the path that the person following the directions should take. Write down your answer on a separate sheet of paper.

"You're here at the gas station on Willow Road. Go east down Oak Street, to the second traffic light. Turn left, go one block to Dogwood, turn right, and the grocery store is on the left."

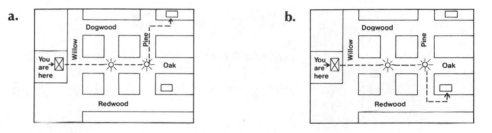

# Activity 6-3:  Parking a Car

The steps listed below give directions for parallel parking. The steps are listed in mixed-up order. Place the steps in correct order. Write your answer on a separate sheet of paper.

**a.** Continue backing up until the front seat of your vehicle is opposite the rear bumper of the vehicle ahead. Then straighten your wheels and keep backing up straight.

**b.** When you are sure your front bumper can clear the car in front of you, turn your wheels sharply to the left. Back up slowly toward the vehicle behind you without touching it. If you have followed the above steps, your vehicle should be about six inches from the curb.

**c.** Straighten the front wheels of the vehicle you are driving. Center the vehicle in the parking space. Set the parking brake. Put the shift lever of the vehicle into "Park."

**d.** Check to make sure that you will not interfere with oncoming traffic. Then turn the wheels of your vehicle all the way to the right. Back up your vehicle slowly toward the curb.

**e.** Choose a parking space large enough for the vehicle you are driving. Signal that you wish to stop. Then pull up even with the vehicle or parking space immediately ahead of you. Your vehicle should be two feet away from the other vehicle.

# Part 7

# Finding Order in Prose Passages

## About This Part...

The word *prose* means the language that people use in ordinary writing and speaking. It usually contains details. In this Part, you will be asked to establish the order of details as they appear in prose passages.

These activities are called *directed reading.* First, you are told your task. Then, you are asked to read the passage. In this way, you read with a definite purpose in mind. The goal is to look for certain details as they *relate* to certain others.

You will be looking for cause-and-effect relationships. The facts, details, items, or events will exist individually. However, their relationships to those that precede and those that follow will also be important to you as you search for meaning in the passage. Knowing the order of the details helps you to understand the meaning.

# Here's How to Do It

As you complete the activities, follow these steps.

1. *Read* the questions carefully.

2. *Glance* through or scan the paragraph. Scanning the passage may help you spot some of the details you are looking for.

3. *Read* the paragraph and note what happens in each sentence.

4. *Find* the details in the paragraph and note the ways the details affect one another.

5. *Think* about the logical order of the details, items, events, etc.

6. *Answer* the questions on a separate sheet of paper.

## Sample Activity:  Hot Air Balloons

Read the following questions. Then, read the passage that follows. Finally, answer the questions on a separate sheet of paper. Use the steps given in "Here's How to Do It."

a. What is the first step in getting a hot air balloon inflated?

b. What kinds of burners are used to finish inflating the balloon once it is just about filled with air?

c. What should be adjusted to cause the balloon to go up and down?

d. What happens to the balloon once it is in the air?

### Hot Air Balloons

Have you ever seen a brightly colored hot air balloon flying over your town? Do you know how the balloon gets into the air? First, air is blown into the mouth of the balloon. Usually, this is done through the use of a power fan. When the balloon is just about filled with air, gas burners finish inflating it. The balloon is now ready for flight. The balloon can go up or down by turning the blast valve on the propane burner. Once in the air, the balloon floats along with the course of the wind. While in flight, the balloon uses over twelve gallons of propane gas per hour. This is enough gas to heat ten houses.

**Answers:** a. Air is blown into the mouth of the balloon. b. Gas burners are used to finish inflating the balloon. c. The blast valve should be adjusted. d. The balloon floats along with the wind.

## *How Did You Do?*

You probably noticed that there was a definite order, or sequence, of events in the passage. In addition, you probably located several cause-and-effect relationships. For example, by adjusting the blast valve on the propane burner (the cause), the balloon can be made to rise or descend (the effect).

# Activities

Complete the activities by following the steps outlined in "Here's How to Do It." Remember to read the questions *first*. This way, you will know what you are looking for. The major purpose of these activities is finding and relating the elements to one another.

## *Activity 7-1:   Pest Poisons*

Look at the following questions. Answer the questions after you read the passages. Write your answers on a separate sheet of paper. Don't forget to follow the steps outlined in "Here's How to Do It."

a.  What are some examples of pest poisons?

b.  What safety precaution should you take before using any pest poison?

c.  What should you do if a pest poison is swallowed accidentally by someone?

d.  When you have finished using a pest poison, what steps should be taken to store the remainder safely?

### Pest Poisons

Pest poisons are used today to eliminate bugs and rats; they are also used extensively to kill weeds. When used, these poisons must be handled very carefully because they can be absorbed into the body through the skin. Before using any pest poison, make certain that your skin is completely covered. Should a pest poison be spilled, sprayed, or dusted onto either the skin or clothing, wash it off at once. If a pest poison should be swallowed accidentally, call a poison center or get medical care immediately. When you have finished using any poison, make sure that it is labeled POISON and stored safely. Since small children typically are not readers and certainly don't have a mature understanding of danger, it is best to store all poisons out of their reach.

## Activity 7-2:  The 65 Percent Solution

Study the following questions before you read the passage. Using the steps listed in "Here's How to Do It," answer the questions on a separate sheet of paper.

**a.** What percentage of your body is water?

**b.** What probably occurs after a person goes without water for longer than a week?

**c.** What role does water play in the processing of food in the body?

**d.** How much water should a person drink each day?

### The 65 Percent Solution

The human body is about 65 percent water. Life depends on water intake. You get water by drinking fluids. You also get some water from foods. You can stay alive for quite a while without eating, but the body can live only for about a week without water. Water is required for processing food. It works with chemicals in your body to change food into energy. Water also plays a role in getting the waste out of your body. This is why you should drink many glasses of water each day.

## Activity 7-3:  Sky Diving

Look at the following questions carefully. Then, read the passage. Finally, answer the questions on a separate sheet of paper. Follow the steps given in "Here's How to Do It."

**a.** What is the first thing one should learn about sky diving?

**b.** How is the arch correctly done?

**c.** What do beginners do before practicing the "Go" position?

**d.** What are some of the things a sky diver needs to learn about chutes?

**e.** How would you probably feel as a first-time jumper?

### Sky Diving

Have you ever thought about sky diving? Thousands of people learn to sky dive each year. The first thing to learn is proper touchdown techniques. That means learning how to fall properly, starting from a four-foot platform. Next, you must learn the arch. This is the proper position for leaving the plane. To do the arch correctly, you must place your weight on your stomach rather than on your back. After examining the airplane to be used for the jump, beginners practice getting into the "Go" position. This is a point at which people sometimes think about whether or not they really want to sky dive. As they step out onto the wheel and hang from the wing strut, the thought of letting go seems scary to the first-time jumper. There's also a lot of information that must be learned about chutes. For example, it's important to learn how to tell if a chute is good or bad, and how to steer the chute. You also must know what to do if a chute emergency occurs. Finally, the sky diver must learn how to overcome the fear that almost always comes with a first jump.

# Activity 7-4:  Amelia Earhart's Last Flight

Read the questions below. Then, read the passage. Finally, answer the questions on a separate sheet of paper. Use the steps listed in "Here's How to Do It."

**a.**  What record did Amelia Earhart set during the twentieth century?

**b.**  What record was she attempting to set in July, 1937?

**c.**  What flight plan did Earhart and her navigator have in mind after leaving New Guinea?

**d.**  What evidence is there that the Lockheed 10E might have run out of fuel?

**e.**  What was the last known radio contact with Earhart's doomed flight?

## Amelia Earhart's Last Flight

Today we refer to Amelia Earhart as a famous aviator of the twentieth century. After all, she did set a record as the first woman to pilot an airplane across the Atlantic Ocean. And, in July of 1937, at the age of thirty-nine, Earhart was attempting to set another record; she and her navigator were on their final leg of flying around the world. After leaving Lae, New Guinea, in their Lockheed 10E, the flight ran into trouble. The site of their next landing was to be Howland Island. About twenty hours after leaving New Guinea, Earhart radioed a ship moored near the island and said that she should be close to the island but couldn't see it. She also said that her fuel was down to thirty minutes. That was the last time that she made radio contact with anyone. More than half a century later, theories still abound about what happened to Amelia Earhart on her last flight.

# Activity 7-5: *Popcorn*

Look carefully at the following questions. Then, read the passage below. Using the steps given in "Here's How to Do It," answer the questions on a separate sheet of paper.

**a.** What facts about the history of popcorn cause people to conclude that popcorn has been popular for a very long time?

**b.** When archeologists discovered corn in North American caves, they determined that it had been popped about how long ago?

**c.** What are some different ways that popcorn has been served or used across history?

**d.** What kind of comments might one hear about popcorn today when entering a movie theater?

**e.** Why is popcorn considered to be a good choice when eaten as a snack?

## Popcorn

Throughout history people from around the world have enjoyed eating popcorn. It's been popular since long before history was recorded. Very old popcorn has been found in North and South America. For example, archeologists discovered corn in North American caves that had been popped more than 5,000 years ago. When the early European settlers arrived in North America, the American Indians gave them gifts, including popcorn. During that same period, popcorn was sometimes eaten as a breakfast dish and served as a soup at other meals.

Today, popcorn is more popular than ever in the United States. It has been associated with movie theaters during this century. As one enters a theater, it is quite common to hear the phrase, "Let's get some popcorn and something to drink." Typically, the popcorn purchased at a theater is served in different sizes: small, medium, or large. And one can order popcorn with or without melted butter. Popcorn is also popped at home and is considered a nourishing snack. More recently, popcorn is receiving recognition for being low in calories when served plain. Those who are less conscious of calories still enjoy making other delights with popcorn. For example, a favorite treat that has spanned the years is Molasses Popcorn Balls. As we think about the future, there's little doubt that popcorn will continue to have a special place in the American diet.

## *Activity 7-6: Chopsticks*

Study the following questions. Answer them only after you have read the following passage. Use a separate sheet of paper for your answers. Follow the steps outlined in "Here's How to Do It."

**a.** Which country in the world is considered to have the oldest continuing civilization?

**b.** How are chopsticks like pincers?

**c.** What are the three basic steps in using chopsticks?

**d.** Which of the two chopsticks remains stationary during use?

**e.** Which of the two chopsticks is held as you would hold a pencil during use?

### Chopsticks

Since its history began around 1500 B.C., China is considered to have the oldest continuing civilization in the world. Long ago in China, civilized people began to eat with chopsticks rather than with their fingers. Today, many other people around the world enjoy the challenge of eating with chopsticks, which are used like pincers. By exercising a little patience and following a few simple steps, this form of eating can be mastered in a short time. First, tuck one chopstick between the end of the thumb and the forefinger; hold it as you would a pencil. Finally, holding the first chopstick in its original position, move the second one up and down to pick up pieces of food.

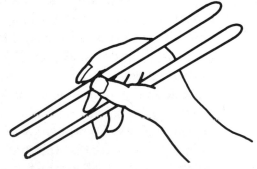

# Activity 7-7: The Moon

Read the questions below. Then, read the passage about the moon.
Answer the questions on a separate sheet of paper.

**a.**   The moon has been compared to many things in early myths. What are some of them?

**b.**   When were telescopes invented?

**c.**   What effect did the invention of the telescope have on the myths about the moon?

**d.**   What role did the moon play in early space exploration?

**e.**   What part of the moon had never been seen before space exploration?

**f.**   Which country was the first to take pictures of the moon's dark side?

**g.**   Who was the first person to walk on the surface of the moon?

**h.**   If you were Neil Armstrong, how would you have felt when walking on the moon?

## The Moon

The moon has been a symbol for mystery and romance for thousands of years. It has been compared to a pearl, to green cheese, and to a lamp. In Oriental legend, it was thought of as a garden with a princess and a rabbit. American children still look for the man in the moon's face. Since the invention of telescopes around 1600, these myths were found to be false. The moon was the target of many early space exploration efforts. In 1961 a Soviet Union satellite took the first pictures of the dark side of the moon, which no one had ever seen. In 1964 a United States capsule took close-up pictures of the surface. On July 20, 1969, Neil Armstrong was the first man to walk on the moon. The moon is still used in songs and poems, but knowing there are footprints on its surface gives them a new meaning.

## Activity 7-8:  Marie Curie (1867-1934)

First, read the questions below. Then, read the passage. Finally, answer the questions on a separate sheet of paper.

**a.**  What caused Marie Sklodowska to leave her homeland of Poland to pursue a higher education?

**b.**  What dream did Marie have for continuing her studies after finishing high school?

**c.**  What two elements did Marie Curie and her husband discover?

**d.**  What kind of recognition did Marie Curie receive for her work as a French chemist?

**e.**  What are some benefits that we have today because of Marie Curie's work as a scientist?

**f.**  What caused Marie Curie's death in 1934?

### Marie Curie (1867-1934)

Marie Sklodowska was born in Poland in 1867. By the age of fifteen, she had finished high school with the highest possible honor. She was encouraged by her family to pursue a higher education, even though at that time only men had such opportunities. Her father realized the extent of her brilliance and offered to help her leave the country to continue her education. Eventually, her dream of going to the Sorbonne, the world-famous university in Paris, France, was realized. In 1895, she married a French research scientist, Pierre Curie, and convinced him to share her work. Together they discovered two new elements: polonium and radium. She was the first major female scientist recognized in modern times. She also won the Nobel Prize in two different sciences: physics and chemistry. Today, benefits such as radiation treatment and X rays are possible because of her life's work. In 1934, she died, the victim of the radium that had been so much a part of her work.

# Part 8

# Multi-Paragraph Jumbled Sequences

## About This Part...

When you read, you notice that the details in the story or the passage are placed in a certain order. These details follow the development of the main idea. If they are out of sequence, the main idea could be misunderstood or lost.

In this Part, you will be asked to reorder jumbled sequences of events in passages with more than one paragraph. You will know the events, or details, ahead of time. This is another example of directed reading. That is, you are reading with a purpose. The sentences you will place in proper order are not worded exactly the same as they appear in the passages. Some have been reworded or paraphrased. That is, closely related details have been combined.

**Here's How to Do It**

Follow this set of steps to complete the activities.

1.  *Study* the details that appear before each passage.
2.  *Glance* through or scan the passage rapidly. Scanning the passage may help you spot some of the details you are looking for.
3.  *Read* the passage. Note what happens in each paragraph.
4.  *Arrange* the details in the same order that they appear in the passage.

## Sample Activity: *Pompeii*

The following details have been pulled from the passage about Pompeii. Study the details, then read the passage. On a separate sheet of paper, arrange the details in the order in which they appear in the selection. Follow the steps outlined in "Here's How to Do It."

a.  Sulfur fumes soon permeated the city.
b.  A shower of volcanic ash covered the street.
c.  In 1748, a peasant discovered a buried wall of Pompeii.
d.  The volcano called Mount Vesuvius exploded.
e.  Much of Pompeii has been uncovered and restored.

### Pompeii

The date was August 24, 79 A.D. The people in the Roman town of Pompeii were going about their daily lives. They were about to suffer a tragedy that would long be remembered. All at once day became night with a giant blast from the top of the volcano, Mount Vesuvius. When the first shower of ash covered the streets, people ran to their homes to be safe. But the explosions got worse. Volcanic stones fell down on the homes. The sky seemed to be on fire.

The people realized their homes were not safe. They loaded carts and hurried to leave the city. Before long, the streets were full. People breathed air filled with toxic sulfur fumes, which soon spread through the city. Buildings fell as the heavy stones crashed down. The people were doomed. Soon Pompeii was buried under lava.

For hundreds of years Pompeii lay buried. Then in 1748 a peasant found a buried wall and told the Italian government. Today, much of the lost city has been uncovered and restored.

If you visit Pompeii, you'll be able to see how life was on the town's last day. The ash that covered the victims hardened. Features of the victims and the shape of their clothes were saved. Many coins were left as people tried to flee the city. Wine jugs and loaves of bread were found just as they had been left in the wine shops and bakery ovens.

## How Did You Do?

Did you notice that the details are not worded exactly the same as they appear in the passage? Were the details harder to find because they have been reworded? Keep the details in mind as you read the passage. When you spot a detail, remember where it is located so you can place it in its proper order.

# Activities

Reordering the jumbled sequence of events is not hard if you read the selections carefully. As you read, keep in mind the order of events as they happen. Follow the steps provided for you in "Here's How to Do It."

## Activity 8-1:  Desert Travel

Study the following details pulled from the passage about desert travel. Then, read the selection. Using the steps listed in "Here's How to Do It," arrange the details in the order in which they occur. Use a separate sheet of paper for your answer.

**a.** When camels get angry, they can be dangerous.

**b.** Some places in today's deserts can best be reached by camel.

**c.** The hump contains fat rather than water.

**d.** Camels have a way of storing water in their bodies.

**e.** They can go for long periods of time without drinking water.

### Desert Travel

To cross most deserts today, one can travel by car, bus, or plane. But four thousand years ago, the only way to make such a trip was to travel by camel. There are still some places in today's deserts that can best be reached by camel. This is because the camel's body is ideal for enduring the heat and sand of the desert.

Camels can go for long periods of time without drinking water. Depending on how bad the weather is, they can go without drinking water for a week to six months. Camels can lose as much as 40 percent of their body weight. They have a system built into their bodies for storing water. Compared to other large pack animals such as oxen or donkeys, camels use water slowly and sweat less. They conserve the water in their bodies, but they do not store an extra supply in their hump, or humps, as most people think. Actually, the hump contains fat rather than water. Another way camels conserve water is through body temperature control. A camel's body temperature rises with the local temperature. Camels also know how to cool themselves on hot days and warm themselves when the weather is cold. They turn their bodies to avoid as much sunlight as possible or to take advantage of the sun's warmth.

One word of warning should you travel the desert by camel. Keep in mind that camels are known for their nasty tempers. Angry camels are often dangerous camels. They even hold grudges!

# Activity 8-2:  Treasure Hunting

The following details have been pulled from the passage about treasure hunting. Study them, then read the selection. On a separate sheet of paper, arrange the details in the order in which they appear in the passage. Don't forget to follow the steps given in "Here's How to Do It."

**a.**   Burt Webber found the sailing vessel *Conception.*

**b.**   Sir William Phips found the sailing vessel *Conception.*

**c.**   The *Conception* remained buried at the bottom of the sea for almost 300 years.

**d.**   In 1641, the *Conception* sank after hitting a coral reef in the Caribbean Sea.

**e.**   Burt Webber shared his findings.

### Treasure Hunting

Have you ever considered treasure hunting as an occupation? How would you like to make the find of the century?

Centuries ago the Spanish galleon *Conception* sank after it hit a coral reef in the Caribbean Sea. When the sailing vessel sank in 1641, it was loaded with tons of gold and silver.

Forty years after the *Conception* went down, it was found by Sir William Phips. He brought up about thirty-two tons of silver and returned to England with his find. In the meantime, his ship's log was somehow mislaid, so Sir William was never able to find the vessel again. The *Conception* remained buried at the bottom of the sea for almost three hundred years.

On November 28, 1978, Burt Webber found the *Conception* after searching with the help of modern equipment. The "pieces of eight" he found were more than three hundred years old and were worth a fortune. Upon further investigation, Webber and his crew discovered that the ship was completely disintegrated and the treasure, worth al least $40 million, was scattered throughout the reefs.

Even though Burt Webber had to share this discovery with his nine-man crew and the Dominican Republic, he certainly was well paid for his efforts. Also, he had lots of fun during the treasure hunt.

# Activity 8-3: Extinct Birds

First, look at the details below. Then, read the selection on extinct birds. Using the steps given in "Here's How to Do It," arrange the details in the order in which they appear. Write your answers on a separate sheet of paper

**a.** The Carolina parakeet was hunted for its feathers.

**b.** Often conservation measures are lax.

**c.** Inquire about what's being done in your area to protect endangered species of birds.

**d.** During World War II, rodents were responsible for killing the flightless rail in Norway.

**e.** Man is guilty for slaughtering birds, too. The passenger pigeon is an example.

**f.** Many birds are threatened as the world becomes more industrialized.

## Extinct Birds

Many birds that once flew in large numbers have vanished completely. Why have so many birds become extinct?

Some birds were killed by animals searching for food. For example, during World War II, the rodents that came to Norway on ships completely destroyed the flightless rail in two years. Sometimes, the vegetation birds need to survive has been destroyed. Rabbits, for example, destroyed vegetation that, in turn, caused the deaths of three-fifths of the birds on an island in the Pacific Ocean. Man, too, is guilty of killing birds. By 1914, the passenger pigeon was extinct even though there had been millions of them in the 1800s. The Carolina parakeet was last seen in 1920 after it had been named a garden pest and hunted for its pretty feathers. Many other birds have been lost forever.

Today, birds are threatened as human populations increase and as the world becomes more industrialized. Factors responsible for this problem include land clearing, swamp draining, contagious bird diseases, and wars. Endangered birds now are somewhat protected from hunters, but conservation measures are sometimes lax. Unless we change our ways, we'll find that endangered birds—such as the whooping crane, the ivory-billed woodpecker, and the California condor—will disappear.

What can you do to help these endangered birds? Begin by inquiring about what's being done in your area to protect endangered species of birds. Then help others become more aware of the problems related to the extinction of birds.

# Activity 8-4: Pyramids

The following details have been pulled from the passage about pyramids. Study the details, then read the passage. On a separate sheet of paper, arrange the details in the order in which they appear in the selection. Follow the steps listed in "Here's How to Do It."

**a.** Flat-topped temples called ziggurats were not as large as the Great Pyramid.

**b.** The most impressive pyramids in ancient Egypt were built about 2600-2100 B.C.

**c.** Pyramids were used by many ancient cultures.

**d.** One example of a ziggurat is thought to be the Tower of Babel.

**e.** The people of the New World also built pyramids.

**f.** You probably are familiar with the pyramids from ancient Egypt.

### Pyramids

Many societies throughout history have shown a passion for pyramids. These structures generally slope from a square base up to a narrow top. They may have either a flat top or a point. This type of building was used by many ancient cultures.

Everyone is familiar with the pyramids in ancient Egypt. The most impressive of these were built as royal tombs and temples around 2600-2100 B.C. The Great Pyramid is the largest, covering thirteen acres.

Another type of pyramid was built in what is now Iraq. These flat-topped temples were not as large as the Great Pyramid. One is thought to have been the Tower of Babel. This type of pyramid was called a *ziggurat*.

The New World also had its share of pyramids. The Maya in Central America built many of them, sometime around 300 B.C. to 800 A.D. Later, the Aztecs continued building temples that were much the same. Some scientists think there may have been 100,000 pyramids in Mexico alone.

# Activity 8-5:   Still Our Best Friend

Carefully study the following details before reading the selection. Then, arrange the details in the order in which they occur. Use a separate sheet of paper for your answers. Follow the steps outlined in "Here's How to Do It."

**a.**   More than forty million dogs eat almost $2 billion worth of food each year.

**b.**   Friendship between people and dogs goes as far back as 50,000 years ago.

**c.**   Canine companions are considered excellent watchdogs.

**d.**   Hunters probably depended on the dog's keen senses to locate small animals for food.

**e.**   In some countries, dogs join their masters at restaurants.

**f.**   Dogs have learned to depend more and more on people for food.

## Still Our Best Friend

Some things haven't changed much over thousands of years. This is the case with the seemingly inborn sense of friendship between people and dogs.

How long has this friendship between people and dogs existed? From studying the cave drawings and paintings of prehistoric times, clear evidence is found. Hunters and their dogs are pictured together as far back as 50,000 years ago! The hunter-dog partnership in all likelihood served both well. Hunters probably depended on the dogs' keen senses of smell and hearing to locate small animals for food, as well as to warn of dangerous animals that approached camps at night. While the dogs were able to hunt for their own food, through the ages they probably learned to depend more and more on people for food. Dogs soon were considered as family members.

Today, men and women still consider their canine companions excellent watchdogs. This holds true for the less-than-three-pound Yorkshire terrier and the more-than-ninety-pound German shepherd. Dogs serve people in other ways. Dalmatians are often seen on fire trucks and seeing-eye dogs walk with the blind. Additionally, dogs act as shepherds, hunters, retrievers, and pets.

Around the world the dog is a favorite friend and pet. In some countries, such as France, it is not an uncommon sight for the family dog to join the family at restaurant dinner tables. In the United States, more than forty million dogs enjoy almost $2 billion worth of food each year. Actually, far more money is spent each year on dog food than on baby food in America. If money spent on dogs is any indication of their worth, there is little doubt that they are highly valued.

## *Activity 8-6:  Dolphins*

The following details have been pulled from the passage, Dolphins. Study them, then read the selection. Using the steps listed in "Here's How to Do It," arrange the details in the proper sequence. Write your answers on a separate sheet of paper.

**a.**   Dolphins are helpless at birth.

**b.**   Sometimes young dolphins are killed by boat propellers.

**c.**   Dolphins often play in the waves in groups of four or more.

**d.**   A dolphin uses its ears to find food.

**e.**   The dolphin is able and ready to protect its young.

**f.**   Dolphins must breathe air at least every five minutes.

**g.**   Dolphins have a few enemies.

**h.**   Dolphins live half as long as humans.

### Dolphins

Dolphins, small relatives of the whale, have much in common with humans. For one thing, both are intelligent mammals. Like human babies, dolphins are helpless at birth. But, unlike humans, dolphins need the care of their mothers for only a couple of years. Although dolphins reach adulthood much sooner than human beings, they live only half as long.

While the dolphin doesn't have many enemies, there are a few. The dolphin's enemies are the killer whale, some sharks, parasites, and some people. Unlike humans, dolphins aren't aggressive toward their own kind. They also are ready and able to protect their young. For example, to protect their young from approaching sharks, dolphins often encircle their babies and form a protective barrier.

In some cases, people have hurt dolphins without realizing it. Sometimes inexperienced young dolphins are killed by boat propellers. Many dolphins drown in fishermen's nets because of a lack of air. Dolphins must breathe air at least every five minutes for survival. In days gone by, so much concern was directed toward not harming the dolphin that superstitious sailors said bad luck would come to anyone who hurt one of these sea creatures.

Dolphins and people see about the same distance under water—

approximately 100 feet. For humans, sight is probably the most important sense. Dolphins, however, "see" better with their ears. The dolphin has a sonar-like process to home in on objects of interest. Many of these objects represent food. The process is especially interesting in that it involves the dolphin receiving and interpreting water-borne vibrations. Sometimes the objects may be as far away as one-quarter mile!

Dolphins have always been known for their friendliness toward humans and for taking from nature only that which is required for their well-being. It's not uncommon to hear an account of a dolphin helping a drowning swimmer. They love to swim beside boats and ships in the ocean. Dolphins have been known to escort ocean vessels for miles. Dolphins are quite the clowns, often entertaining spectators with their leaping tricks. They enjoy surfing and sculling. Because of dolphins' powerful tails, they can stand almost two-thirds of their body length out of the water for seconds at a time. Usually, dolphins frolic in the waves in groups of four or more. There's little question about their ability to relax and play.

# Activity 8-7: Bicycles

Look at the details below. Then, read the selection on bicycles. Arrange the details in the order in which they appear. Write your answers on a separate sheet of paper. Follow the steps outlined in "Here's How to Do It."

a. Bicycling doesn't create any pollution.

b. The world's best cyclists compete in the famous bicycle race, *Le Tour de France*

c. In 1839, a blacksmith invented a different kind of bicycle.

d. When purchasing a bicycle, pay special attention to the condition of the brakes.

e. The early bicycle had to be propelled by the rider's feet pushing along the ground.

f. The frame of the bike should be strong enough to hold the rider's weight.

## Bicycles

The concept of a bicycle dates back to ancient times in Babylon, Egypt, and Pompeii. To move the early bicycle, a rider had to push his or her feet against the ground. Then, in 1839, a Scottish blacksmith named

Kirkpatrick Macmillan invented the first bicycle that riders could propel without touching their feet to the ground.

Today, bicycling is popular in many countries. One reason for this is that it is a good form of exercise. It is also a good means of transportation, for it requires no fuel and, therefore, doesn't create any pollution. Of course, if you need to get somewhere in a hurry, you'll need to allow plenty of time unless you're unusually fast at cycling.

Cycling also is considered a sport, especially in Europe where the famous bicyle race, the *Tour de France*, takes place. There, the world's best cyclists meet the challenge of a 3,000-mile road course.

If you'd like to get into cycling and need to buy a bicycle, give careful consideration to the following suggestions:

1. Buy the size that is right for you. Be sure you can reach the pedals and handlebars while sitting on the seat.

2. Double-check the frame to make certain it is perfectly straight and sturdy.

3. Make sure there are reflectors on the bicycle. Ideally, they should be on the front, back, sides, and pedals.

4. Put a light on the bicycle, especially if you plan to ride at night.

5. Attach a bell or horn to the bike.

6. Check the brakes to make sure they will hold, especially if you buy a bicycle with handbrakes.

# Activity 8-8: *The Miracle Machine*

Carefully study the following details before reading the selection. Then, using the steps in "Here's How to Do It," arrange the details in the order in which they occur. Use a separate sheet of paper for your answers.

a. In 1642, Pascal developed a machine with numbered dials that could be turned to add or subtract.

b. The abacus was an early "computer-like" tool.

c. The "up" and "down" patterns from the Jacquard loom were adapted to the "on" and "off," or 1 and 0, system used in all computer languages.

d. Many people have never heard the history of the computer.

e. The Jacquard loom, made in 1801, was controlled by preplanned patterns in paper cards.

f. The Babbage "engine" was built to solve many number problems.

**g.**   Microcomputers and pocket calculators are used today.

**h.**   Although the first digital computers built were larger and slower than today's models, they were very useful during the 1930s and 1940s.

## The Miracle Machine

Computers affect the lives of many people, from things as minor as digital watches to those as major as controlling the economy. Computers have changed from huge rooms full of equipment used by a few scientists to handy little tools that can be carried anywhere. Many people have never heard the history behind this miracle machine that is changing the way we work and play.

The idea that a machine could be built to add and subtract was an early step. The abacus, a gadget with beads on wires, was developed long ago to help do this. In 1642, Blaise Pascal developed another machine. This one had numbered dials that could be turned to add or subtract columns of numbers.

Another "thread" in the history of the computer was the invention of looms that were controlled by punched paper tape or cards. The most advanced of these was the Jacquard loom, invented in 1801. The holes in the cards moved up and down to create the pattern in the cloth. These "up" and "down" patterns were adapted to the "on" and "off," or 1 and 0, system that is the basis for all computer languages.

These two areas were combined by Charles Babbage in 1834. His "engine" could have been used to solve many number problems. However, the machine designed by Babbage was beyond the manufacturing abilities of that time. His "analytical engine" was never built.

The first true digital computers were built during 1934–1946. At the end of this time span, the ENIAC was able to perform 5,000 additions per second. This machine weighed about thirty tons and filled a large room. This is large and slow by today's standards. It is the grandfather of all of the microcomputers and pocket calculators used today.

# Part 9

# Arranging Details in Sequence

## About This Part...

The ability to arrange details in sequence is an important skill. It will help you to better understand the main idea in the passages you read. The activities in this Part are designed to help you master this skill. Be persistent in your work, and try to complete all of the activities. Soon you should be able to arrange details in sequence in your mind as you read.

Because the selections are longer, read them carefully. Some passages will contain more details than are asked for. List only the most obvious details. Use your own words when you write the details. Try not to copy the phrases from the passage. Once you have listed the details, arrange them in the order in which they occur in the passage.

## Here's How to Do It

Follow this sequence of steps to complete the activities.

1. *Read* the passage carefully.
2. *List* the details in your own words.
3. *Arrange* the details in the same order in which they appear in the passage.
4. *Check* your work by rereading the passage.

## Sample Activity:  Amazing Look-Alikes

First, read the following passage. Then, list three details from the selection on a separate sheet of paper. Finally, arrange the details in the same order as they appear in the passage.

### Amazing Look-Alikes

Did you ever try to pick up a twig that walked away? Or watch a moth first land on a tree trunk and then seem to vanish? Many insects survive by looking like something else. Some escape being eaten by not being seen. The walking-stick insect, for instance, looks like a twig when it stands still. Some insects also may fool enemies by looking like different kinds of insects. For example, some butterflies that birds would eat look like other types of insects that birds will not eat. There are also some harmless insects that look menacing. For example, some flies look like stinging wasps. The ways such small creatures are able to survive can be amazing.

**Answer:** a. Some insects, such as the walking stick insect, escape being eaten by looking like something else. b. There are harmless insects, like some flies, that look menacing. c. Some of the ways insects are able to survive are amazing.

## How Did You Do?

Did you notice that listing the details in your own words is harder to do than listing them as they appear in the passage? It takes practice to write the details in your own words. Until you can master this skill, you may wish to reread the passage.

# Activities

As you work through the following passages, you will notice that the reading becomes longer and more challenging. Take your time when reading the selections. Some details may be easy to spot; others may be hidden within the passage. The steps outlined in "Here's How to Do It" should make your task easier.

# Activity 9-1:  Early Burials

Read the following passage about early burials. Select three details and list them on a separate sheet of paper. Then, arrange the details in the same sequence as they appear in the selection.

### Early Burials

As far as we know, people have buried their dead for at least 70,000 years. The way the Neanderthals buried their dead suggests they had religious beliefs. They buried the bodies with food and tools. This means they may have believed in life after death. Many bodies have been found in sleeping positions. In one case, soil tests showed that the body had been encased with wild flowers and pine branches.

# Activity 9-2:  Diamonds

Read the passage below carefully. On a separate sheet of paper, list four facts you have learned about diamonds. Arrange them in the same order as they appear in the passage.

### Diamonds

A diamond is one of the loveliest gems known. Many people know that diamonds are very hard and tough. They are not used just for rings and necklaces. They also are used in industries and the space program. Many of the world's diamonds come from mines in South Africa. First the soil is removed down to layers of gravel and rocks that contain the rough diamonds. The rocks are crushed to the size of the gravel. This is passed through a dark area where an X ray is used. Diamonds will shine in a certain way. They are then removed from the gravel. After sorting, they may become cut gems or be used in other forms.

# Activity 9-3:  Quicksand

Carefully read the selection below about quicksand. On a separate sheet of paper, list six things you should do if you fall into quicksand. Arrange them in the same order as they appear in the passage.

### Quicksand

On the movie screen, a victim is being swallowed up by quicksand. The person struggles desperately but to no avail. Fiction would have us believe that once entrapped by quicksand, little hope for survival exists. This is simply not true.

Quicksand, usually found near the mouths of large rivers or along streams where pools of water can't drain, is deceiving in its appearance. It resembles solid sand formations, but it can't support much weight. Most objects sink into the mass of loose sand mixed with water unless they are light enough to float.

A person who falls into quicksand *can* survive. The key is knowing how to escape. Keep in mind that one can float on quicksand. Struggling is a mistake.

Should you find yourself trapped in quicksand, try to keep calm and avoid jerking motions. The best thing to do is to remain still, keeping your arms outstretched. You will stop sinking once your weight equals the weight of the displaced sand. This usually occurs about the time the quicksand reaches your armpits. Then use the arms in a swimming motion and keep the feet perfectly still. Try to ease your body into a horizontal position. Your goal will be to roll from the surface of the sand to firm ground. Should there be help, a stick or branch can be used to introduce air below your feet. This air can break the vacuum that is sucking you down further and holding you in the quicksand.

# Activity 9-4:  Positive Mental Attitude

The following addresses positive mental attitude. After reading the passage, list four examples of how imagination can be used to develop a positive mental attitude. Arrange them in the same order as they appear in the selection. Use a separate sheet of paper for your list.

### Positive Mental Attitude

We all are forced to face many problems in our lives. Some are simple; some are complex. Of course, we'd like to deal with each one successfully. One of the best ways of facing problems is with a positive mental attitude.

The key to developing a positive attitude is imagination. We all behave according to what we imagine to be true. For example, you behave one way if you think you look nice on an important occasion. You behave differently if you think you look awful. What happens to your behavior if you dwell on how bad you look? You become more and more negative. You might even begin avoiding others, so they think you aren't interested in talking with them. They feel snubbed, and the situation worsens. On the other hand, you can use your imagination and picture a good image of yourself. You then project a far more appealing personality to others. You will enjoy yourself so much that you become less concerned with how you look.

We need to realize that our actions are based on our own images and beliefs. By mentally visualizing ourselves in a certain way, we have the chance to practice new behavior. For example, if you feel nervous when speaking in front of a group, just picture yourself succeeding in that kind of situation. This will actually help you become less nervous. Positive mental practice helps you because you're concentrating on "I can" rather than on "I can't."

In one study, persons who mentally practiced throwing darts actually improved their dart-throwing ability. By imagining the act as successful, they were helped in completing the act with greater success. In another experiment involving sinking baskets with a basketball, those who "pictured" success were almost as successful as those who actually practiced.

While you imagine yourself in various situations important to you, role-playing also will be helpful. As you picture the situation, think about how you will handle it. Anticipate what you'll actually say and do. For example, if you're trying to sell a product, think about the different types of customers. If you know how to deal with questions and objections they might raise, you'll make more sales. Create situations in your mind before they happen. Practice what to do and say. You'll be preparing yourself for success as you practice these role-playing situations. You'll be developing your confidence.

Sometimes we underestimate ourselves and our abilities. If we are to reach our fullest potential, we need to help ourselves to grow. Creating a positive image and role-playing that new image are bridges to personal growth.

# Activity 9-5: The Oldest Creature

Read the selection below about the opossum. On a separate sheet of paper, list five reasons why this creature is the oldest on this continent. Arrange your reasons in the same sequence as they appear in the selection.

## The Oldest Creature

Do you know what animal is the oldest on this continent? This animal is also the only marsupial (a mammal that has a pouch for carrying its young) in North America. It's the Virginia gray opossum, a creature that some people say dates back 70 million years.

Why has the opossum survived through the ages when other creatures have come and gone? The reasons are numerous. The opossum's birthrate is one factor. Their breeding occurs twice a year. They can have large litters within only a thirteen-day period. The opossum also has the most teeth. With fifty teeth and a wide-ranging appetite, opossums do not go hungry. They can (and do) eat almost anything, including insects, berries, and rotting wood. The opossum also is able to run quickly for short distances, is a skillful climber of trees, and is a fairly good swimmer.

The opossum does have enemies. These include certain owls and foxes. Often, though, the opossum escapes by hissing and showing its long, sharp teeth.

Even more interesting is what has been learned about the opossum's will to survive. They have been known to recover from broken bones that would have resulted in death for other animals. Also, opossums have lived through extremely cold temperature by biting off frostbitten body parts such as tails. Even though the opossum has been labeled a coward, it has been known to pursue food persistently.

The opossum has a reputation for playing dead when danger is near, then scurrying off when the danger has passed. Some experts believe that this act is used by the opossum to escape danger. Others suggest that the animal may simply faint as a result of certain stimuli. Regardless of which view is correct, playing dead has helped the opossum survive.

Where does the opossum make its home in this day and age? It is likely that one will see an opossum in the wild. The opossum can and does live comfortably in a variety of places. It often lives in tree hollows, caves, and dens left by other animals. The opossum likes to make its home cozy and does so by placing leaves in its nest. Because the opossum has keen night vision, it has become known as one of the night's creatures. It is not uncommon, though, to hear reports of opossums being seen in the daytime.

The opossum is a tough, adaptable little animal that has the potential to remain on the earth a long time. The next time you see an opossum, pay your respects.

# Activity 9-6:  The Sinking of the Titanic

Carefully read the following. On a sheet of paper, list the major events that occurred the night that the "unsinkable" ship sank. Arrange the events in the same sequence as they appear in the selection.

### The Sinking of the Titanic

The date was April 10, 1912. The largest and most luxurious ocean liner ever built at that time was setting out for its first voyage. It was 882 $\frac{1}{2}$ feet long and could carry as many as 2,500 passengers as well as a crew of 900. The British-built ship was named the Titanic and was said to be "unsinkable." The passenger list for that first voyage included society's elite of that day. As the ship left the port at Southampton, England, with New York as its destination, passengers were unusually comfortable as they enjoyed the many extras on board. For example, there were Turkish baths, a gymnasium, and even a French sidewalk café.

Before midnight on April 14, 1912, a lookout in the crow's nest spotted an iceberg in the ship's path and called the bridge. "Iceberg right ahead," exclaimed Frederick Fleet. But it was too late to avoid disaster. When the liner collided with the mammoth iceberg southeast of Newfoundland, the hull was ripped open. The ship began to tilt to one side. Yet, because the liner had been declared "unsinkable," many people still refused to accept that they were in any real danger. However, many survivors reported that they had heeded the instructions of stewards who told them to get their lifebelts and their children and rush up on deck.

What about lifeboats? Surely a luxury liner would have ample lifeboats for every person on board. This was sadly not the case. As women and children were encouraged to take the available spaces, many families were separated. By 2:00 A.M. on April 15, 1912, it was obvious to all concerned that the ship was sinking. The waters were calm as the Titanic vanished into 13,000 feet of cold dark water. More than 1,500 people met their deaths as the seemingly impossible happened.

From expeditions that took place in 1985 and 1986, it is now clear that the ship split in two as it sank; the bow and the stern were found on the ocean floor more than 600 yards apart. Much has been learned about the actual sinking of the Titanic from thousands of photographs that were taken during these underwater expeditions.

# Activity 9-7: Tecumseh

Read the following about an Indian warrior. On a separate sheet of paper, list five events that occurred in his life. Arrange the events in the same sequence as they appear in the selection.

### Tecumseh

Tecumseh was a Shawnee Indian warrior who was born in Ohio in 1768. He saw little peace during his life, but he never gave up his dream of getting all the Indian nations together to protect their land.

When Tecumseh was only six years old, white settlers started flocking onto land belonging to the Shawnee. His father, who was the Shawnee war chief, was killed by the settlers.

After being adopted by Chief Blackfish and learning all he could about warfare, Tecumseh fought against the settlers in 1790. He was determined to do what he could to stop frontiersmen from taking more and more land belonging to Indians. In 1792, he became the Shawnee warriors' leader, battling the settlers in Tennessee, Georgia, Florida, Alabama, and Mississippi.

Tecumseh knew that the Indians didn't have a chance unless they united. So he spent the next twenty years traveling and speaking for Indian unity. He covered thousands of miles across the country, sharing his dream with thousands of other Indians. He did all he could to persuade them to unite. The dream seemed impossible, but Tecumseh didn't give up hope. By the early 1800s, the name of Tecumseh was known throughout the land.

Then, in 1812, war broke out between the Americans and Great Brittain. Hoping to get back some of the land taken by the settlers, many Indians sided with the British. Tecumseh fought with great courage, and in 1813, he died during one of the battles.

Tecumseh's dream was never realized, but his memory has not been lost. He stood firm, fighting for his beliefs.

# Finding Expressed Main Ideas

# Part 10

# First-Sentence Paragraphs

## About This Part...

Sentences in a paragraph are not placed there at random. They are placed in a deliberate order. When you think about *all* the sentences, you realize they are about one subject. That subject is *the main idea* of the paragraph.

In Section Three, you'll concentrate on *expressed main ideas.* This means you'll work on finding main ideas in the passages you read. To start finding main ideas, you'll begin by reading one-paragraph passages. In this Part, the key sentence, which contains the main idea, appears at the beginning of the paragraph. When the main idea is located at the beginning, the paragraph is called *deductive.* The main idea is followed by sentences that help to *explain, clarify,* or *develop* its meaning.

Keep two things in mind:

1. All paragraphs in this Part start with a key sentence.

2. Don't stop reading after the first sentence. The sentences that follow *develop* the main idea.

## Here's How to Do It

When you read a deductive paragraph, follow these suggested steps.

1.  *Read* the first sentence slowly and carefully. Remember, this sentence contains the main idea of the passage.

2.  Write down the key words and phrases in the first sentence that tell you what the paragraph is about. Use a separate sheet of paper for this.

3.  *Read* the rest of the paragraph. As you do, notice how each succeeding sentence helps to *develop* the main idea.

4.  *Refer* to a dictionary to learn the meaning of any word you can't define immediately.

5.  When you finish reading the paragraph, close your book and *think* about the paragraph you have just read.

6.  *Write* a sentence of your own that tells what the paragraph is about. Then open your book and compare your sentence with the key sentence in the paragraph.

## *Sample Activity:  U.S. Historical Sites*

Find the main idea in the first sentence. Then, read the rest of the paragraph. Follow the six steps listed on page 97.

### U.S. Historic Sites

Many of the great moments in our history occurred in small places. The fight for U.S. independence began near the little village of Concord, Massachusetts, in 1775. We won that war in 1781, when the British surrendered in Yorktown, a tiny place in southeast Virginia. A great war cry was once raised: " Remember the Alamo." It came from the slaughter of U.S. defenders by the Mexican Army in 1836 at a Franciscan mission called the Alamo, near San Antonio, Texas. The deciding battle of the Civil War, fought in 1836, was staged in another small town: Gettysburg, Pennsylvania. In 1876, George A. Custer, a famous general, was defeated by his Native American opponents at the Little Big Horn River in Wyoming. Today, there are shrines raised at each of these sites to remind visitors of what happened there.

**Answer:** Students' answers will vary. A possible key sentence could be: "Many of the great moments in our history occurred in small places."

# Activities

Read each of the following passates carefully. The sentence that contains the main idea always appears first in each passage. This sentence is also called the main idea statement. Read main idea statements carefully. Follow the steps outlined in "Here's How to Do It." For each of the paragraphs you read, you must write *your own* key sentence.

## Activity 10-1:  A Separate Peace

The following passage is about a John Knowles novel. Following the steps in "Here's How to Do It," write your own sentence on a separate sheet of paper.

### A Separate Peace

John Knowles's novel *A Separate Peace* is mostly about friendships among teenage boys. It is set in a New England boys' school. The boys are working toward graduation. World War II is on, and the boys will join the service when they graduate. Phineas, the main character, is very bright and clever. His best friend, Gene Forrester, admires him. Their friendship is very close. The other boys in the school also admire Phineas. One day, Gene accidentally pushes Phineas out of a tree. The boy is badly hurt. He eventually dies. His death greatly affects the friendships of all the boys in the school.

## Activity 10-2:  Situation Comedies

The passage below is about sitcoms. Follow the steps outlined in "Here's How to Do It." After you have read the selection, write your own key sentence that tells what the passage is about.

### Situation Comedies

The situation comedies (sitcoms) we see on television have a very long history. The first sitcoms go back to the fourth century B.C. In that period, Athens, Greece, was a busy, wealthy place. People had active social lives, and they liked entertainment. Much of this came in the form of plays. While some of the plays were very serious, others were lighthearted. A man named Menander (Men-an-der) wrote many light plays or sitcoms. The best known one is called "Dyskolos" (Dis'-kol-os), which means "the ill-tempered man." The play is about a grouch who has lots of money. Many people in Athens don't like him and like to play tricks on him. The tricks make Menander's character mad, but they made the audiences of fourth-century Athens laugh. That's what the situation comedies of today do for us.

# Activity 10-3:  Need to Win

The selection below is about some people's need to win. Follow the steps listed in "Here's How to Do It." Then, write your own key sentence on a separate sheet of paper.

### Need to Win

Although everyone wants to win, the need to win can cause problems. People who win all the time can get the feeling that they are too big and important. They expect others to bow down to them just because they are winners. This can damage friendships. Others need to win so badly that they will break any rule to come out on top. Every year some school or college gets a penalty for breaking the rules in order to put out a winning team. Still other persons can harm their bodies and minds. They do this because they want to perform better in the contest. They force their bodies to perform beyond endurance. Some pretend they haven't hurt themselves, even though they are in pain. None of these decisions is good for the winner in the long run.

# Activity 10-4:  The Personal Computer

The following paragraph introduces the personal home computer. Find the main idea stated. Follow the steps in "Here's How to Do It."

### The Personal Computer

The personal home computer is a box that takes in, stores, analyzes, transfers, and puts out information. It can receive large amounts of information from the operator. In computer talk, this person is called "the user." The user can direct the computer to store the information for any period of time. When needed, the computer can "output" (give out) that material in a number of ways. In addition, the user can direct the computer to transfer almost any amount of information to other computers. This exchange can usually be completed quickly and easily.

## Activity 10-5:  St. George Island

The passage below is about an island off the coast of Florida. Following the steps in "Here's How to Do It," write your own key sentence on a separate sheet of paper.

### St. George Island

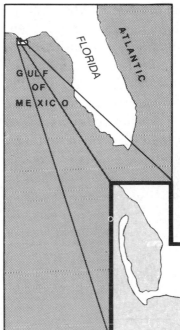

On the Gulf of Mexico, off the coast of Florida, lies St. George Island, which poses a serious problem in human living. It has almost fifteen miles of beautiful beaches and a mild climate. People can swim, boat, and fish there most of the year and they also can lie on the beach. Because of all this, land developers want to build cottages, motels, and condominiums all over the island. They want to provide places for thousands of vacationers. They also want to make a lot of money. The local people, who live near the island, are against this. Many of them fish for a living. They fish in the bay of St. George Island. Out of this bay come tons of shrimp and oysters every year. The people who fish there are afraid that the land development will poison the shrimp and oyster beds. Each group wants to make its living. How to please each group is the problem. It is a problem going on all over the world today.

## Activity 10-6:  Consumer Protection

The passage below discusses some of the things Ralph Nader has done to protect consumers. Follow the steps outlined in "Here's How to Do It." After you have read the selection, write your own key sentence.

### Consumer Protection

Ralph Nader has spent most of his adult life studying ways in which consumers are cheated. His main worry is about poor people and the faulty products they are persuaded to buy. Several years ago, he wrote a book called *Unsafe at Any Speed*. It was about the things wrong with modern autos. Since that book, all American car producers have done much to improve their cars. Nader went from cars to many other products. He studied appliances to see if they were safe and workable. He watched projects to see if they harmed the environment. He looked at those activities of politicians which had to do with consumer protection. His work has caused many producers of goods and services to be more careful and honest.

## *Activity 10-7: Early Newspapermen*

After reading the passage on early English newspapers, find the main idea
statement. Follow the steps in "Here's How to Do It."

### Early Newspapermen

Joseph Addison and Richard Steele were the first big-time newspapermen
for English-speaking people. They were British citizens who lived in
London in the early eighteenth century. London was a very large city then.
There was a lot going on there, and improvements in the printing press
made it easy to produce cheap copy. Addison's paper, "The Tatler," began
first. It covered political gossip and social events. Later on, Addison got his
friend Steele to produce "The Spectator." Steele invented a character, Sir
Roger de Coverley. It was Sir Roger who reported on, and often made fun
of, the best-advertised people, places, and events in London of that day.
While in print, both papers were big sellers.

# Activity 10-8:  The Curse

After reading the passage on the baseball book, find the main idea statement. Follow the steps outlined in "Here's How to Do It."

### The Curse

In his book, *The Curse of the Bambino*, Will McDonough states his belief that when the Boston Red Sox sold Babe Ruth to the New York Yankees in 1918, an everlasting curse fell on the Boston ball club. Certain events have led many Boston fans to wonder about the curse. In 1946, the Red Sox lost the final game of the World Series to the St. Louis Cardinals when their great shortstop, Johnny Pesky, held the ball as the winning run scored. The team then lost a one-game championship playoff to the Cleveland Indians in 1948. In that game, the Boston manager left his best pitcher sitting on the bench. The very next year, the Yankees defeated the Sox for the pennant on the last day of the season. In that game, the winning runs scored when a pop fly fell among three Boston fielders. The final (seventh) game of the 1975 World Series went down as a victory for the Cincinnati Reds when Boston's second-best pitcher couldn't hold a three-run lead. Another one-game playoff, in 1978, was lost to those same hated Yankees when a weak hitter named Bucky Dent smashed a late-inning home run. The most famous example of the curse, however, occurred in the 1986 World Series' sixth game with the New York Mets. With the Sox holding a two-run lead in the last inning, a usually reliable first baseman named Bill Buckner let an easy ground ball go through his legs, which led to the scoring of the winning run. The Mets then won the next game—and the World Series—and prolonged the curse.

# Activity 10-9:  Dramatic Monologues

Some of Robert Browning's dramatic monologues are discussed below. Write your own key sentence by following the steps outlined in "Here's How to Do It." Use a separate sheet of paper for your sentence.

### Dramatic Monologues

The English Victorian poet Robert Browning wrote a number of poems that are called *dramatic monologues.* In these poems, the speaker tells someone about his or her thoughts, interests, feelings, or actions. Because the person who is listening never replies, the term *monologue* is used. It means that only one person is speaking. In "My Last Duchess," for example, the speaker is a nobleman who is telling someone just how and why he killed his first wife. The speaker in "Soliloquy of the Spanish Cloister" is a holy monk. He is telling someone why he hates one of his fellow monks and how he fools him. In "The Laboratory," a woman is the speaker. She is asking a druggist to prepare a killer potion for her. She says that she wants to use it to poison her husband's girlfriend.

# Activity 10-10:  Driver's Licenses

The passage below discusses some ways people can lose their driver's licenses. Follow the steps in "Here's How to Do It." After reading the passage carefully, write your own key sentence on a separate sheet of paper.

### Driver's Licenses

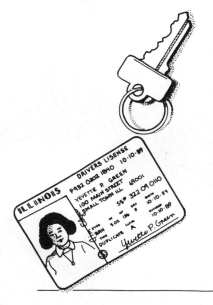

People who own driver's licenses can lose them for a period of time (suspension) or for good (revocation). They may lose their licenses for up to twelve months. Suspensions are given to drivers who have received too many points during a certain time. Most points are assessed against a driver's license for moving violations. Speeding, not stopping at stop signs, and illegal passing are examples of violations. People can lose licenses for more serious offenses. Revocation can occur because of drunk driving, leaving the scene of an accident, or giving the police false information.

## Activity 10-11:  Environmental Pollution

The following passage is about pollution. Using the steps outlined in "Here's How to Do It," write a key sentence of your own on a separate sheet of paper.

### Environmental Pollution

Today, one of the greatest dangers to life on earth is the wholesale pollution of the environment. This can create serious health problems for people. Most city residents must breathe foul air. Industrial waste and fumes pour into the air. Rivers and lakes are being filled with waste products which endanger all forms of life. Testing of nuclear weapons has spread much contamination. Plutonium is difficult to dispose of. Overcrowded living quarters add to the problem. Too many people in a small area create tremendous amounts of waste and trash.

## Activity 10-12:  Changes in Radio Programming

The following paragraph discusses the changes in American radio. Follow the steps in "Here's How to Do It." Then, on a separate sheet of paper, write your own key sentence.

### Changes in Radio Programming

American radio is now dominated by the music industry, but in the past, radio was the primary source of entertainment. Evenings brought adventure stories, dramas, and comedies. A show called "Lux Presents Hollywood" offered one-hour summaries of current films. Afternoon listeners got caught up in dramatic fifteen-minute serial dramas about domestic life. Because laundry soap makers sponsored most of these, they were known as "soap operas." Radio broadcast major sports events to fans across the nation. During World War II, Armed Forces Radio carried Bowl games, the Kentucky Derby, the World Series, and other major sports events to soldiers throughout the world. By the late 1940s, TV had changed all that, so that now radio is dominated by popular music. Most stations play rock and country music. Some offer "easy listening," the popular ballads of the past. A few stations, mostly National Public Radio, broadcast classical music. AM stations usually broadcast news or talk shows all day. FM stations often broadcast news and local weather on the hour. Because of TV, radio has had to redefine its role.

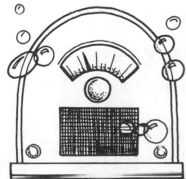

# Part 11

# Finding and Relating Supporting Details

## About This Part...

In the activities you did in Part 10, the main idea always appeared in the first sentence of each passage. The sentences that followed provided *supportive details.* They were there to develop, or support, the main idea statement. In this Part, you will learn how supporting details add to your understanding of the main idea.

**Supporting details have three purposes:**

1. They make the general idea more specific.

2. They expand the idea in your mind.

3. They clarify the idea for you.

In identifying the meaning of each paragraph in this Part, your job will be to *find* the supporting details. Then, you must relate the supporting details to the main idea, which is located in the key sentence. In other words, you must connect them to the subject. The steps outlined in "Here's How to Do It" will help you with this task. Learning how to find and relate supporting details is a necessary skill if you are to become an effective reader.

## Here's How to Do It

To find and relate supporting details, follow these steps:

1. *Look* at the first sentence carefully. This key sentence contains the main idea.

2. *Write* the key words that you find in the key sentence on a separate sheet of paper.

3. *Read* the rest of the sentences in the paragraph. Find the supporting details in them.

4. *Write* down each detail as you see it. Next to each detail, write the word or phrase in the key sentence it supports.

5. *Refer* to a dictionary to learn the meanings of any unfamiliar words.

6. *Reread* the whole paragraph. Review the main idea and the details that support it.

## Sample Activity:  Alcoholic Beverages

The following paragraph contains a main idea in the first sentence and is followed by several sentences with supporting details. To find and relate the supporting details, carry out each of the steps listed in "Here's How to Do It." Write down your replies on a separate sheet of paper.

### Alcoholic Beverages

People who drink a lot of alcoholic beverages place themselves in danger. For one thing, too much drinking is the number one cause of auto accidents in this country. Not only that, alcohol has adverse effects on the body and the brain. The heart works harder when one drinks. Thus, many heavy drinkers develop high blood pressure. Heart disease often follows. The kidneys also are placed under more strain. When they give way, death is almost a certainty. The same can be said for the liver. Cirrhosis of the liver is a common result of too much alcohol. Then, too, alcoholic beverages contain a large number of calories. It is hard for a heavy drinker not to gain excess weight.

**Answer:** The key words in the first sentence are *people who drink* and *danger.* The supporting details are that the heart, kidneys, and liver work harder; heavy drinkers develop high blood pressure, heart disease, or cirrhosis of the liver; and heavy drinkers also gain weight.

## How Did You Do?

Did you notice that there is a *cause-and-effect* relationship in the main idea sentence? It says, in simplest language, "If you drink, bad things can happen." The "If you drink" part is the cause; the "bad things can happen" is the effect. Then the rest of the paragraph contains details which support the effect. That is, they spell out the "bad things." You will work more closely with cause-and-effect relationships in Section Four.

# Activities

Below you will find a number of paragraphs, some long and some short. Each has a main idea in its first sentence. Follow the steps listed in "Here's How to Do It" to find and relate the supporting details. Write down your responses on a sheet of paper.

## Activity 11-1:  Uses of the Computer, I

Read the paragraph about ways in which the computer can be used to receive information. Then find the key sentence. Finally, identify the details which tell us more about input.

### Uses of the Computer, I

The computer can receive input of information from many sources. Some of the more commonly used ones are the keyboard, the "mouse," and the optical scanner. From the keyboard, the user can type documents to be stored inside the computer, and programs can be written. A program is a special set of instructions the computer follows when it is performing its various tasks.

## Activity 11-2:  Turnpikes

The passage below is about turnpikes. Follow the steps outlined in "Here's How to Do It." Find the supporting details and relate them to the key sentence. Use a separate sheet of paper for your responses.

### Turnpikes

For people who must drive long distances, turnpikes offer a well-planned and safe route of travel. There must be four and sometimes six driving lanes. There must be wide shoulders for drivers who have car trouble. Also, there must be service areas for gas, food, and repairs. Exits must be well marked, and signs giving distances to points down the road must be found easily. Drivers can get on turnpikes only at certain places, and there can be no abrupt or hidden intersections. Bad spots on the road must be repaired quickly.

## Activity 11-3:   The Canterbury Tales

The following selection is about a famous poem. Using the steps listed in "Here's How to Do It," find the supporting details and relate them to the key sentence. Write your responses on a separate sheet of paper.

### *The Canterbury Tales*

In the Prologue to his famous poem, *The Canterbury Tales*, Geoffrey Chaucer describes the interesting characters who are making a pilgrimage. Even though they are all on this religious trip, they are very different people. One, the Pardoner, wants to make money by saying prayers for people. He also wants to sell them phony relics. Another, the Squire, thinks he is a heartbreaker. He is looking for lovely women. The Wife of Bath is looking for a husband. She's already had five. Now, she's getting older, but she's still interested. The Clerk is a holy man. He is also a good teacher. The Miller and Reeve are just going along for a good time. These are only some of the characters going to Canterbury as holy pilgrims.

## Activity 11-4:   Uses of  the Computer, II

Read the paragraph on the mouse. Find the key sentence and then relate the details which follow and support it.

### Uses of the Computer, II

The mouse is a widely used source of input for the computer. It is a small hand-held device with wheels on its underside. As it is moved around on the table, an arrow moves around on the computer screen. The user can press a button on the mouse to select items he or she sees on the screen. The mouse is just one of the many devices that simulate direct input to the computer by way of pointing and physical movement.

## Activity 11-5:  *English Satire*

Read the passage below. Find the key sentence. Then identify the details which support it. Follow the steps in "Here's How to Do It."

### English Satire

In English literature, the early eighteenth century is known by some as the Age of Satire. Satire is the use of irony or sarcasm to attack some form of human behavior. One writer who liked to poke fun at his society in poems was Alexander Pope. Another writer, Jonathan Swift, used essays and novels as well as poems to present his criticisms. His book, *Gulliver's Travels,* is a good example of satire. John Gay wrote a famous play called *The Beggar's Opera* to express criticism in a musical drama. It was light in tone, but the attacks were sharp. Two newspaper writers, Joseph Addison and Richard Steele, published the first two English newspapers. Most of the pieces in those newspapers were satirical descriptions of the ways in which London citizens of that day behaved.

## Activity 11-6:  *Product Warranty*

The following is a warranty on an electric shaver. Find the supporting details and relate them to the key sentence using the steps outlined in "Here's How to Do It."

### Product Warranty

We warrant that each Super Electric Shaver (except for its cord) has no defects in materials used in it or in its workmanship. This warranty is for one year from the date of its purchase for use. We also agree to repair or replace any faulty parts, without charge. The shaver's return must be *postpaid* to the nearest Super Electric service station or the nearest authorized service station. (See enclosed booklet.) This return must be made within the one-year period. In packing the shaver for shipment, please wrap it carefully for protection. *Important:* be sure to enclose $1.00 to cover the costs of insurance and shipping. This warranty is in lieu of all other warranties expressed or implied. No responsibility is assumed for any consequential damage which might occur from accident, abuse, or lack of reasonable care, loss of parts, or using the shaver on any but the prescribed voltage.

## Activity 11-7:  Uses of the Computer, III

Read the passage on the scanner. Find the key sentence it contains. Then find the relevant details that describe its use in computer work.

### Uses of the Computer, III

The hand-held optical scanner is a new addition to the rapidly changing supply of input devices on the market today. The device is used to read text from a printed sheet of paper and transfer this information to the computer. The scanner usually has a wide surface that is placed directly on the sheet of paper, then scrolled across its length as it reads the information. It's not hard to see that this direct input from paper to computer is much more efficient than typing all the words with the keyboard. Some scanners currently in use can capture highly detailed graphic displays and even photographic images.

## Activity 11-8:  Credit for Women

Follow the steps outlined in "Here's How to Do It." On a separate sheet of paper, list the supporting details and relate them to the key sentence.

### Credit for Women

The law specifies that a woman has a right to her own credit if she is creditworthy. If you are a woman getting married, remember that you can maintain your own credit accounts and credit record. There are several things that a creditor may not do. (1) A creditor may not refuse to grant you an individual account because of your sex or marital status. (2) He or she may not refuse to open or maintain an account in your first name or maiden name, or your first name and your husband's surname, or a combined surname. (3) He or she may not ask for information about your husband or ex-husband unless you are relying on his income, or using his account, or are liable for his account, or unless you're relying on income from alimony or on community property to support your application. (4) He or she may not require a cosigner or the signature of your spouse because you are a woman or married. If your *marital status changes,* a creditor also *may not* require you to reapply for credit, change the terms of your account, or close your account unless there is some indication that you are no longer willing or able to repay your debt. But, a creditor *may* ask you to reapply if your ex-husband's income was counted on to support your credit.

## Activity 11-9:  Loss of Hearing

This passage discusses some of the causes of hearing loss. Find the supporting details and relate them to the key sentence. Use a separate sheet of paper for your responses. Don't forget to follow the steps in "Here's How to Do It."

### Loss of Hearing

Doctors are increasing their warnings to young people to take care of their hearing. Recently, many cases of hearing loss in young people have been reported. Much of the damage has been caused by exposure to very loud noise over a long period of time. People who go to rock concerts listen to very loud music. Hearing damage gradually builds up until it becomes severe. Just as damaging are portable cassette/radios with earphones. When the volume is loud, the noise directly hits the eardrums. Other noises also are harmful. Doctors have found cases of hearing loss caused by motorcycles and dirt bikes, video arcades, and cordless telephones. The biggest problem of all is not the noise itself. It is that people do not take precautions—such as wearing earmuffs or turning down the volume—until after their hearing has been damaged or destroyed.

## Activity 11-10:  The Upper Midwest

Read the passage below. Find the key sentence. Then identify the details which support it. Follow the steps in "Here's How to Do It."

### The Upper Midwest

If you can cope with very cold winters, which usually bring lots of snow, the five states of the Upper Midwest are good places to live. The state of Wisconsin, called "America's Dairyland," has rolling hills, lovely lakes, and lots of other beautiful scenery. Its largest city, Milwaukee, is the home of two professional teams: the Bucks basketball team and the Brewers baseball team. The Green Bay Packers football team also plays some home games there. Minnesota is called "The Land of 10,000 Lakes." It is a water wonderland in its north country. The winter sports of skating, skiing, tobogganing, snowmobiling, and ice fishing are very popular there. The nation's corn belt is centered in Iowa, which has some of the richest soil anywhere in the country. Iowa also can boast an outstanding school system, from kindergartens to universities. North Dakota is the site of some of the greatest Indian battles of the last century. It is rich in history. Its Red River Valley is also a great agricultural area. In South Dakota, the Badlands reveal a strange, desolate space that has attracted tourists for almost 100 years. South Dakota is also the location of Mt. Rushmore, a huge cliff that has the faces of four great American presidents carved on it. A great deal of typical American life can be found in the region.

## *Activity 11-11:  Read the Fine Print*

Read the warranty statement below. Find the key sentence. Then identify the details that support it. Follow the steps in "Here's How to Do It."

### Warranty

If you require service during the warranty period, you must contact an authorized service center to arrange for repairs. The service center must be allowed to keep defective parts. After the first ninety days of the warranty period, the cost of transportation to and from the service center and service labor are your responsibility. Warranty service will be performed by an authorized service center. We suggest that you contact your dealer. If your dealer does not operate an authorized service center, he or she will direct you to the authorized service center that services the product he or she sells. If you reside in an area where we have a factory service center, you can contact the center to schedule a convenient time for an in-home service call.

## *Activity 11-12:  Slogans and Emblems*

Follow the steps outlined in "Here's How to Do It." Find the supporting details and relate them to the key sentence. Use a separate sheet of paper for your responses.

### Slogans and Emblems

Several states in the United States are known for their state emblems and slogans. Some are known by the pioneering people who settled them. Examples are North Carolina (the Tarheels), Pennsylvania (the Quakers), and Oklahoma (the Sooners). More are known by the food products they produce. Wisconsin, for example, is famous for its cheese. Citrus fruits—oranges and grapefruit—are the main symbols of Florida. Neighboring Georgia has long been called the Peach State. Kansas grows a lot of wheat. Next door to Kansas, the people of Nebraska carry the title "the Beef State" on their auto license tags. Maryland is known nationwide for its seafood pulled from Chesapeake Bay. In Vermont, residents are proud of their maple sugar and syrup. Louisiana advertises its creole dishes, most of which are seafood. You can tell a lot about states by their slogans and emblems.

# Part 12
# Last-Sentence Paragraphs

## About This Part...

Key sentences don't always come at the beginning of a paragraph. Frequently they are placed at the end. The chief reason is that the writer wants to lead up to the main idea. This kind of paragraph is known as an *inductive* paragraph.

An *inductive* paragraph begins with a set of facts or details and leads to a general statement (key sentence). Careful readers note each detail and relate it to the other details until they reach the key sentence at the end.

As you read the paragraphs that follow, be aware that the supporting details come first. Remember that they are leading to a key sentence at the end.

Keep two things in mind:

1.  Relate supporting details to the main idea.
2.  Watch for cause-and-effect relationships. Sometimes the details will be the causes and the main idea will be the effect.

# Here's How to Do It

As you complete the following activities, follow these steps.

1. *Look* at the detail discussed in the first sentence. On a separate sheet of paper *write* down the key words.

2. *Do* the same thing for each succeeding sentence up to the last one.

3. *Refer* to a dictionary to learn the meanings of any unfamiliar words.

4. *Look* at the key words you wrote down and *guess* where the passage is leading before reading the last sentence. *Write* your idea of what the passage is about in a brief sentence.

5. *Read* the last sentence of the paragraph carefully.

6. *Write* on your paper the key words and phrases in the last sentence.

7. *Relate* these key words and phrases to the key words you listed in Steps 1 and 2. That is, look at the key words and phrases together. Do you see a connection?

8. *Look* at the sentence you wrote in Step 4 and compare it with the main idea statement in the last sentence of the actual paragraph. Are they similar?

## Sample Activity:  Vocational Training

Remember, the following is an inductive paragraph. The main idea is in the final sentence. Following the steps outlined in "Here's How to Do It," find the details that support and relate to the main idea.  Be sure to write all your answers on a separate sheet of paper.

### Vocational Training

Plumbers now make more money than many college professors and news writers. There is a shortage of people who know how to do wiring. Employers, such as home builders, always need such workers. Good carpenters can just about name their price. A look at the jobs section of any newspaper shows a big demand for skilled auto mechanics. The electronics industry constantly needs help. Many young men and women go into vocational-technical training programs. They know that there will be high-paying jobs waiting for them when they graduate.

**Answer:** Key words are: plumbers make more money; a shortage of people; employers always need workers; big demand for skilled mechanics; industry needs help; and many go into training. A possible guess sentence could be: Because of the demand for skilled workers, students in vocational-training programs have a bright future.

## How Did You Do?

Did you notice that the supporting details gave you clues as to what the main idea is about? *Plumbers making more money, a shortage of people, employers always need workers,* and all of the other details relate to the key sentence. That is, they support the main idea.

# Activities

The following activities contain a variety of inductive paragraphs. Read each one carefully. Note that the main idea is in the last sentence. Notice the supporting details. Follow the steps in "Here's How to Do It." Write all your answers on a separate sheet of paper.

## *Activity 12-1:  Dialect Differences*

The following paragraph is about different ways we speak English. Follow the steps in "Here's How to Do It." Look carefully for the main idea statement.

### Dialect Differences

On the shelves of supermarkets and convenience stores all over the United States, you will find a bottled beverage called "club soda." Some customers have shortened its name to "soda." In certain geographic areas, primarily in the Midwest, the same product is referred to as "charge water" or just "charge." In still other regions, it is commonly known as "seltzer." The people who live in the Far West, or Pacific Rim as it is called, have labelled it "fizzy." Many residents of southeastern states ask for "sparkling water." The several names given to this well-known product reflect the fact that Americans speak the English language in a number of *dialects*.

## *Activity 12-2:  The Theater*

The passage below discusses the theater. Follow the steps listed in "Here's How to Do It" and find the supporting details; relate them to the key sentence. Use a separate sheet of paper for your responses.

### The Theater

People of all ages like to act in plays. They may never become Hollywood movie stars or appear in Broadway shows. Still, they love the theater and enjoy being a part of it. Of course, every play needs a director and a stage manager. They keep things running smoothly. Other people who enjoy plays can design and paint sets. Some sew costumes or help work the lighting. Some are even happy to sell tickets or hand out posters and programs. All of them simply like being part of a stage production. Community theater groups give people of all ages and skills a chance to enjoy the excitement—and hard work—of the theater.

# Activity 12-3:  Interactive Fiction

The following discusses interactive fiction. Find the supporting details and relate them to the key sentence. Use a separate sheet of paper for your responses. Don't forget to follow the steps listed in "Here's How to Do It."

### Interactive Fiction

You have entered a dark, mysterious tunnel. Suddenly a shadow looms before you. You can do one of two things: you may continue through the tunnel or you may turn and run. No, you are not really in danger. You are reading *interactive fiction*. In this kind of fiction, you are the hero or heroine. You decide how the story will proceed by making choices at different points. These stories can be found in book form or as computer software. In a book, you make your choice and then turn to a specified page. On the computer, you push a button to enter your choice, and a new screen appears. Interactive fiction has become a popular form of entertainment in recent years.

# Activity 12-4:  Stephen Crane

Using the steps outlined in "Here's How to Do It," find the supporting details and relate them to the key sentence. Use a separate sheet of paper for your responses.

### Stephen Crane

Stephen Crane, an American fiction writer, wrote some stories about the western frontier. One, "The Bride Comes to Yellow Sky," is about a showdown between two gunfighters. He also wrote about the sea. "The Open Boat" describes how men feel when faced with the problem of survival. It provides some good examples of courage in the face of great odds. His best known book, *The Red Badge of Courage,* is the story of a young man's actions and feelings during his first brush with combat during the Civil War. The author, however, was never a gunfighter, a seaman, or a soldier. In his life story, Crane tells how he learned about courage. He states that during his days as a high school and college football player, he learned all he ever knew about human courage.

## *Activity 12-5: Rite of Passage*

Read the following paragraph about growing up. Then find the key sentence telling what it is all about. Follow the steps in "Here's How to Do It."

### Rite of Passage

Huckleberry Finn, the main character in Mark Twain's novel, *The Adventures of Huckleberry Finn,* was a young person on the verge of becoming an adult. In this book, written in 1884, Huck saw a number of adults act in ways that bothered him. They were drunken, cruel, cheating, and unfriendly. They made him question what becoming an adult would be like. Some forty years later, Ernest Hemingway wrote a short story collection entitled *In Our Time.* The main character in these stories was a boy named Nick Adams. He saw many of the same adult behavior traits that Huck had seen. He was equally turned off. In her novel, *Roll of Thunder, Hear My Cry,* Mildred Taylor's central character Cassie Logan was a young African American struggling to understand the prejudice leveled against her in the Mississippi of the 1930s. All these young people felt doubt about how they would get along with their fellow adults once they came of age. This whole process of growing up and worrying about adult life has often been called "the Rite of Passage," and is the topic of many well-known American novels.

## *Activity 12-6: Life Struggles*

Read the passage about the struggles young people have in growing up. Then find the key sentence. Follow the steps in "Here's How to Do It."

### Life Struggles

In *The Red Badge of Courage,* a novel by Stephen Crane, a young soldier named Henry Fleming struggles with his fears during his first combat experience. The same is true of Lieutenant Henry in Ernest Hemingway's *A Farewell to Arms.* In *Lord of the Flies,* William Golding describes the character Ralph as having a lot of trouble learning to lead a group of frightened teenage boys. Ralph and his followers have just survived a nuclear disaster and a plane crash on a deserted island. Alfred Brooks, a teenage high school dropout from Harlem, decides to try his hand at boxing in Robert Lipsyte's novel, *The Contender.* Many books written by American authors feature the theme of young people struggling to succeed in an activity usually reserved for adults.

## Activity 12-7:  Food Business

Follow the steps listed in "Here's How to Do It." Find the supporting details and relate them to the key sentence. Use a separate sheet of paper for your responses.

### Food Business

There are pizza places in the smallest town today. Tacos, burritos, and enchiladas can be bought in quick food service shops from coast to coast. Chow mein and egg rolls are commonly found on menus in towns like Kansas City, Louisville, and Atlanta where once they only appeared in certain restaurants in Boston and San Francisco. Lox, bagels, matzoth, and gefilte fish are much more common than they used to be. Also, crêpe and escargots, which were once found only in a few places, are now found in many areas. The ethnic food business is really booming in this country.

## Activity 12-8:  Destruction of Our Environment

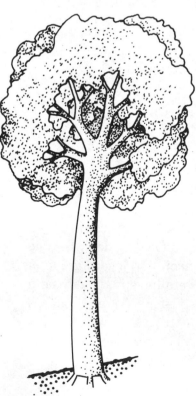

The passage below is about our environment. Following the steps listed in "Here's How to Do It," find the supporting details and relate them to the key sentence. Use a separate sheet of paper for your responses.

### Destruction of Our Environment

Some big factories pour toxic waste into water, killing fish and endangering the water for drinking. Offshore oil drilling is harming life in the sea. Careless people who drop litter transform public parks into dumps. Burning garbage turns the air foul for miles around. Junkyards, full of used, useless cars, can be found in large numbers throughout the countryside. Yes, signs of destruction of living space can be found everywhere.

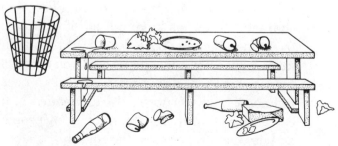

## Activity 12-9:  Athletes and Steroids

Read the passage on athletes trying to improve their athletic performance by using drugs. Find the key sentence. Then relate the supporting details. Follow the steps in "Here's How to Do It."

### Athletes and Steroids

Distance runners want to run faster. Shot putters, discus, and javelin throwers strive for distance records. Sprinters will do almost anything to improve their burst of speed. In football, defensive linemen feel the need to be bigger, stronger, and quicker than their opponents. Baseball players crave the added power that will make them big-time home-run power hitters. To lift at ever-higher levels, weight lifters seek to increase their musculature and body mass. Gymnasts analyze all available means of assistance as they attempt to attain Olympic-level performances in their chosen events. The desire for superior athletic achievement has led hundreds, even thousands, of men and women to endanger their health by taking anabolic steroids.

## Activity 12-10:  Satire

The following discusses one way writers make people laugh. Find the supporting details and relate them to the key sentence. Use a separate sheet of paper for your responses. Follow the steps outlined in "Here's How to Do It."

### Satire

As human beings, we all have faults and quirks that make us unique but at the same time make us like all other humans. Writers often use these faults and quirks to make people laugh. However, beyond the laughter, they want us to see how these shortcomings can create problems. By exaggerating the behavior of an individual or group of people, writers can create humorous situations that also make us wonder whether what we are laughing at is very close to the truth. From the Roman poets to contemporary writers, this device has been used in countless literary works. These works are called *satires,* and their purpose is to criticize problems to improve society.

## Activity 12-11:  Wars in the Twentieth Century

Read the passage on modern wars. Find the key sentence. Then relate the details which support it. Follow the steps in "Here's How to Do It."

### Wars in the Twentieth Century

In 1917, the U.S. joined the Allied countries fighting Germany and the Central Powers in World War I. When Japan bombed Pearl Harbor on December 7, 1941, and efforts to maintain a lasting peace failed, we again joined the Allies to oppose the Axis powers of Germany, Italy, and Japan in WWII. Our role in World War II lasted from 1941 to 1945. Our support of what is now known as the United Nations led us to participate in the Korean War (1950 to 1953) against the North Koreans and the Chinese Communists. The war in Vietnam began slowly in the early 1960s, but by 1970, thousands of American troops were fighting in South Vietnam. American ground troops withdrew in 1973, and in 1975 the Communist North Vietnamese took Vietnam. Two very brief wars, Grenada in 1983 and Panama in 1990, preceded a full-scale encounter with Iraq in 1991 when the war called "Desert Storm" was fought. The twentieth century has seen the United States send its troops all over the world to advance its government's aims.

## Activity 12-12:  Terrorism

Follow the steps listed in "Here's How to Do It" and find the supporting details. Then, relate them to the key sentence. Use a separate sheet of paper for your responses.

### Terrorism

In modern times, many small nations oppose the policies of larger, more powerful nations. They know, however, that they cannot engage these superpowers one on one. Some of these smaller countries are controlled by religious fanatics, who will stop at nothing to fulfill their goals. Some may inspire their followers with the belief that dying for their country is a direct ticket to heaven. To such people, the lives of innocent citizens are not important, and if these innocents are killed, that's the way it is. Leaders of this type also want publicity for their causes, and they know they can get it on TV. To get media exposure, they train their soldiers to commit acts of murder and sabotage. They also provide these soldiers with supplies and money. Through all this, terrorism has become the newest form of warfare throughout the entire world.

# Part 13

# Interior Sentence Paragraphs

## About This Part...

If you have been successful at finding the main idea positioned at either the beginning or end of a paragraph, you are becoming a flexible reader. If you also have been successful at finding and relating supporting details to those main ideas, then you are learning another important skill. Congratulations! You probably have greatly improved your reading comprehension.

Now you are ready for the toughest main idea search of all: finding the key sentence *somewhere* in the passage. This time you will have to look carefully at *all* the sentences to find it. You also need to look extra hard for supporting details. They can be *anywhere* in the paragraph.

After you find the key sentence, review the other sentences so that you can relate their details to the main idea. Then, you will write a short title that *restates* the main idea. This means writing a title that tells what the passage is about. Your work will be harder. Some of the paragraphs will be longer. Read each one slowly and carefully.

## Here's How to Do It

Follow these steps to help you find the key sentence in the following activities.

1. *Read* the first sentence, looking for important words and phrases. Write these details down on a piece of paper.

2. *Repeat* Step 1 with each succeeding sentence.

3. *Remember* that the key sentence, or main idea statement, will never appear first. When you find it, write down its details.

4. *Read* the sentences that follow the main idea statement. Write down the important words or phrases for each of these sentences. These are your supporting details. Now, relate the supporting details to the details in the main idea statement (Step 3). Do this by drawing a line on your paper from each supporting detail to the appropriate details in the main idea statement. In this way, you can see how the sentences are connected to each other.

5. *Review* the whole paragraph. Note, again, the main idea, the details you found in Steps 1 and 2, and the supporting details.

## Sample Activity:  Effects of TV

Read the paragraph below. Using the steps listed in "Here's How to Do It," find the main idea and its supporting details. Then, restate the main idea as a title using five words or less. Write your answer on a separate sheet of paper.

There is a rise in the crime rate among teenagers. Parents who don't care is often given as one reason. The thrill of doing something different is another. A reason which is being heard more and more, however, is that of violence on television. Today's young people see violence on the screen every night. Gangs of all kinds clash. Hundreds of police chase dozens of robbers. Men and women shout, brawl, chase, and kill. People in all walks of life are portrayed as having bloodthirsty instincts.

**Answer:** The statement *A reason which is being heard more and more, however, is that of violence on television* is the key sentence of the passage. The details *violence on the screen; gangs clash; police chase; shout, brawl, chase, and kill;* and *bloodthirsty instincts* all support the main idea. A possible title for this passage could be "Television and Teenage Crime."

## How Did You Do?

Did you notice that the *fourth* sentence is the main idea sentence? When you saw the key words *reason, more and more,* and *however,* you were able to realize that this, indeed, was the direct statement of the main idea of the paragraph.

Review the entire paragraph, noting how the main idea is set up or introduced by the first three sentences and then developed and supported by the last five sentences.

# Activities

Below you will find a number of paragraphs. Read each paragraph with care. Find the main idea located somewhere within the paragraph. There *always will be one.* Find the supporting details and relate them to the main idea. If you have trouble, follow the steps provided for you in "Here's How to Do It."

## Activity 13-1:  *The Service Alternative*

First, read the selection below. Then, using the steps listed in "Here's How to Do It," find the main idea and its supporting details. Write your answer on a separate sheet of paper.

Going to college after high school is what some students choose to do. Many others prefer to find a job. For those who aren't sure whether to go to school or find a job, the military service might be the answer. The Army, Navy, Marines, Air Force, and Coast Guard all offer careers and provide schooling. A person can learn a trade in the service. This can become a career while in the service, and it may also be a career once that person returns to civilian life. Lengths of service run from two to six years, depending on which branch you join. These terms can be renewed. For those who finally want to go to college, the service can be used as a time for growing up and saving money.

## Activity 13-2:  *Convenience Stores*

Read the following passage. Find the main idea and its supporting details. Follow the steps listed in "Here's How to Do It."

If you want to save time in your grocery shopping, there are convenience stores all over this country. They don't have a wide range of goods, but you can get what you need in a very short time. For variety and customer service, the big supermarkets are where you need to go. They have a wide range of products, not just groceries. They also have lots of brand names. When saving money is your goal, however, the discount food store is the place for you. The prices there are much lower than those in convenience stores. They also have a wider variety of products. They are cheaper than the supermarkets as well. They don't offer much customer service, though. For instance, you must bag your own purchases.

## Activity 13-3:  Views of General Custer

Read the passage on a famous U.S. general. Find the key sentence. Then relate the details which support it. Use the steps in "Here's How to Do It."

### View of General Custer

In 1941, there appeared a movie called *They Died with Their Boots On*. It starred the famous hero actor Errol Flynn and told about the defeat of General George Armstrong Custer by the Sioux at the Little Big Horn River. That film portrayed Custer as a brave, loyal U.S. soldier. His fight against the "evil" enemy was lost only because of overwhelming odds. He fought to the death. Thirty years later, another movie was made about Custer. It was called *Little Big Man* and starred Dustin Hoffman. He played the role of a white who was raised as an Indian and later became one of Custer's scouts. This film depicted the general as an egomaniac who didn't live in the real world and who enjoyed ordering his troops to kill women, children, and old people. Then, in 1990, a Hollywood producer named Bill Armstrong did a truly historical film on this famous general and his last battle. After living near the site of that battle for many months, Armstrong came up with what is probably the most accurate picture of this famous leader. It shows him as neither a hero nor an over-ambitious wacko. Instead, Custer is portrayed as a hard-driving, loyal army officer who got carried away with his mission to defeat the enemy. For his documentary, Bill Armstrong was voted into the Cowboy Hall of Fame in Oklahoma City in 1991.

## Activity 13-4:  Samuel Johnson

Carefully read the passage below about the eighteenth-century writer. Find the main idea and its supporting details. Write your answer on a separate sheet of paper.

Samuel Johnson, an eighteenth-century English writer, is well known as a literary critic. All the English writers of his era looked to him for judgments of their work. Johnson gathered around him some of the most learned men of his time. His group, called "Johnson's Circle," included some of the most notable English writers, artists, and political figures of the 1700s. Johnson was best known, however, for having produced the first English dictionary. Completed in 1755, it was the result of many years of hard work. It showed the author's great knowledge of Latin and Greek. It also laid down many rules of English grammar. This inspired the first English grammar books, which were published in the early 1760s.

# Activity 13-5:  Changing Names

Read the following passage about team names. Then find the sentence which most clearly expresses its main idea.

### Changing Names

In the first half of this century, high school, college, and professional athletic teams chose their names without much serious thought. If Duke University, for example, wanted to call its team the "Blue Devils," nobody seemed to care very much. In the latter half of the twentieth century, however, concern for the feelings of minorities and special interest groups has changed all that. Because of fear that they would offend people, numerous teams have either changed their names or been urged to do so. In the early 1970s, Stanford University changed its team's name from the "Indians" to the "Cardinals." Shortly after that, Virginia Tech University replaced the name "Gobblers" with "Hokies." In Florida, pressure has been placed on Dixie Hollins High School (St. Petersburg) to drop their team's name, the "Rebels." During the 1991 World Series, groups of Native Americans picketed the Atlanta Braves baseball team, trying to persuade the team to change its name.

# Activity 13-6:  The Wild 1960s

Carefully read the selection below. Using the steps listed in "Here's How to Do It," find the main idea and its supporting details.

Americans saw a lot of changes during the 1960s. For example, many saw the war in Vietnam grow. The United States became involved in this war. And in 1967, the U.S. played an even greater role. Many young people opposed this move. Scores of young men burned their draft cards. In the meantime, race riots were spreading in big cities across the country. In 1968, all of these problems were brought to a head. The enemy in Vietnam launched a surprise attack on Saigon, the capital city. This was called the Tet Offensive, because it occurred during the Tet holiday (New Year) in January. Two months later, President Lyndon Johnson announced that he would not run for re-election. Less than a month after President Johnson's announcement, the civil rights leader, Martin Luther King, Jr., was shot to death in Memphis, Tennessee. This caused riots in a number of cities. Then in June of 1968, Robert Kennedy was assassinated as he sought the nomination for Presidency. In August, the Democratic convention was the scene of a bloody fight between demonstrators and the Chicago police.

## Activity 13-7:  The Novelist's Style

Read the following. Find the main idea and its supporting details. Use a separate sheet of paper for your answers. Write a title for this passage.

Occasionally, authors use different formats for their novels. Rather than write a novel in chapters, the traditional way, they use other means to tell their characters' stories. One format is to tell a story through the entries in a diary. Another is to tell the story through letters. *The Color Purple* is a novel by Alice Walker that uses the format of letters. The story of the daily life, heartaches, troubles, and hopes of a black woman and her sister is told through their letters. The reader learns about the innermost thoughts and feelings of Celie and Nettie. The format was successful. Alice Walker won the Pulitzer Prize in 1983 for her novel. The novel was made into a film.

## Activity 13-8:  Ex-Presidents

Read the passage about presidents' activities after they leave office. Find the key sentence. Then relate the details that support it. Follow the steps in "Here's How to Do It."

### Ex-Presidents

Most of our presidents take life easy once they leave office. Lyndon B. Johnson went back to his ranch in Texas to relax. Dwight D. Eisenhower put in more time on the golf course playing the game he enjoyed. So did Gerald R. Ford. Former President Jimmy Carter, however, began a whole new career of service by founding Habitat for Humanity. Mr. Carter and his wife, Rosalynn, started gathering groups of volunteer citizens to build houses for the poor and homeless. Today, this effort has grown into a big-time enterprise. Thousands of volunteers participate in this program. Some people from other countries travel long distances to join in. Building supplies are donated by large corporations, small businesses, and individuals who want to pitch in. The owners-to-be get involved as well. Because of this effort, hundreds of people down on their luck now own their own homes.

# Activity 13-9:  A Traitor's Name

Read the passage about Vidkun Quisling. Find the key sentence. Then relate the details that support it. Follow the steps in "Here's How to Do It."

### A Traitor's Name

Throughout history, the names of certain people have become associated with ideas, character traits, or philosophies. The name "Horatio Alger," for example, has come to mean a great ending to a story, one in which the good guy wins. Actually, Alger was a popular, late-nineteenth-century American author. Small men with big eyes and a desire for power are sometimes called "Little Napoleons" after the famous nineteenth-century French military leader. We all know what a Judas is. A name that came to mean traitor in this century, however, is "quisling." It comes from the deeds of a Norwegian politician named Vidkun Quisling. He couldn't get elected in his own country in the 1930s, so he traveled to Germany in 1939 where he met Hitler. The two made a deal in which Quisling returned to Norway to become a Nazi spy. He helped set up Hitler's invasion of Norway in 1940, which ended with a Nazi victory there. Quisling, as head of the only political party acknowledged by the Germans, became Norway's premier in 1942, but he was always hated by his country's citizens. When Norway became free in 1945, Quisling was arrested and shot as a traitor. His name, however, lives on.

# Activity 13-10:  Staying Warm

First, read the passage below. Find the key sentence that expresses the main idea.

In cold weather people put on warmer clothing and stay indoors. They can turn on the heaters in their cars or other vehicles. Wild animals, however, find a variety of ways to survive in cold weather. Some leave for a warmer climate. Others crawl into caves or other shelters and sleep until spring. Others store food in advance, to prepare for winter. Many grow heavier coats of fur. Animals seem well-equipped to survive even under conditions of extreme cold.

## Activity 13-11:  Mrs. Stowe's Novel

Read the passage about a sermon that inspired the writing of *Uncle Tom's Cabin.* Find the key sentence. Then relate the details that support it. Follow the steps in "Here's How to Do It."

### Mrs. Stowe's Novel

Bowdoin College is a small liberal arts school located in Brunswick, Maine. Established in 1794, it has produced some famous American authors. The novelist and short-story writer Nathaniel Hawthore was one of these. Another was the poet Henry Wadsworth Longfellow. Probably the most famous book written at Bowdoin, however, was *Uncle Tom's Cabin,* by Harriet Beecher Stowe. With her husband, a Bowdoin professor, Mrs. Stowe attended the First Parish Church on campus each Sunday. One Sunday in 1850, Mrs. Stowe heard a passionate sermon there on the evils of slavery. It disturbed her so much that when she went home she began writing a novel. It was published in 1852 and, by 1854, *Uncle Tom's Cabin* was a best seller in the U.S. and Great Britain. More important, it had a great impact on thousands of people who were concerned about living in our "land of the free." Thus a number of historians believe that Mrs. Stowe's novel helped change people's perceptions about slavery.

## Activity 13-12:  Paying on Time

First, read the following passage carefully. Then find the key sentence that best expresses the main idea.

The buyer may fail to make any agreed-upon payment. He or she may fail to comply with one or more of the previously stated terms or conditions. Proceedings in bankruptcy, receivership, or solvency may be instituted by or against the buyer or the buyer's property. Or the seller may have reasonable cause to believe that the property is in danger of misuse or confiscation. Or the buyer may fail to comply with the other terms of this agreement. Or said required physical damage insurance (whether procured by the seller or the buyer) may be cancelled by the insurer prior to its expiration. In any of these situations, the seller shall have the right, at the seller's or the corporation's election, to declare the unpaid balance, together with any amount for which the buyer shall have become obligated hereunder, to be immediately due and payable.

# Part 14
# Putting It All Together

## About This Part...

Throughout Section Three, you have been doing *directed reading* activities. Directed reading means that the task is stated first and then the reading selection is provided. You have worked with main idea statements, always knowing where the key sentence would be located. Now, in this Part, you are going to review the skills you have learned.

In the activities that follow, there always will be a key sentence. Sometimes it will be at the beginning of the paragraph; sometimes it will be at the end; and at other times, it will be somewhere in the middle. Your job will be to find the key sentence in each paragraph *without help*. When you do so, remember that it is good reading practice to relate the supporting details in each paragraph to the main idea they support.

There is no Sample Activity for this Part because the activities combine the things that you have been doing all through Section Three. If you need to review the techniques to use in finding main ideas and supporting details, you can find them in the "Here's How to Do It" instructions on the following pages:

# Activities

When you have finished reading a passage, decide which sentence is the key sentence. Was it the *first sentence, last sentence,* or an *interior sentence*? On a separate sheet of paper, write down the key sentence. Good luck in your searches!

## Activity 14-1:  Ted Williams

Read the following paragraph. Then, find the key sentence. Use a separate sheet of paper for your answer.

### Ted Williams

Ted Williams, one of the greatest hitters in baseball history, had a lot going for him. He began his big league career at the age of eighteen, and he played for many years. This enabled him to earn a great deal of money. He was tall and slender. This gave him a lot of range in swinging the bat. He had very strong wrists and arms, which provided power with the bat. He loved to hit and would practice for hours. He also had amazing eyesight. He could follow any ball from the pitcher's hand to the plate. He could pick up the speed of a fast ball and know just when a curve would break. Ted Williams had skills few hitters have possessed before or since.

# Activity 14-2:  The Granite State

Carefully read this paragraph about a beautiful state. Find the key
sentence, located somewhere in the paragraph. Refer to the steps in
"Here's How to Do It."

## The Granite State

Although Vermont has the smallest population of all the states in the
Northeast, it is one of the most attractive for tourists. Its summers are long
and cool with lots of sunshine. Its winters are cold and snowy, making it
a perfect place for those who enjoy skiing. Its autumns are among the most
beautiful in the world, with the foliage displaying vivid reds, oranges, and
yellows for many weeks. The Green Mountain Forest with its craggy,
granite hills, provides an ideal range for hiking, camping, climbing, and
exploring. Two-thirds of Lake Champlain lies in Vermont (the rest in
Canada) and offers water sports for boaters, swimmers, and skiers.

# Activity 14-3: English Literature

First, read the passage. Then, find the key sentence. Use a separate sheet of paper for your answer.

### English Literature

In the early stages of recorded English literature, most poems, plays, and stories were about important and powerful people. There was *Beowulf,* which is about a great hero. There were the legends of King Arthur and his Knights of the Round Table. There was the romantic tale, *Sir Gawain and the Green Knight.* Geoffrey Chaucer was the first known English writer to portray the common man in his work. His long poem, *The Canterbury Tales,* describes people from all walks of life. He does include nobles, but he spends time and space describing millers, teachers, apprentices, country priests, and the like. The uniqueness and value of everyday human beings is offered with wit and sensitivity in his great poem from the Middle Ages.

# Activity 14-4:  Read the Fine Print

Read the passage about what you can claim from E-Z Mailing Service. Then find the key sentence in the paragraph. It may be anywhere in the paragraph.

### Loss or Damage Claims

Unless declared above, the maximum value for each parcel does not exceed $100.00. Sender agrees to hold E-Z Mailing Service and the carrier blameless for damage or loss to any parcel or contents caused by improper packaging by the sender. Determination of proper packaging shall be made by the carrier whose decision will be final. All damaged materials must be returned to E-Z Mailing Service for inspection. Sender agrees that parcels may be opened for inspection at any time to determine contents/packaging. Claims for loss or damage must be made in writing to E-Z Mailing Service within ninety days from date of shipment, otherwise they will be considered waived.

# Activity 14-5:  State Prison

The following is a narrative about a state prison. After reading the passage, find the key sentence. Use a separate sheet of paper for your answer.

### State Prison

There is a mood of tension around the entire prison. Groups opposing capital punishment march around the walls, carry placards, and shout slogans. Newspaper men and women come and go, and television cameras appear everywhere. Inside the prison, the guards perform their routine tasks. The prisoners are almost without exception grim-faced and quiet. On Death Row itself, the execution chamber stands ready. A prison chaplain moves to the cell of a man condemned to death. With the return of the death penalty in the U.S., the day of an execution is a grim, tense one at the appointed state prison.

## *Activity 14-6:  Creditworthiness*

Read the passage below carefully. Then, find the key sentence hidden in the selection. Use a separate sheet of paper for your answer.

### Creditworthiness

Suppose you and your husband apply for a loan and your application is denied because of "insufficient income," *but* your salary was not considered. Suppose you are single and want to buy a home. The bank turns you down for a mortgage loan even though you feel sure that you meet its standards. Suppose your charge account is closed when you get married, and you are told to reapply in your husband's name. What do you do? In each case, you may file a complaint under the Equal Credit Opportunity Act, a federal law which prohibits discrimination against an applicant for credit on the basis of sex, marital status, race, color, religion, national origin, age, and other factors. The Equal Credit Opportunity Act does not give anyone an automatic right to credit but it does require that creditors apply the same standard of "creditworthiness" to all applicants equally.

## *Activity 14-7:  Biology*

The following discusses some of the things students learn in biology. After reading the passage, find the key sentence. Use a separate sheet of paper for your answer.

### Biology

Once, in high school biology courses, most of the time was spent studying zoology, or animal life. Students focused their attention both on one-celled animals and complex animals, such as humans. The growing popularity of houseplants, however, has caused more interest in the study of botany. Now, more time than ever before is spent in the classroom studying plant life. The nature, growth, care, and diseases of plants are getting attention. Students enjoy field trips to observe and record the plants they find. This interest in plants has created business for garden centers and nurseries. More important, it has caused a balance in biology courses as students learn about all living things.

# Activity 14-8:  Credit Risk

First read the selection. Then, find the key sentence using the skills you have
learned. Write your answer on a separate sheet of paper.

## Credit Risk

Creditors choose various criteria to rate you as a credit risk. They may ask
about your finances: how much you earn, what kinds of savings and
investments you have, or other sources of income. They may look for signs
of reliability: your occupation, how long you've been employed, how long
you've lived at the same address, or if you own or rent your home. They also
may examine your credit record: how much you owe, how often you've
borrowed, and how you've paid past debts. Creditors want to be assured
of two things: (1) your ability to repay debt and (2) your willingness to do
so. The Equal Credit Opportunity Act does not change this standard of
creditworthiness.

# Activity 14-9:  Harry S Truman

Carefully read the passage below about Harry S Truman. Using the skills you have
learned, find the key sentence. Write your answer on a separate sheet of paper.

## Harry S Truman

Initially, Harry S Truman may have seemed to be a small, unimportant
person, but he may well stand out as one of the great American presidents.
Taking over the presidency in 1945 after the sudden death of Franklin
D. Roosevelt, Truman was immediately faced with the decision of drop-
ping the first atomic bomb. He did so and thereby ended World War II.
Many objected to his move, but it probably saved millions of lives which
otherwise would have been lost in battles. The next winter the coal miners
threatened to strike. President Truman nationalized the coal industry,
which didn't make him popular with labor leaders but did ensure that
northern families were warm during the winter. When the Russians
blockaded all routes into Berlin in 1948, President Truman ordered an
airlift, which provided the people in the surrounded city with the necessi-
ties of life until the blockade was lifted. In 1950, North Korean forces
moved across the South Korean border. Truman ordered U.S. forces into
combat and led the United Nations resistance to the Communist takeover.
He might not have always been right, but President Truman never backed
away from a tough situation.

## *Activity 14-10: A Latin American Author*

Read the following about a Latin American author. Then, find the key sentence in the passage. Use a separate sheet of paper for your answer.

### A Latin American Author

Some of the most exciting literature in the twentieth century has come from Latin American authors. One such author, who has many fans in the English-speaking world, is Gabriel García Márquez. In his novels, he combines reality and fantasy to create special worlds. His most famous novel, *One Hundred Years of Solitude,* is an excellent example of his rich imagination. The story takes place in Macondo, a fictitious town in Colombia. The fast-moving story of the people there keeps the reader wondering what could possibly happen next.

## *Activity 14-11: Creditors*

First, read the passage. Then, find the key sentence using the skills you have learned. Write your answer on a separate sheet of paper.

### Creditors

Creditors use various systems to arrive at the balance on your credit card account on which they assess finance charges. Some creditors assess finance charges after subtracting your payments for the billing period. This is called the *adjusted-balance method.* Other creditors give you no credit for payments made during the billing period. This is called the *previous-balance method.* Under a third method—the *average daily-balance method*—creditors add your balances for each day in the billing period and then divide by the number of days in the billing period. Under this method, your purchases made during the billing period may or may not be added to the daily balance.

# Activity 14-12: Verbs in English

Read the selection about changes in verb forms in English. Then find the key sentence. It may be anywhere in the paragraph. Thus you must read each sentence carefully.

### Verbs in English

For a long time, in our language, the only past tense of the verb "strive" was "strove." Today, if you look in the dictionary, you can find its past tense form listed as "strived." Also, though it may sound a little unnatural, the past tense form of "drag" used to be "drug." It is now listed in the dictionary as "dragged." Some day, therefore, the past form of "think" may be "thinked" rather than "thought." Because the past tense of English verbs is usually formed by adding "-d" or "-ed," and because verbs using this method are easier to learn, more changes like this may occur. Such changes are all part of the normal process of making language forms in the English language more consistent and less confusing.

# Part 15

# Multi-Paragraph Statements

## About This Part...

So far, in Section Three, you have been working with one-paragraph passages. Since most of the reading you do, in or out of school, consists of more than one paragraph, it's time to move on to longer passages. In this Part, you will focus your attention on finding main ideas in passages longer than a single paragraph.

Passages composed of several paragraphs usually contain a *unifying statement*. This acts as the key sentence in the passage and gives the main idea. It tells, in a nutshell, what the *entire* passage is about. In the following set of activities, the unifying statement always will appear in the first paragraph. Each of the remaining paragraphs has a main idea of its own. These paragraphs expand, clarify, and further explain the unifying statement.

As you work on the following passages, remember these points:

1.  Each long passage has a unifying statement.

2.  Each paragraph in the passage has a key sentence.

3.  Each paragraph relates, in some way, to the unifying statement for the passage as a whole.

As you can see, the task of comprehending what you read becomes more complicated here. Read these longer passages carefully!

## Here's How to Do It

Use these steps for the activities in this Part.

1.  *Read* the entire passage.

2.  *Read* the first paragraph and find the unifying statement for the whole passage. Write it down on a separate sheet of paper.

3.  *Read* the next paragraph and find its main idea and write it down.

4.  Repeat Step 3 for each of the remaining paragraphs.

5.  Review your work when you have finished. Be sure the unifying statement describes the content of the whole passage. Check to see if each paragraph's main idea relates to the unifying statement.

## Sample Activity:  Books for Teens

Read the following about books for teens. Follow the steps outlined in "Here's How to Do It." Find the unifying statement and the main idea of each paragraph. Use a separate sheet of paper for your answers.

### Books for Teens

Books that honestly deal with young people entering into adulthood are a valuable part of a literary education. Such books must "tell it like it is" about growing up. Certain aspects of the growing-up years are painful to go through and not easy to express. A fearful reader finds books that shy away from these matters. Books that are straightforward about growing up discuss topics that some people do not like school children to read.

For many years, teenagers had little more than books showing sweet, obedient little girls and serious, well-mannered little boys. Then, in the early 1950s, a novel that appeared was more to the point. It described a rich teenage boy named Holden Caulfield who was kicked out of an upper-class prep school and then went underground in New York City for a few days. Holden's adventures made most adults look rather silly and clumsy. The novel, the *Catcher in the Rye,* by J. D. Salinger, captured the imagination of the young reading public because it told their story honestly.

Books that do a good job of describing teenage lifestyles can pose problems, however. One involves the use of obscene language. Another is the description of sexual activity. *The Catcher in the Rye* included both and, in doing so, angered many parents. In 1958, the publication of John Knowles's *A Separate Peace* provided an alternative, since it spoke honestly about teenage relatioships but didn't contain bad language or sex activity. Knowles's treatment of the friendship of two boys was frank and believable. He portrayed an honest picture of serious aspects of growing up which young readers enjoyed. He also avoided some of the topics that got the Salinger book in trouble.

Judith Guest's more recent *Ordinary People* is an open, humorous, sensitive, and honest book about kids growing up. It does use bad language and describes some sex. It deals with boy-girl relationships and high school friendships. It also pays attention to problems of adults relating to young people. There is much concern with son-mother and son-father situations. There is also a lot of description of how husbands and wives struggle to get along with each other. In general, it is as honest as the other two earlier books but covers more of life than they do.

**Answer:** The unifying statement is the *first* sentence in the paragraph. The following are the key sentences in the remaining paragraphs: In the second paragraph, it is the *last* sentence; in the third paragraph, it is the *fourth* sentence; and in the fourth paragraph, it is the *first* sentence.

# How Did You Do?

Did you note that the first sentence in the first paragraph is the unifying statement? It tells what the whole passage is going to be about. In the last sentence of the second paragraph, you find out that the book being described is by J. D. Salinger. Then, in the next paragraph, the fourth sentence introduces John Knowles's book. Finally, the last paragraph begins with a key sentence that states the qualities of Judith Guest's novel.

# Activities

You will find a number of multi-paragraph passages on the following pages. They all have unifying statements at the beginning of the first paragraph. Read the first sentence carefully. The paragraphs that follow all have key sentences, but they are not always in the first position. Note them as you read through the passage. You may wish to write down key sentences as you see them. Notice especially their positions in each paragraph. For dealing with the entire passage, follow the steps listed in "Here's How to Do It."

## Activity 15-1:  Using a Floppy Disk

Read the passage about using a diskette to store computer information. Find the key sentences. Then relate the details that support them. Follow the steps in "Here's How to Do It."

### Using a Floppy Disk to Store Computer Information

Once the user has inputted important information into the computer, this information should be recorded or "backed up" for future reference. One of the storage areas should be somewhere outside the computer in case the drive fails. If such a failure occurs—and the user has no "backup"—the information is lost. This can be extremely frustrating to someone who has spent many hours creating important documents or other computer data. Storing computer information efficiently and inexpensively is a rapidly evolving area of computer technology. In the early years of the personal computer revolution, using cassette tapes was the primary way to record computer data. Now, diskettes are the usual means of storage. The diskette, or floppy disk, is a widely used method of storing computer data. A box of floppy disks can be purchased at most stores that sell computer

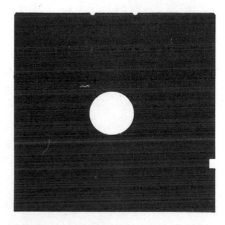

equipment. These small disks are relatively inexpensive, lightweight, and easy to store.

Shaped like a small square, the floppy disk contains a paper-thin disk of magnetic film, much like that in a cassette tape. To back up data, the user inserts the diskette in the disk drive device of the computer and gives the computer the command for backing up information. The computer drive can both record to the diskette and retrieve information from it. The physically magnetic properties of the disk inside the diskette casing allow for the storage of magnetic charges onto its surface. The information in the computer is translated and recorded onto the disk by the computer's disk drive, which charges certain areas of the disk. It leaves other areas without a magnetic charge. The drive can read the information from the diskette by sensing the charges and translating them back into the letters, numbers, and symbols that people can understand. Each diskette can hold between 55 and 450 typed pages of text, depending on the size of the magnetic surface, the density at which data is compacted, and whether both sides can be used to store information. The floppy disk is a great invention for efficiently backing up and storing important computer information.

# Activity 15-2:  Preparing for a Test

The passage below discusses some of the ways you can prepare for a test. On a separate sheet of paper, write the unifying statement for the passage and the main idea for each paragraph.

## Preparing for a Test

Taking an important test requires preparation and effort. There are things you can do to prepare for specific tests. You should review the required readings and go over your notes. A good night's sleep also helps. There are, however, some things you can do during a test to help improve your performance.

Don't panic when you first get your test paper. Relax in your chair. Make yourself read the directions first, slowly and carefully. Read any directions which are written on the board. Listen closely to what the instructor says when the test is distributed. Ask questions if you're not sure what the important ground rules are. Don't be afraid to ask if you're not sure of something. Finally, begin reading test items or writing when you're sure you know *what* you're supposed to do, *how much* you must complete, and *how long* you have to finish the test.

Read each test item slowly, thinking as you read, and reread it at least once before answering. Finish one question before going on to the next. Think only about the issue in the question. Recall what you know about it. Answer it slowly. Then look at your answer. Do the items one at a time and only concentrate on the question you're working on.

Look for key words in all items. Watch and see how words such as *always, never, everyone, the most, without exception,* and other such terms are used. Sometimes they are tossed in to provoke your thinking about the circumstances of a topic. Good test questions are worded very carefully. Train yourself to look for key words and phrases, especially those you have seen or heard the instructor use at different times in class.

Don't become stumped by questions concerning topics you think you know nothing or little about. Read through the item. If nothing comes to your mind, pause. Then, read the item again. If it's still a mystery, leave it immediately. Read another item as described before. If you can handle it, do so. If you can't, drop it and find one you *can* answer. Then work carefully on that one. Come back later to the ones which you have not been able to answer. When you read them again, you'll be surprised how many aren't that far out of your scope of knowledge after all. By doing the easier questions first, you have helped yourself prepare for the harder ones.

## Activity 15-3:  Grammar

Read the following passage. Using the steps outlined in "Here's How to Do It," find the unifying statement for the passage and the main idea of each paragraph. Write your answer on a separate sheet of paper.

### Grammar

The study of the grammar of a language has to do with how its systems function. All languages have certain ways of forming words to mean various things. Forms of words help change their meanings, such as from singular to plural (*boy to boys*) or from present to past (*touch to touched*). Also, the particular ways in which words are placed in a sentence may determine the meaning of a sentence. Any time you study one or more such systems in a language, you are studying its grammar.

Some people mistakenly think that grammar study consists of finding out what and what not to say in a language. This isn't true. Choices in language, such as saying "he is" rather than "he isn't" or "the children were" rather than "the children was," depend on fashion and style in the language at a particular time. Such choices change as people's fashions change. The study of these fashions and styles, and the ways in which they change, is called *usage*.

Closely related to the study of usage is the study of dialects of a language. Speakers of a language don't all speak it the same way. *Dialect* study concerns itself with the way in which the use of language varies according to geography and social class. The particular ways in which people use their language are affected by the geographic region in which they live, the kinds of jobs they have, the schools they attend, and the neighborhoods in which they live.

# Activity 15-4: High-Tech Movies

Read the following passage. Then find the key sentences in each paragraph.

## High-Tech Movies

Over the past twenty years or so, a number of movie types have been created. One movie will be a smash hit, such as *The Godfather* (1972), Then a series of sequels will appear: *Godfather II, Godfather III*, etc. Also, a number of movies about Mafia or Mafia-like gangland activities have emerged. A highly popular type of new movie is the high-tech, bloody, adventure film. *Alien* was a good example and, as of 1992, has been followed by two sequels. The same can be said for *Lethal Weapon*. There are now *The Terminator* I and II. The popularity of *The Hunt for Red*

*October* could well signal the beginning of a cluster of post-cold-war, high-tech thrillers.

The fast-action, technology-oriented films have been accompanied by a group of young male actors who have become high-tech heroes. Arnold Schwarzenegger may be the best known of these. Bruce Willis may well rival Schwarzenegger in this category.

The team of Mel Gibson and Danny Glover ranks high on this list. Chuck Norris has starred in several films as a modern-day combat soldier. And, of course, Harrison Ford has done several of these films since his success in *Star Wars*. Even a relatively old-time star such as Sean Connery, the James Bond of earlier days, has tried his luck at a high-tech adventure or two on the silver screen.

# Activity 15-5: The Courts

Read the passage on the nature of courts in our country. Then find the key sentence in each paragraph.

## The Courts

A court is an institution that is set up by the government to settle disputes through a legal process. Disputes come to court when people can't agree about what happened: Did Bill Jones run a red light before his car ran into John Smith's, or was the light green, as he says it was? Did Frank Williams rob the bank, or was it his twin brother, Joe?

Courts decide what really happened and what should be done about it: If the accident *was* Jones's fault, how much should he pay Smith for the damage he did? If Williams did rob the bank, how should he be punished?

Courts play an important role in our society for a number of reasons. They decide whether a person committed a crime and what the punishment should be. They also provide a peaceful way to decide private disputes that people can't resolve among themselves. A court decision can affect people other than the individuals who are involved in the lawsuit. For example, in 1965 three high school students in Des Moines, Iowa, were suspended from school for wearing black arm bands to protest the war in Vietnam. They went to court to have the rule against arm bands declared invalid. When the Supreme Court decided in *Tinker v. Des Moines School District* that the rule violated the students' constitutional right of freedom of expression, that decision affected the rights of public school students all over the country to express their views in a nondisruptive manner. The Supreme Court's 1954 decision in *Brown v. Board of Education* had an even more widespread effect. The case settled a dispute between the parents of Linda Brown and their local board of education in Topeka, Kansas. The Supreme Court decided that requiring white children and black children to go to separate schools violated the U.S. Constitution.

Since political leaders appoint judges in America, the philosophy of the courts has changed from time to time. In 1988, for example, the U.S. Supreme Court rendered its now-famous *Hazelwood* decision, in which it determined the speech of students could in fact be restricted if school administrators felt students' statements were not consistent with the school's "basic educational mission." This decision represented a very different point of view from the one handed down in *Tinker*. The majority of justices voting for the school administration in Hazelwood had a different understanding of the Constitution from those of twenty years before.

# Activity 15-6:  Special Checks

Carefully read the selection below. Follow the steps given in "Here's How to Do It." Find the unifying statement on the passage and the main idea of each paragraph. Write your answers on a separate sheet of paper.

### Special Checks

In addition to the checks you normally use, there are special types of checks that you may find useful periodically.

Traveler's checks can be purchased at banks for a small fee and can be used anywhere around the world. Denominations are $10, $20, $50, or higher. At the time you buy traveler's checks, you must sign each one in the upper left-hand corner; this enables the person cashing it to compare two signatures—the signature in the corner with the one you complete as you finish making a purchase.

Certified checks are required for certain financial transactions such as real estate closings. The bank can certify one of your personal checks by using a special ink stamp; the amount of the check is then set aside from your account and is released only when the check is received for payment.

Cashier's checks are drawn by the bank on itself at your request; you pay the bank for the amount of the check, plus a small fee. Cashier's checks are of unquestioned value and can be used if you are making an important payment where you are not known.

# Activity 15-7:  Problems in the New Peace Era

Read the passage on ways in which the end of the Cold War has created problems. Find the key sentences. Then relate the details which support them. Follow the steps in "Here's How to Do It."

### Problems in the New Peace Era

In November 1989, citizens of West and East Berlin began to tear down the Berlin Wall, which marked the beginning of the end of the Soviet Union's control of Eastern Europe. In rapid order, countries of Eastern Europe threw out their Communist governments and began to erect new ones. The people in the U.S.S.R. soon joined this movement. Today there is a number of independent republics there. Some of these republics have joined together to form a nation called the Commonwealth of Independent States. The Communist dictatorship known as the Union of Soviet Socialist Republics is gone, after lasting almost seventy-five years.

These amazing events brought an end to what we Americans had called "the Cold War" for about forty-five years. Our foreign policy, our economy, and much of our thinking about the future had been deeply affected by that powerful opponent, the U.S.S.R. One of its leaders, Nikita Khrushchev, had said about the U.S. in 1961, "We will bury you." Today, the power of that huge country is spread out over a number of smaller ones that are trying to figure out how to survive and are no longer a major military threat.

However, the end of this long period of worry about a nuclear war with the Soviets has brought some problems for many Americans. Our economy has depended on defense against Communism since the end of World War II. When that threat ended, a number of Army, Navy, and Air Force bases in the U.S. were considered to be no longer needed. As plans were made to close them, the problem of people's jobs became a real one. Many military personnel faced the loss of their careers. Civilians working on the bases were told they were no longer needed. The towns, often small ones, where military bases were located depended heavily on the military people living on these bases to shop there. Many of the local businesses had to close down. This put even more people out of work, most of whom had no place to go.

Weapons manufacturers lost a lot of business when the Cold War came to an end. Hit just as hard were the major airplane makers such as Lockheed and Boeing. They depended on contracts with the U.S. military for their survival. Electronics companies, which supplied the systems for hundreds of military products, saw a sharp reduction in their contracts. So did garment firms that made uniforms and other clothing for the Army, Navy, Marines, Air Force, and Coast Guard. The entire U.S. economy has taken some heavy losses as the country has begun to adjust to a peaceful way of life.

Not only bases in the U.S., but those military installations operating overseas have been affected by the sudden end of the Cold War. A large number of bases all over the world are now in the process of "drawing down," the military term for closing. One of the main features of these bases has been the Department of Defense's schools, which have taught the children of U.S. service personnel for more than forty years. These schools must close, too. Their teachers find themselves out of work for the time being. Secretaries, janitors, and other school workers are also laid off. Many of these people are citizens of the host country, such as Germany, Spain, and Turkey. They are having trouble finding new jobs. The school buildings are now useless and will probably be torn down. Thousands of U.S. school children will be relocated, most back home where they will have to adjust to new schools, teachers, courses, and classmates. The "New Peace" is not without cost.

# Activity 15-8:  American Writers

Read the following passage. Follow the steps outlined in "Here's how to Do It." Find the unifying statement for the whole passage, then the main idea of each paragraph. Write your answers on a separate sheet of paper.

### American Writers

*Real* American literature did not emerge until after the Civil War. Before that period, most American writers imitated British authors; after the war, people began migrating west, however, and a new breed of writers appeared whose subjects were American places, people, interests, and themes and whose styles were authentically American rather than British. Foremost among them was the folksy journalist, storyteller, and novelist Mark Twain, whose famous novel *The Adventures of Huckleberry Finn* is considered by many scholars the first truly *American* literary work.

One of America's first great poets was Walt Whitman, a vigorous, active man who enjoyed travel and outdoor life. His first poem, "Song of Myself," published in 1871, is a very long work describing many things Whitman loved: physical activity, love, the American frontier, courage, exploring new places, and similar themes. Whitman's poems are almost all lengthy and full of stories, descriptions of the new country, exaggerations, and profane language; they reflect the public's love for movement, action, and adventure.

Like Whitman, Emily Dickinson created her most famous poetry after the Civil War. Dickinson spent her entire life in New England, a very private person who never married, had few close friends, and seemed to prefer solitude. Dickinson's quiet, formal nature is reflected in her poems, most of which are very short and deal with personal feelings and themes like privacy and loneliness in a restrained, almost cryptic way that leaves the reader much to interpret. Dickinson's language is proper and precise, never given to exaggeration. Thus she was a very different person and writer than Whitman, though together they established what truly can be called *American* poetry.

## Activity 15-9:  Technology and the Radio

Carefully read the passage below. Write the unifying statement for the whole passage on a separate sheet of paper. Then, write the main ideas of each paragraph.

### Technology and the Radio

Modern technology has satisfied the cravings people have for listening to music by making radio portable. Music has become an important part of everyday life. Throughout the country, people now listen to music at home, at work, and at play.

There was a time when radio could only be found in affluent homes. Today, most home owners now can tune in to music while gardening, cleaning, and exercising. Technology and the low cost of producing radios made it possible for more people to own radios.

Outside the home, people can be seen toting a radio, listening to music while jogging, walking, or just sitting in a park. Technology made radio portable, which made it possible for people to listen to music almost anywhere. Portable radios come in various sizes and could be as small as a wallet or as large as a briefcase. Most portable music systems are equipped with headsets.

In the workplace, there are some offices that broadcast music for their employees. Some people, however, may prefer to listen to a different type of music. Technology made it possible for people to bring a portable radio into the workplace.

## Activity 15-10:  The Modem:  A New Computer Capability

Carefully read the passage below. Write the unifying statement for the whole passage on a separate sheet of paper. Then, identify the main ideas of each paragraph.

### The Modem: A New Computer Capability

A modem is a device that allows a computer to exchange information with another computer or device using regular telephone lines. The modem converts the data to be sent into audible tones. These tones, which sound a little like high-pitched chirping, are transmitted over the telephone lines until they are received by the modem on the receiving end. The modem in the receiving device or computer then converts the tones back into a format that the user can understand.

Modems have become popular in today's computer market. Businesses find them extremely helpful. For example, an office manager who is at home can gain access to information that is stored in his/her office computer. Modems can also be used to transfer files, programs, documentation and records to computers all over the world. Those involved in research can exchange their latest findings without having to wait for the publication of a journal article, which might take weeks or even months.

Frequently, modems are used for everyday household matters, social interaction, or just plain fun. For example, if someone wishes to share a list of recipes with a friend or relative, the list can be sent quickly from one computer to another. Without a modem, the recipes would have to be copied or printed, then mailed or delivered. Using a modem, the list goes quickly and efficiently over the telephone lines from computer to computer. Using a modem to participate in multi-player games from the privacy of one's own home is a lot of fun and can be highly competitive. More and more users regularly turn to their modem just to "chat" with people who have similar interests and concerns. In this way, modems create friendships among people who have never met in person.

## Activity 15-11: *More on Computers: Bulletin Board Systems*

Carefully read the passage below. Write the unifying statement for the whole passage on a separate sheet of paper. Then, identify the main idea of each paragraph.

### Bulletin Board Systems

Bulletin board systems, called *BBSs* for short, are becoming commonplace in the United States, even in small towns. A BBS is a computer with phone lines and modems "dedicated" to receiving calls from other modem users who subscribe to the system. Bulletin board systems serve as a connection point or clearinghouse for their subscribers, who generally live in a given area, such as a city or town. Files and messages can be stored temporarily on the BBS computer until subscribers call the BBS to retrieve them.

Bulletin board systems are usually available twenty-four hours per day. This is very convenient for those who are away from home for a large part of the day at school, work, or on vacation. Why is a BBS useful? If, for example, a user who has a modem is not at home—with the computer turned on—when a message is sent, he or she could *not* receive it. As a BBS subscriber, however, he or she can call in to the BBS at any time to see if there are any messages. If there *are* messages, the user can quickly retrieve them.

# Finding Meaning in Figurative Language

# Part 16

# Working with Figurative Language

## About This Part...

Suppose your uncle explains how cousin Jerry ate his dinner by saying, "Jerry ate like a pig." When your uncle compares Jerry to a pig, he expects you to picture how a pig eats. Then, you compare what you know about a pig's eating habits with the way Jerry ate his dinner. Your uncle is using *figurative language* to describe Jerry's behavior.

Figurative language includes *simile* and *metaphor*. A simile is a comparison using the words *like* or *as*. A metaphor is a comparison that does *not* use such words.

Figurative language is commonly used in writing and speaking. It makes the ideas conveyed more interesting and vivid. But sometimes it is difficult to understand what the writer or speaker means if you don't understand the figurative language. In this Part, you'll practice a three-step process to find figurative meanings.

## Here's How to Do It

Finding meaning in figurative language is a problem-solving process that has three steps.

1. *Find the figurative language.* As you read, find the word or phrase the author uses to compare the idea with something he or she *hopes* is familiar to you.

2. *Try its literal meaning.* Does the exact meaning of the word or phrase make sense? In the example used earlier, does Jerry look like a *real* pig? The answer is "of course not." You need to look for other aspects of the word or phrase in addition to its first, most literal, or most familiar meaning.

3. *Find its intended meaning.* Compare what you know about the word or phrase with what the writer or speaker is trying to convey. For example, compare what you know about pigs (they eat sloppily) with the way in which Jerry ate his dinner. The intended meaning is that Jerry ate sloppily.

Sometimes the sentence or passage may contain "clues." Context clues may help you find the intended meanings of figurative language. So read the sentence or passage carefully.

## Sample Activity: Tim and the Coach

Read the following passage. Find the figurative language in *Tim's sentence*. Then, on a separate sheet of paper, write the literal meaning and the intended meaning. Follow the steps outlined in "Here's How to Do It."

**Tim and the Coach**

It's been a while since Tim has played in a football game. He asks his coach why he hasn't been given the chance to play. Coach Rose talks about how neat Tim is, now hard he has been working, how much he has improved, and so on. Finally, Tim interrupts him and says, "I wish you'd stop beating around the bush."

**Answer:** 1. Find the figurative language: beating around the bush.
2. Try the literal meaning: Is the coach literally beating around a bush?
3. Find the intended meaning: Tim wants the coach to stop stalling and answer him in a straight manner.

# How Did You Do?

Did you notice the context clues? Rather than answering Tim's question, the coach talks about "how neat Tim is, how hard he has been working, how much he has improved..." These clues tell you the coach is not giving Tim a straight answer.

Sometimes, however, you need more than context clues to help you find the intended meanings. The figurative language must be in your *language experience*. In the example above, the coach understood what Tim meant because he knows what the verb *beating* means, and he knows what a bush is. He also knows that Tim is really asking him to quit stalling.

## Figurative Language Not in Your Experience

One of the biggest problems in understanding what you read is to be able to figure out the intended meaning in the figurative language. If the figurative language is not in your experience, you must find the information you need in a reference source.

In the story *A Christmas Carol* by Charles Dickens, three ghosts visit the rich miser, Scrooge, on Christmas Eve. In the final chapter, Scrooge has a terrifying dream; the ghost of Christmas Yet to Come leads Scrooge to a deteriorated cemetery. There they find a gravestone bearing the name "Ebenezer Scrooge." When Scrooge wakes up, he realizes that he *isn't* dead, that this *is* Christmas Day, and that he *does* have a chance to amend his cheap and unpleasant ways. After Scrooge awakes, Dickens describes him in this manner. "He frisked into the sitting room, making a perfect Laocoön of himself in his stockings."

The question is this: How did Scrooge look when he realized that he wasn't dead and had a chance to live a better life? Well, the fact is that he looked like Laocoön. The big question is, of course, *who* is Laocoön, and how did *he look*? Try the three-step process.

It's easy to complete the first step by noticing the name "Laocoön." The identity of this person is probably *not* in the language experience of many people. So key is the *second* step: "Try its literal meaning." Most people cannot accomplish this because there are two unknowns: (1) the subject (Scrooge), and (2) the *supposedly* familiar person that the subject is compared to (Laocoön). When you have two unknowns in a metaphor, you have problems.

What do you do? First, you have to find out about the thing to which the subject is compared. Who is Laocoön? You learn that he was a priest, a holy man in the myth of the Trojan War. One day, during the ten-year war, Laocoön was performing a religious ceremony in his temple on a hill outside the walls of Troy. Because he had supernatural powers, Laocoön realized that there were Greek soldiers inside the horse. To warn his fellow Trojan citizens, he ran down from the hill yelling, "Don't take the wooden horse into the city! I fear the Greeks even when they bear gifts!" When he reached the bottom of the hill, two large snakes came out of the sea. The snakes entwined themselves around Laocoön and his two young sons. Laocoön and his sons struggled frantically as they were dragged to their death in the sea. The Trojans, feeling this was a sign that Laocoön was wrong, took the horse into the city. That night, the Greek soldiers came out of the horse. They opened the gates to let in their fellow Greeks who were waiting outside the walls. They destroyed the Trojan city.

Now, think back to the figurative language. How did Scrooge look on Christmas morning? "He looked just like Laocoön." How did Laocoön look? He struggled frantically with the sea serpents' coils, trying to free himself. That's the way the excited Scrooge looked —all tangled in his long stockings. This is the part of the Laocoön story you need to understand. Of course, it helps to know the whole story, but at least you need to know the part about the struggle with the serpents to reach step three in the problem solving process.

Try using the three-step process again. In the following passage, you will see the metaphor "meet our Waterloo." You can only understand the meaning if you know the historical reference.

It was late in the football season before I realized that the team was facing an uphill battle in its goal to play a bowl game. Not only had members of the team been injured in the last two games, but the most promising quarterback that we had seen in five years was caught for cheating on an exam. The suspension that he faced was sure to be crucial. It was almost certain we would meet our Waterloo as a team unless the tide turned in some unpredictable way.

To completely understand what the metaphor "meet our Waterloo" means, you need to know the history about Waterloo. Napoleon Bonaparte, Emperor of France, lost an important battle to the Duke of Wellington of England in 1815 at Waterloo. Many thought the battle was a crushing defeat for Napoleon. This battle became known as the Battle of Waterloo.

Now, let's go back to the passage. Knowing the history about Waterloo, you now understand that the writer fears the football team might lose the upcoming game.

The passage below contains some figurative language that probably is familiar to you. One metaphor, however, may be unknown to you. Again, use the three-step process to help you find the intended meaning.

At the beginning, the adventure seemed like a dream come true. Actually, having the opportunity to travel to another galaxy was something I had fantasized about as a youngster, never seriously thinking that I'd be making such a trip in my lifetime. The mission was one of mercy; and that was the drawing card for me as a physician. With a surplus of us on Earth, I knew that I was needed in areas that were just being pioneered. My goal was to serve humankind, and it made little difference to me that I'd be doing that several light years away from my native planet.

So, late in the twenty-first century, I placed my John Henry [signature] on the agreement and set out to meet the challenge like a knight in shining armor. Little did I know what was in store for me during the next six months. Even though I was only attempting to help people, the "powers that be" made life impossible for me. My self-image was rapidly becoming one of a rebel against the great injustices around me. However, it wasn't long before I realized that I was *Prometheus bound* with little hope of being freed.

How did the writer feel at the end of the passage? First, identify the metaphor, *Prometheus bound.* Using context clues, you *can* understand that all is not well. To fully understand the passage, though, you really must know the story of Prometheus. Therefore, you need to do some research and find out about Prometheus. Who was he? Why is the writer comparing himself to Prometheus?

Prometheus was a Titan in Greek mythology who cared a great deal for men long before the creation of women. Prometheus stole fire from heaven as a gift for man. He also arranged for man to get the best part of animals sacrificed, while the gods received the worst parts. Zeus, in his anger, first punished men by giving them women and then punished Prometheus for favoring man, even though Zeus was indebted to Prometheus for his help in conquering the other Titans. Prometheus was bound to a rock by chains that were unbreakable and was told that he would not have a moment's peace. Not only did Zeus want to punish Prometheus for his gifts to man, but he also wanted to force Prometheus to tell a secret related to the future. Prometheus refused to tell the secret to Zeus' messenger, Hermes.

Zeus sent an eagle to tear at his body. Still, Prometheus remained silent. He realized that his body was chained to the rock, but his spirit was free. Prometheus knew in his heart that he had done what was right by caring about mortals in their helplessness and that he had been good to Zeus all along. Prometheus never yielded. Later on, he was delivered from his bonds with the help of Hercules and Chiron.

In the fifth century B.C., the Greek author Aeschylus wrote a play about Prometheus and his punishment. The play is entitled *Prometheus Bound.*

Now, return to the metaphor. By knowing the story of Prometheus, you are better able to understand how the author felt when he compared himself to Prometheus. You now know that he was experiencing great suffering rather than a little discomfort like acid indigestion; you also know that, like Prometheus, the author sees little relief in the near future.

When you read passages that contain figurative language, you need the whole story! If you have trouble trying its literal meaning (step two), you must find the information you need to fill in the picture. Some reference sources will give you *a thumbnail sketch* (Did you *catch the figurative language?*) of the topic for which you need background. Others will not be as helpful. Don't depend solely on the dictionary; be prepared to look at other sources. In this Part, you'll have practice working with figurative language for which you won't need help with step two.

As you read, you may encounter other allusions (indirect references) that are not in your language background. Be sure to take a few minutes to find the information by using the resources in your library. The knowledge you gain from your research will aid you greatly in understanding allusion. This skill, in turn, can help you become a better reader.

# Activity

In the sentences below, you will have an opportunity to use the three-step process to find meaning in figurative language. The three-step process is listed in "Here's How to Do It" on page 157. Many of these are expressions that almost have been worn out through overuse. When such overuse occurs, the expressions are referred to as clichés.

## Activity 16-1:  Using Figurative Language

Using the steps outlined in "Here's How to Do It," 1) find the figurative language; 2) try its literal meaning; and 3) find the intended meaning. Write your responses on a separate sheet of paper.

**a.**    I'll do what you ask, but just remember that I'm going out on a limb for you.

**b.**    After a good night's sleep, I felt like a million dollars.

**c.**    When Elaine first started helping paint the house, she felt like a square peg in a round hole.

**d.**    The book sold like wildfire and was on the bestseller list in no time flat.

**e.**    Everyone wanted Ken on the swim team because he could swim like a fish.

**f.**    Some people can't keep a secret; they let the cat out of the bag.

g.  They agreed to salt away enough money for the education of each family member.

h.  Mary must have a memory like an elephant because she remembers everyone she ever meets.

i.  Jennifer was such an independent thinker that her closest friends realized she marched to the beat of a different drummer.

j.  Pedro said the upcoming math quiz would be a piece of cake for him because he had studied so much over the weekend.

k.  Ann is working extremely hard at her new job because she knows that hard work is the key to moving up the ladder.

l.  When you are doing something you enjoy, time flies.

m.  The news of his inheritance came out of the blue.

n.  Stop killing time and get to work!

o.  Dan says he is a great basketball player, but I think he is just talking through his hat.

p.  It's no surprise that he got his walking papers, since he has been coming into work late.

q.  Many people believe that putting one's best foot forward is important when interviewing for a job.

r.  The evidence the police found in her home nailed her to the wall.

# Part 17

# Figures of Speech

## About This Part...

Much of the language we read or hear every day is understood on a *literal* level. That is, the words and sentences have a single, clear meaning. But frequently, language has a *figurative* meaning that may not have much to do with the exact definitions of the words used. The meanings conveyed by figurative language are usually clear only to certain persons—those who share the history and culture in which the figurative language is relevant. For example, someone from the other side of the globe may not understand the figurative meaning of "tickled pink." The literal meaning certainly would not make sense. Figuratively, the phrase means the person is pleased.

Words or phrases with figurative meanings are called figures of speech. There are many kinds of figures of speech. In this Part, you'll work with similes, metaphors, personification, and hyperbole. You'll use the three-step process you learned in Part 16. Your job will be to select the intended meaning.

# Working with Similes

A simile compares two unlike things using the words *like* or *as*. When the use of a simile is effective, it makes you see something in a different way. For instance, "His thoughts were as jumbled as clothes in a dryer" compares a person's thoughts with clothing. Literally, this person's thoughts were probably not being rotated in a drum. But figuratively, you picture the bouncing, turning thoughts in that person's mind.

Learning how to identify a simile is a useful skill. It will help you to understand better the intended meaning in passages you read.

## Here's How to Do It

Finding the intended meaning in similes is a problem-solving process with three steps. The following are similar to the three steps you worked with in Part 16, Working with Figurative Language. The difference is that you don't need to *find* the figurative language in the activities. The figure of speech is identified for you. You also are given a choice—you *select* the intended meaning from a list of possible choices.

1.  *Read* the passage and look at the simile carefully.

2.  *Try* its literal meaning.

3.  *Select* the intended meaning from a list of possible choices.

Remember, the passage may contain *context clues* that will help you find the intended meanings of figurative language. Read the passage carefully.

## Sample Activity:  Working with Similes

Look at the following sentences. The simile in each sentence is identified for you. Try the literal meaning. Then find the intended meaning. In this activity, you are *not* given a list of choices. The purpose is to see how well you do in finding the intended meanings.

a.   Dale's smile was *as bright as sunshine.*

b.   Trying to find the lost ring in the lake was *like looking for a needle in a haystack.*

**c.** By exercising daily, she soon felt *as fit as a fiddle.*

**d.** It feels *like a month of Sundays* since we last went to the park.

**Answers:** a) Intended Meaning: Dale's smile appeared friendly and attractive.
b) Intended Meaning: Looking for the lost ring will be difficult.
c) Intended Meaning: She felt healthy.
d) Intended Meaning: It's been a long time since they last went to the park.

# How Did You Do?

Did you notice how the simile made the description more vivid? For example, instead of stating that Dale has a nice smile, the writer compares her smile to a *bright sunshine.* Instead of stating that it's been a long time since they went to the park, the writer compares the time to a *month of Sundays.*

# Activities

In each of the following activities, you will be asked to first read the passage and look at the simile carefully. The simile is identified for you. After reading the passage, try its literal meaning. Then select the intended meaning from a list of possible choices. Write your answers on a separate sheet of paper. Don't forget to follow the three step process listed in "Here's How to Do It."

## Activity 17-1: Weather Problems

Read the short passage and look at the simile carefully. Try the literal meaning. Then, select the intended meaning from a list of possible choices. Follow the steps listed in "Here's How to Do It." Write your answer on a separate sheet of paper.

### Weather Problems

There had been no rain for months and all the crops were dead. Some parts of the farm were beginning to look *like a desert.*

### Possible Choices

The phrase *like a desert* means a place

**a.** with no noise at all

**b.** too dry for most things to grow

**c.** where no one lives

## *Activity 17-2: Jerry's Bike*

Read the short passage below about Jerry's bike. Look at the simile carefully. Then try the literal meaning. Finally, select the intended meaning from a list of possible choices. Write your answer on a separate sheet of paper. Don't forget to follow the steps listed in "Here's How to Do It."

### Jerry's Bike

Jerry's bike had disappeared from his front yard. After his bike was stolen, he bought a bike lock. His father said, "That's *like closing the barn door after the horse has been stolen.*"

### Possible Choices

The phrase *like closing the barn door after the horse has been stolen* means

**a.**   deciding not to get another horse

**b.**   making sure other things are safe

**c.**   doing something when it's too late

## *Activity 17-3: Buying Jeans*

Emily compares a pair of jeans to something else. First, read the selection and look for the simile. Next, try the literal meaning. Finally, select the intended meaning from a list of possible choices. Write your answer on a separate sheet of paper. Follow the steps outlined in "Here's How to Do It."

### Buying Jeans

The salesperson was trying to help Emily choose a pair of jeans. She told Emily that the baggy legs were in style, but Emily did not agree. "They fit *like socks on a rooster,* and I don't want them."

### Possible Choices

The phrase *like socks on a rooster* means

**a.**   the jeans have an interesting fit

**b.**   the jeans fit loosely

**c.**   the jeans look funny

## *Activity 17-4: Study Habits*

Read the following to find out how the study habits of Gerald and Rick are different. Look for the simile and try the literal meaning. Select the intended meaning from a list of possible choices. Write your answer on a separate sheet of paper. Don't forget to follow the steps listed in "Here's How to Do It."

### Study Habits

Gerald said, "I typically study about two or three hours every night during the school week. If I have an exam, I tend to reserve the night before for review. Of course, I study a lot more most weekends."

"Well," declared Rick, "I study just when I don't have anything else to do. Maybe that's why your grades are always better than mine. It would appear that our study habits are *as different as night and day.*"

### Possible Choices

The phrase *as different as night and day* means the students' study habits were

   **a.** nearly the same

   **b.** not alike at all

   **c.** similar in a few ways

# Working with Metaphors

A metaphor makes a direct comparison, but does so without using the words *like* or *as.* The word *metaphor* comes from the Greek word *metapherein,* which means "to transfer." This means that one thing is expressed in terms of another, "transferring" the qualities of one object to another object that is not really the same.

**Here's How to Do It**

To find the intended meaning in sentences that contain metaphors, follow this three-step thinking process.

1. *Read* the selection and look at the metaphor carefully.

2. *Try* its literal meaning.

3. *Select* the intended meaning from a list of possible choices.

Look for context clues in the passage. They may help you find the intended meanings.

## Sample Activity:  Working with Metaphors

Read each of the following sentences and look at the metaphors. Try the literal meaning for each metaphor. Then *find* the intended meaning. Again this Sample Activity does not give you a list of choices. Try your best. Record your answers on a separate sheet of paper.

**a.**    Sara feels as if *dark clouds were hanging over head*, refusing to move.

**b.**    Peter woke up in the *small hours of the morning* and could not go back to sleep.

**c.**    The rain has been *coming down in sheets* all day.

**d.**    If you hear news *through the grapevine*, it's possible there will be little truth in it.

**e.**    Carmen said she had the key to the problem.

**Answers:** a) Intended Meaning: Sara has been feeling gloomy.
b) Intended Meaning: Peter woke up very early.
c) Intended Meaning: It's been raining hard and steady.
d) Intended Meaning: The news, which has been passed along from one person to the next, has changed.
e) Intended Meaning: Carmen had the answer to the problem.

## How Did You Do?

Did you find the intended meanings?  Following the three-step thinking process in "Here's How to do It" makes your task easier. What were your reactions?  For example, dark clouds hung over Sara's head. Literally, you picture seeing Sara sitting under dark clouds. Can you imagine how that would make you feel? There you are getting up in the morning and right over your head is a black cloud. What did the writer intend when using the metaphor?  Dark clouds may make you feel gloomy, and you infer that Sara is feeling similarly.

If a problem is like a locked door, having a key is like unlocking the problem. That's what Carmen can do. She has the key to the problem. Literally, you picture a key like the one you use to unlock your front door. To solve the problem, Carmen has a "figurative" key—an *answer* to unlock the problem just as a key unlocks your door.

# Activities

In this set of activities, you are given passages that contain metaphors. The metaphors are identified for you. After reading each passage and studying the metaphor, select the intended meaning from a list of possible choices. Write your answers on a separate sheet of paper. Using the steps listed in "Here's How to Do It" will help make your task easier.

## Activity 17-5:  Musical Talent

Read the following to find out what one fan said about the musician's performance. Look at the metaphor, then try its literal meaning. Select the intended meaning from a list of possible choices. Follow the steps outlined in "Here's How to Do It." Write your answer on a separate sheet of paper.

### Musical Talent

"The concert was exceptional, particularly the guitarist," exclaimed the fan. "He's sure to *set the world on fire* with unique talent like that."

### Possible Choices

The phrase, *set the world on fire,* means

**a.**  to do things the right way

**b.**  to show unconditional approval

**c.**  to achieve much success

## Activity 17-6:  Elizabeth Blackwell

Carefully read the short passage about Elizabeth Blackwell. Look at the metaphor. Using the steps listed in "Here's How to Do It," try the literal meaning, then select the intended meaning from a list of possible choices. Write your answer on a separate sheet of paper.

### Elizabeth Blackwell

Elizabeth Blackwell became the first woman doctor in the United States in 1849. Her sister, Emily, *followed in her footsteps* and also became a doctor. They opened a small hospital that later became a large training place where women could become physicians.

### Possible Choices

The phrase *followed in her footsteps* means Emily

**a.**  used her as a model

**b.**  walked right behind her

**c.**  borrowed her shoes

# Activity 17-7: Waxing Cars

Read the selection below and look at the metaphor in the second sentence. Follow the steps in "Here's How to Do It," and try the literal meaning. Then, select the intended meaning from a list of possible choices. Write your answer on a separate sheet of paper.

## Waxing Cars

The fund-raising idea of waxing cars on Saturdays seemed like a great idea initially. In reality, the actual work was taking much more time and *elbow grease* than the club members imagined. Even when the best wax was used, vigorous rubbing was necessary to make the cars shine.

## Possible Choices

The phrase *elbow grease* means
a. Strenuous physical effort
b. a futile endeavor
c. rapid, circular movement

# Activity 17-8: The Oregon Trail

Read the following to find out about travel on the Oregon Trail during the 1800s. Look at the metaphor in the first sentence, and try its literal meaning. Then, select the intended meaning from a list of possible choices. Don't forget to follow the steps in "Here's How to Do It." Write your answers on a separate sheet of paper.

## The Oregon Trail

The inconveniences associated with travel today are just a drop in the bucket compared to those 100 years ago. For example, pioneers during the middle 1800s crossed the challenging, 2,000-mile wilderness from Missouri to Oregon by walking, riding horses, or in wagons pulled by mules or oxen. The particular path to the Pacific Ocean, which became known as the Oregon Trail, often had travelers on foot pushing their belongings in wheelbarrows. Hardships on the Oregon Trail included diseases such as cholera, serious problems related to wagon maintenance and care for the needs of the livestock used to pull the wagons, crossing mountains during bad weather, and food shortages. Many pioneers never finished the long trip, which often took up to six months to complete. Deaths were common along the trail. Some turned back rather than continue; others broke away from the trail to settle and build their homes in areas that seemed appealing. Unlike travel today, each day on the trail was full of uncertainty.

## Possible Choices

The phrase *a drop in the bucket* means
a. insignificant
b. insurmountable
c. innovative

# Working with Personification

In *personification*, an inanimate (lifeless) object or idea is given some characteristic of a person. This can create a more vivid picture, or give an unusual twist to the way the reader or listener thinks of something. For example, read the following sentence:

"The moon peeked over the mountains, then shyly hid his face behind a cloud."

In this sentence, the moon is given the characteristics and emotions of a person. This shows a much stronger and more interesting image than "The moon came up over the mountain and then a cloud blew in front of it."

A figure of speech very similar to personification is called *anthropomorphism*. This also is giving human characteristics to something not human. But this type of figurative language is used more typically when an animal is spoken of as having human emotions. You will not work with this type of figure of speech in this book.

In this set of activities, the three-step thinking process has been changed slightly. Instead of using the phrases "literal meaning" and "intended meaning" the book will use the terms "literal object" and "intended image." The changes will help make understanding personification easier.

### Here's How to Do It

To find the intended image in passages that contain personification, follow this three-step thinking process.

1.  Read the passage and look at the personification carefully.

2.  Find its literal object. What is the object the writer is using?

3.  Find its intended image. To what is the object being compared?

## Sample Activity:  Working with Personification

In each of the following sentences, the personification is identified for you. Using the three-step process outlined in "Here's How to Do It," find the literal object and the intended image. Write your answers on a separate sheet of paper.

a.  The leaves *whispered cheerfully* to each other, *gossiping* about the wind that blew around them.

b.  The boat rocked *gently* in the *arms* of the ocean.

**Answers:**
a) Literal Object: leaves making noise; Intended Image: a large group of people talking about someone else
b) Literal Object: the boat moving; Intended Image: a mother rocking her baby to sleep

## *How Did You Do?*

Did you recognize to what the literal object in each sentence is being compared? For example, what did you picture in your mind when you read the words *rocked gently* and *arms?* You probably pictured someone rocking a baby to sleep. Can you see how personification adds vividness and interest in writing?

# Activity

Apply the three-step method listed in "Here's How to Do It" to the following sentences. Again, the figure of speech, personification, is identified for you. Your job is to find the literal object and the intended image. Write your answers on a separate sheet of paper.

## *Activity 17-9: Working with Personification*

Each of the following sentences contains a personification. Using the steps given in "Here's How to Do It," find the literal object and intended image for each figure of speech. List your answers on a separate sheet of paper.

**a.** As the sun rose, the garden seemed to *stretch* and *smile to greet* the day.

**b.** The plants *begged* for water when the family returned from their long trip.

**c.** The hurricane *shouted* and *raved madly* around the lighthouse.

**d.** The telephone is *sitting* on the table, with *its face turned to the wall,* so I can't see it *sneer.*

**e.** Make sure you open the door when opportunity *knocks.*

**f.** Research *tells* us about the dangers of drug abuse.

**g.** In some countries it seems that justice *wears blinders.*

**h.** We watched the heavens *weep* through our bedroom window.

**i.**    The bird's nest was safe in the *arms* of the oak tree.

**j.**    Just then, a gust of wind *slapped* my face.

# Working with Hyperbole

The last type of figurative language we will discuss is *hyperbole* (hi-PER-bo-lee). Like other figures of speech, hyperbole is meant to create a vivid picture or have a strong effect. It does this through exaggeration or overstatement. Here are some examples of hyperbole that you may have heard (or used) before:

Alice was *on top of the world* when she got her raise.

He was so angry that he blew up *like an atomic bomb*.

Our new supercomputer can do the calculation *a million times* faster.

Hyperbole is frequently meant to be humorous, but also can be serious. Hyperbole can be much like a simile or metaphor. The phrase *on top of the world* could be a metaphor; and the phrase *like an atomic bomb* could be a simile. It is the great exaggeration, carrying the comparison to ridiculous extremes, that makes these examples of hyperbole.

Some expressions that are hyperbole in one sentence may be fact in another. In the phrase *a million times* the expression is probably fact.

**Here's How to Do It**

To find the intended meaning in passages that contain hyperbole, follow the three-step thinking process below.

**1.**    *Read* the passage and look at the hyperbole carefully.

**2.**    *Try* its literal meaning.

**3.**    *Select* the intended meaning from a list of possible choices.

## Sample Activity:  Working with Hyperbole

Read the following sentences. The hyperbole is identified for you. However, you are not given a list of choices to select the intended meaning. Do your best to find the intended meaning. Write your answers on a separate sheet of paper.

**a.**    Lee is *scared to death* of spiders.

**b.**    That bug is *as long as my arm!*

## How Did You Do?

Can you picture how Lee must look when he sees a spider? Can you imagine seeing a bug as long as your arm? You will notice how the use of hyperbole gives a more vivid picture of what the writer is trying to convey. Did you also notice that the phrase as *long as my arm* could be a simile? Remember, it is the great exaggeration that makes a figure of speech a hyperbole.

# Activity

As with the previous activities, your task is to find the intended meaning of each hyperbole. Following the steps outlined in "Here's How to Do It" will make your task easier. Use a separate sheet of paper for your answers.

## Activity 17-10:  Working with Hyperbole

Each of the following sentences contains a hyperbole. The figures of speech are identified for you. Using the three-step thinking process in "Here's How to Do It," find the intended meaning for each one. Write your answers on a separate sheet of paper.

**a.**    I've told you a *million times* not to touch that!

**b.**    The train whistle was loud enough to *wake the dead.*

**c.**    When I last saw Jessica, she was eating a *mile-high* banana split.

**d.**    The food portions in that restaurant are so small you need *a magnifying glass* to find them.

**e.**    Samantha was *scared to death* during the last part of their climb along the narrow cliff.

**f.**    The suggestion to sing songs at the party went over like a *lead balloon.*

**g.**    This home-baked bread is *as heavy as a brick!*

**h.**    Alice nearly *dropped dead* when she won the lottery.

**i.**    It's been *raining cats and dogs* for the last two days.

**j.**    Sheldon *hit the ceiling* when he learned his car had been stolen from the parking lot.

## Putting It All Together

In the previous activities, you practiced finding the intended meaning in passages that contain figurative language. You used the three-step thinking process outlined in "Here's How to Do It" as your guide. Now it's time to use what you have learned in a different way. This time, you will not use pencil and paper. Use only your thinking skills. For the passages here, you are to *think* about your responses. Then compare them to the comments given. You will be able to use context clues within sentences as well as between sentences of the paragraph. Carefully read the sentences before and after the one containing the figure of speech. Remember that the context may influence the meaning. For example, look at the difference between the following two sentences:

Everyone wanted Randy to come to the party because he's such a live wire.

Aaron's as dangerous as a live wire around water.

The expression "live wire" has a different meaning in each situation. It is crucial that you use the context to determine the meaning intended.

In this part of the book, there is no Sample Activity, but the following steps listed in "Here's How to Do It" will help make your task easier.

**Here's How to Do It**

As you know, there are three steps to finding meaning in figurative language. In this part of the book, there is a fourth step.

1.    *Read* the passage and look for the figurative language. Although the figure of speech is identified for you, the passages are longer, making it harder for you to quickly find the figurative language.

2.    *Try* its literal meaning in your mind.

3.    *Find* the intended meaning and think about it.

4.    *Compare* your answer to the response given.

As you read each passage, look for context clues that may help you find the intended meanings.

# Activities

Read the following passages. In each case, the figure of speech is identified for you. Follow the steps outlined in "Here's How to Do It." Try the literal meaning of the figurative language in your mind. Find the intended meaning and think about it. Then, compare your responses to the comments that follow each selection. Try not to read the comments until *after* you have thought about your responses.

## *Activity 17-11:  Jay's Garden*

Read the passage carefully and look for the figurative language. Then, try the literal meaning. Finally, *think* about the intended meaning. Compare your responses below. Follow the steps outlined in "Here's How to Do It."

### Jay's Garden

After returning from his vacation to the mountains, Jay *made a beeline* for his vegetable garden. Just as he had feared, his garden was showing signs of neglect. Jay was determined to save every plant so he wasted little time putting his *green thumb* to work.

### The Results

1. *Find* the metaphors *made a beeline* and *green thumb.*

2. *Try* their literal meanings. Is it possible that Jay is really a bee or that he has a green thumb?

3. *Find* the intended meaning. Context clues help immensely at this point. You know that if Jay has been away for some time, it's likely that he'd rush to see how his garden is surviving. By using the metaphor "made a beeline," the author tells you that Jay went straight to the garden with great speed, just as a bee might.

    It isn't likely that Jay has a green thumb, or that his thumb has been in green paint. It is more likely that Jay has a talent for making plants grow.

## Activity 17-12:  The Beauty of Friendship

In the following passage you will read about Gail and Katie, two close friends who are facing the reality that they will be separated geographically when one of the families move. Read the passage carefully. Using the steps given in "Here's How to Do It," look for the figurative language and try to determine the literal meaning. Then, find the intended meaning and think about it. Compare your responses to the ones below.

### The Beauty of Friendship

The two girls had maintained a steadfast friendship *through thick and thin* since childhood. Gail asked, "What's to become of our friendship now that my family is *pulling up stakes*? How can we continue to share our lives when I'll be living on the other side of the country?"

Katie reassured her with a loving expression on her face and the words, "I'll carry the wonderful memories we've created together in my heart. Besides, we can write, telephone, and visit during holidays."

### The Results

You can find the metaphors *through thick and thin* and *pulling up stakes*. As you try the literal meanings, you are able to visualize an actual physical obstacle and removing of sticks or posts used to mark the boundaries of property. Are the girls actually facing some physical obstacle in their friendship? Do you think Gail's family will literally have their property marked with stakes or sticks and then pull them up when they leave?

The answer is *no* in both cases. So, you continue searching for the intended meanings. By using context clues, you can infer that their friendship has been constant over time in spite of any difficulties and that the upcoming move to another part of the country will not cause the friendship to be put in jeopardy. In spite of any problems the girls may encounter, we feel confident their friendship will continue to be a beautiful one.

## Activity 17-13:  The Football Team

Mel and Danny are talking about their football team. Follow the steps listed in "Here's How to do It." Read the passage and carefully look for the figurative language. Then, try the literal meaning. Finally find the intended meaning and think about it. Compare your answers to the ones below.

### The Football Team

Mel and Danny had *high hopes* for the football team this year. "I don't think we have a thing to worry about," said Mel. "That new quarterback has a fantastic arm."

Danny nodded his head and smiled. "You might say that *his arm is worth its weight in gold*," he agreed.

### The Results

Were Mel's and Danny's hopes really *high* or *tall?* Of course not. Not in a literal sense—but their hopes were big. They had confidence that the football team had a good chance of doing well during the season.

Is anyone's arm really worth its weight in gold? How valuable is gold? For centuries, people have considered gold to be very valuable. The new player's arm is not really gold, but it is extremely valuable, *like* gold. Obviously, this hyperbole means the new quarterback is a great passer.

## Activity 17-14: *The Class Presidency*

Many of Marilyn's friends thought she would be perfect for the class presidency. Read the selection to find out if Marilyn agrees to think about becoming a candidate. Using the steps outlined in "Here's How to Do It," look for the figurative language and try its literal meaning. Then, find the intended meaning and think about it. Compare your responses to the ones below.

### The Class Presidency

"Marilyn, your friends and classmates would like for you to become a candidate for the class presidency," offered Anatoli. "We believe you will provide the kind of leadership that is so needed at this time."

"I sincerely appreciate the confidence you've shown in me, and I will give serious thought to *throwing my hat in the ring*," responded Marilyn. "I'll let you know my decision soon."

### The Results

Do you think Marilyn will let Anatoli know her decision by throwing a hat into some ring, such as those used by boxers or wrestlers? Do you think it is more likely she will tell him her decision in person or over the telephone? The intended meaning of the figurative language is much clearer once we understand that, in days gone by, challenges were accepted by throwing one's hat into a ring.

# Activity 17-15:  Learning to Dance

First, read the passage and look for the figurative language. Then, try its literal meaning, Finally, find the intended meaning and think about it. Compare your answers to the ones below. Don't forget to follow the steps given in "Here's How to Do It."

## Learning to Dance

"What an experience," exclaimed Russ. "I had no idea learning to dance would be so much fun. Of course, I'm just starting to *get into the swing of things*."

"Well," chuckled Anne, "I think I'll enjoy the class more when I *get the lead out of my feet*."

"I hope you two will *hang in there*," said the instructor with an encouraging smile on his face. "After all, *Rome wasn't built in a day*."

## The Results

The figurative language in the passage is to *get into the swing of things, get the lead out of my feet, hang in there,* and *Rome wasn't built in a day.* Try literal meanings and ask questions such as the following: Does the literal meaning of to *get into the swing of things* come close to its intended meaning? Does its intended meaning address the level of comfort Russ is feeling as his ability to dance improves?

Do you believe Anne's feet are as heavy as lead or that her shoes contain lead? Perhaps Anne is expressing her frustration with her own slow pace. Is the instructor trying to get them to hang something somewhere? Why might the instructor compare the building of a city, such as Rome, to learning to dance? When searching for intended meanings, you use your skills with context clues. As we read that the instructor has an encouraging smile, we are aware the instructor is trying to get them to stick with their dancing class. With the reference to building a city, we realize such an undertaking would be very time consuming; this would be particularly true for the building of a great city, like Rome.

## *Activity 17-16: Changing Schools*

The following selection discusses what Donna thinks about changing schools. Read the passage and look for the figurative language. Try its literal meaning. Find the intended meaning and think about it. Finally, compare your responses to the ones below. Follow the steps outlined in "Here's How to Do It."

### Changing Schools

Changing schools in the middle of the year presented a problem for Donna in many ways. First of all, she would have to leave all her good friends 500 miles behind. She would have to give up her part-time job at the jewelry store. Worst of all, she would have to face a school full of strangers. She feared she would feel *like a fish out of water* for some time.

Fortunately, she made the decision to *wash her hands* of any negative thoughts. She knew most people would treat her the way she acted. So, taking a deep breath, she smiled as she continued packing.

### The Results

Begin by imagining a fish out of water. Perhaps a goldfish is flopping helplessly beside a fish bowl. Or visualize fish that have been washed up on the beach. As you search for the intended meaning, take the literal helplessness and apply that to Donna. She feels as helpless as that fish beside the fish bowl. Sounds awful! As you continue examining the metaphors, you read that she's going to wash her hands of any negative thoughts. Does Donna go to the sink to wash away thoughts with soap and water? Not likely! She's obviously going to forget any negative thoughts.

# Activity 17-17:  Bamboo

Read the following about the many uses for bamboo. Look for the figurative language. Try its literal meaning. Then, find the intended meaning and think about it. Compare your answers to the ones below. Don't forget to follow the steps listed in "Here's How to Do It."

### Bamboo

It may sound like *a drop in the bucket* to some of you, but I'm impressed by the fact that a variety of bamboo in India grows as much as three feet in a twenty-four-hour day. It grows up to 120 feet and has a hollow stem that is a foot thick. Bamboo already has a variety of uses. For example, it is used for food, building materials, furniture, and fishing poles. While we don't want *to count our chickens before they hatch,* bamboo may prove to be a viable solution to the energy problem. Some scientists say it is possible to make fuel from this fast-growing plant.

### The Results

Picture one drop of water in a bucket. The author is telling you that this is not much.

How do you count chickens before they hatch? Find a hen's nest with eggs, count the number of eggs, and then guess how many will hatch. Just as you cannot be positive about how many eggs will hatch, the author is saying you shouldn't count on bamboo as a fuel source until it is available as fuel.

# Activity 17-18:  Totem Poles

Read the passage carefully to learn more about totem poles. Look for the figurative language. Then, try the literal meaning. Finally, think about the intended meaning. Compare your responses to the ones below. Use the steps in "Here's How to Do It."

### Totem Poles

"The Native Americans of the Northwest carved totem poles as an art form," explained Jason. "Long before metal was introduced by explorers from other parts of the world, they used stone tools to carve red cedar into their totem poles. Contrary to what many people think, the Indians never worshipped their totem poles."

"As an art collector, I'd give *a pretty penny* for one," said Benjamin. "I'd even *eat my hat* if I could get the story associated with it. It's fascinating to me that each of the pole's elements represents part of the owner's personal story."

"Well," teased Jason, "I don't think it's very likely you'll get a story *straight from the horse's mouth,* given the age of those totem poles."

### The Results

The figurative language in the passage is *a pretty penny, eat my hat,* and *straight from the horse's mouth.* Do you believe it would be possible to purchase much of anything with a penny, even for a very shiny, bright, new penny? Valuable art forms certainly would cost a lot more than one cent! They tend to be expensive, particularly when they are rare and old. In isn't very likely the art collector means he will literally eat his hat. Since he doesn't believe he'll have much luck in getting the personalized story for the totem pole, he feels safe to make the statement about eating his hat if he did. Can horses really talk? Jason is doubtful that a reliable source for obtaining information about exact meanings for the totem poles is still available; he is questioning if there is truly someone in the know, given the age of the totem poles.

## Activity 17-19:  *Koala Bears*

Read the following selection about koala bears. Using the steps in "Here's How to Do It," look for the figurative language. Try its literal meaning. Then, find that intended meaning and think about it. Compare your responses to the ones below.

### Koala Bears

Have you every wondered why you rarely see koala bears at a zoo? Well, the answer is rather simple. They are hard to care for because of what they eat. Koala bears, which aren't bears at all, need a fresh supply of eucalyptus leaves each day. Unfortunately, these leaves don't grow in many places, and so koalas are rarely found outside of Australia.

Why is the koala bear so popular with zoo goers? There are many reasons. The koala, which is a marsupial, is *like a kangaroo.* After the birth of a baby, which is about an inch long, the baby crawls into the mother's pouch and lives there for about six months. Many people have never seen marsupials except in a zoo. A koala is appealing because it is *like a teddy bear* many people recall from their childhoods. Finally, a koala is fun to watch when it is sleeping; because of its keen sense of balance, it can easily perch on a branch even when asleep. A koala usually chooses a safe spot where the branches come together *like the closed end of an open safety pin.*

### The Results

As you read about the koala bear, you begin to use the similes in the second part of the passage to help you visualize the animal. Even if you have never seen a koala at a zoo or in a picture, finding meaning in the similes helps you visualize the animal. You are told the koala is like a kangaroo in that both have pouches to carry their young. You are told that the koala is not a bear at all; so there is the simile *like a teddy bear,* and you know the author is not talking about the bear such as the grizzly, which is large and powerful. A teddy bear is small and cuddly; one would hardly play with a grizzly bear. Finally, you located the simile, *like the closed end of an open safety pin.* You know it is not likely that even a small koala can literally sit on a safety pin. As you sought the intended meaning, you visualized tree branches similar to those described through the simile.

# Activity 17-20:  Greta

Carefully read the passage about how hard Greta worked to prepare for a race. Using the steps listed in "Here's How to Do It," look for the figurative language. Then, try its literal meaning. Finally, find the intended meaning and think about it. Compare your answers to the ones below.

## Greta

It was almost spring. Greta realized there was a tremendous challenge ahead of her. For the past three years she had run in the annual foot race that her school sponsored to raise money. Each year she had come in second. This year she was more determined than ever to win the race, especially since she would be graduating and would never have another chance. Hard work was the answer. Practice, practice, practice, she thought to herself as she sat contemplating how she would feel if she won. With a hopeful heart, she began working toward her goal. Greta worked *like a bee;* in fact, she could almost have *managed the hive single-handedly.* When the moment was finally at hand, Greta *faced the music* with confidence. "Did she win the race?" you ask. Of course she did and in record time.

## The Results

After reading the passage and studying the sentences surrounding the one with the metaphor about a bee, you know Greta is directing much energy to her goal of winning the foot race. How much energy? How busy is a bee? Worker bees are very busy. They need only short rests between long hours of work. They make and store honey at all hours of the day and night. Since you know the author is not saying that Greta is a bee, but is comparing her to a bee, you have an idea about how hard she is working.

As you continue looking for the intended meaning, you read about Greta being so efficient she could manage a hive by herself. That would be quite an undertaking since worker bees gather nectar, communicate with other bees, feed and care for the queen, watch over developing bees, build new cells, cool the hive by fanning it with their wings, fight off other bees who come to steal honey, and clean and repair empty cells so they can be used in the future. So, you know Greta is not only busy but capable of meeting the challenges. Did Greta really face the music when the moment for the race occurred? What music are you thinking about? Perhaps you imagine soft stereo music playing or maybe a band. By returning to the context, you realize that Greta faced her challenge bravely.

# Part 18

# Figurative Language in Longer Passages

## About This Part...

Up to now, you've been finding and analyzing figurative language in single sentences and short paragraphs. Now you will apply the skills you have learned to longer passages. You still will work with the three-step thinking process introduced in Part 16, Working with Figurative Language. You will have to look more carefully to find the various figures of speech. Because the passages are longer, identifying the figurative language becomes more challenging.

# Here's How to Do It

Finding meaning in figurative language is a problem-solving process.

1. *Look* for the figurative language. Although the figures of speech are identified for you, the passages are longer, making it harder for you to quickly find the figurative language.

2. *Try* the literal meaning for each figure of speech.

3. *Select* the intended meaning from a list of possible choices.

4. *Reread* the paragraph where the figure of speech appears if you are unsure about its intended meaning.

## Sample Activity:  The Last Game

Read the following passage carefully. List your responses on a separate sheet of paper. Check your responses with the comments that follow the paragraph.

The figures of speech are identified for you. In this Sample Activity, you are not given a list of choices to select the intended meaning. Try your best to *find* the intended meanings of each figure of speech.

### The Last Game

The end of the football season was *close at hand*. Only three days remained before the big game. Coach Brag was worried, and for good reason. Two days earlier his star quarterback had been injured in a scrimmage and could not practice. Knowing that scouts from the opposing team usually check out their competition, Coach Brag decided all practice sessions would be closed to the public. Otherwise, the *Achilles' heel* of the team might be discovered. Tension among the players was so thick it could have been *cut with a knife*. Coach Brag conferred with Dr. Hopeful about whether the injured quarterback could play in the upcoming game. The doctor told Coach Brag it would be about *as likely as Florida snow in August*. You would have thought Coach Brag had *lost his last friend* when he hear that dismal news. As you may have guessed, it was *curtains* for the team without their quarterback playing in the game.

**Answer:** *Close at hand* meant the end of football season was near. *Achilles' heel* meant the weak spot of the team. *Cut with a knife* meant the tension was obvious. In the phrase *as likely as Florida snow in August*, the doctor meant the quarterback would not be able to play. *Lost his last friend* meant Coach Brag felt badly. *Curtains for the team* meant the team was bound to lose the game.

# How Did You Do?

Did you notice that finding meaning for some of the figures of speech is easier than for others? The ease depends on your bank of background experiences. For example, look at the literal meaning of *close at hand;* picture something being near to one of your hands.

*Achilles' heel* is more difficult, even with context clues, because there is a need to know a mythological story about Achilles' heel. Does your research agree with the following information?

When Achilles was born, his mother, Thetis, wanted to make him completely invulnerable. She attempted to do this by dipping him in the River Styx, which would protect whatever it touched. However, she was not careful to make sure his whole body was touched by the river's waters; she held him by the foot, and the water did not touch that part of his body. Therefore, Achilles' vulnerable spot was his heel. If anything happened to him, it would be the result of an attack on his heel. So, when the author makes reference to the Achilles' heel of the team, you know the weak spot is the injured quarterback.

Can a person really cut the tension with a knife? The answer is "of course not." The figure of speech makes it clear that the tension is obvious.

You know the quarterback probably won't play when the doctor says it's about *as likely as Florida snow in August.* How often does it snow in Florida in August? This hyperbole makes clear that the doctor's diagnosis was "No."

Did Coach Brag really lose his last friend? Probably not, but he felt that badly. By using context clues, you can find meaning in the metaphor *curtains for the team.* You know they are bound to lose if the quarterback can't play, and that's just what happened. (*Curtains coming down* means the end of a show.)

As you continue to find meaning in figurative language, you will become more aware of how frequently this kind of language is used.

# Activities

The following three short stories have been written not only for your enjoyment, but also to challenge your ability to interpret figurative language in a different kind of context. The figures of speech have been identified for you. After each short story is a list of possible choices. Your task is to select the intended meaning for each figure of speech. Don't forget to use the three-step thinking method outlined in "Here's How to Do It."

## Activity 18-1:  Mystery of the Bermuda Triangle

Carefully read the short story below. The figures of speech are identified for you. After reading the selection, you will be asked to select the intended meanings of the figures of speech from a list of possible choices.

### Mystery of the Bermuda Triangle
#### by Barbara C. Palmer

"Lost somewhere over the Bermuda Triangle," she said. "That's *the long and short of it;* that's all I remember about my father."

"Didn't they tell your family more details than that?" he asked. "Try to tell me all you remember."

So she began the painful story that had puzzled her for almost thirty-five years. "It was a *run-of-the-mill* flight on a clear December afternoon in 1945. My dad, along with the four other Navy pilots, had flown that kind of mission time after time. When it was almost time for their return, a radio call reached the base. It was from Lt. Charles Taylor, the lead pilot. People at the base said he sounded *as if he'd seen a ghost* and probably knew he was a *goner*. Realizing they were lost, Lt. Taylor asked the base to guide them back safely. Suddenly all radio contact was lost. It was lost forever. And, so were the pilots."

"Wasn't there a search party?" he asked.

"Of course," she answered. "Hundreds of planes and ships searched the Atlantic Ocean. They covered the area of the triangle from South Florida to Bermuda to Puerto Rico. Some even looked beyond that triangle. But it was worse than *looking for a needle in a haystack*. Nothing was found—not even a life jacket. Finally, after months and months of searching for any sign of my father, the family gave up all hope of ever seeing him again."

"Then why have you returned here after all these years?" he asked. "And how can I be of help to you?"

"I'm going to *speak my mind*," she answered. "And, if you *buy my story*, I want to *retrace my father's footsteps* with you as my copilot. My plan is to fly the same course he did. You see, I sense a missing piece of the puzzle will be found if I make this flight."

"Are you saying this flight will solve the mystery of the Bermuda Triangle?" he asked with eager eyes.

"Perhaps it will for me," she answered. "And that's why I've come to you. I'm *banking on* your experience over the triangle. Even though I've flown for years, I've avoided facing the triangle. While there's always the thought that it might *do me in*, the *price is worth paying* if I find what I believe I will."

"How soon would you like to leave?" he asked. "I wouldn't miss a trip like this *for love nor money*."

"Exactly four days from now," she replied. "Let's hope this December afternoon will be *as clear as crystal*."

Those four days seemed to move *as quickly as a second hand on a watch*. During the last hours before the day of the flight, talk about the mystery of the Bermuda Triangle was constant. It was almost as if they could talk of nothing else. They were both suddenly aware of a feeling that they were being drawn to the triangle by some unknown force.

Now into the triangle she flew, knowing she'd probably *meet her maker*. Continuing to follow her father's path, she hit an air pocket. It was almost *as if death were knocking at her door*. She had to go on. After all, what was an air pocket to an experienced pilot? Suddenly, strange things began to happen to the instrument panel. Was some magnetic force causing the instruments to behave strangely? Then, *out of the blue*, white foam seemed to cover the water beneath the plane. The foam was *like a giant blanket* over the ocean as far as one could see. She thought of her father. Was this what he went through? Then, she felt her hand reaching for the radio; every moment had to count now. As she pushed the button down to send her message, a ringing noise began. It was *as shrill as a siren*. She began to feel beads of sweat roll down her face. Louder and louder the sound continued. She was going down. The force was pulling at the wings of the plane. Down! Down! Down! And she could tell no one. Just before the plane crashed into the water, she woke up from the terrible nightmare. The alarm clock had finally awakened her from a dream that seemed too real.

As she dressed for breakfast, the dream flashed through her mind. Was the dream an omen? Was it a warning about what the day would bring? Should she go ahead with her plans? The decision was made. She would tell no one about the dream. However, she would make the flight alone just in case.

As the plane left the runway, she took a long look at the beauty of the clear day and the earth beneath her. She wanted to soak it all in *like a sponge*. Even the smallest detail of the day had to be captured for she knew she would never make this flight again.

The Bermuda Triangle was now directly ahead. There would be no turning back on the planned mission. With determination she followed her father's path. Everything felt *as smooth as silk*. The plane was gliding quietly, and there was a sense of peacefulness in the soft-looking clouds. Deeper into the triangle the plane hit an air pocket. As she remembered the air pocket in her dream, the muscles in her neck tightened *like a stretched rubber band*. She immediately looked at the control panel. All was well there. Yet, she sensed a force surrounding her. She no longer felt alone in the plane, although her common sense told her she was very much alone. Then she was sure she heard a voice say, "Child, I am here with you. I am here to let you know that I am at peace in my world and that I want you to be at peace in yours."

"Father, is that you?" she thought.

"Yes," was her answer. "You have found the missing puzzle piece. And I am proud of your courage. Now return with a peaceful heart."

She reached for the radio and announced her plans had changed. She wished to return ahead of time. Her mission was complete. Finally she knew her father was at peace.

Before she could unfasten her seat belt, her friend rushed out to the plane *like a gust of wind*. "You're early! What happened?" he asked.

"I found that piece of the puzzle we talked about a few days ago," she answered.

"Then you have solved part of the triangle's mystery," he said.

She paused for a moment. "Yes," she said, "at least I found what I hoped to find."

"Did you find some sign of your father?" he asked.

"You might say that," she answered. "Let's get a cup of coffee and I'll tell you all about it."

## Possible Choices

The following are the figures of speech used in the story "Mystery of the Bermuda Triangle." Try the literal meaning for each one. Then, select the intended meaning from a list of possible choices. Use the steps given in "Here's How to Do It."

**Example:** *Banking on* means

> **a.** buying    **b.** selling    ©.trusting

1.  *The long and short of it* means
    **a.** many strange facts    **b.** an entire story    **c.** all new ideas

2.  *Run-of-the-mill* means
    **a.** regular    **b.** special    **c.** unusual

3.  *A goner* means a
    **a.** lonely pilot    **b.** hopeless case    **c.** worried person

4.  *Speak my mind* means to talk about something
    **a.** properly    **b.** angrily    **c.** completely

5.  *Buy my story* means
    **a.** pay me    **b.** listen to me    **c.** believe me

6.  *Do me in* means
    **a.** cause my death    **b.** change my plans    **c.** lose my money

7.  *As quickly as a second hand on a watch* means that time passed
    **a.** quietly    **b.** swiftly    **c.** finally

8.  *Meet her maker* means she might
    **a.** lose her life    **b.** have an accident    **c.** make a mistake

9.  *Smooth as silk* means really
    **a.** light    **b.** perfect    **c.** calm

10. *Like a gust of wind* means
    **a.** eagerly    **b.** quickly    **c.** silently

# Activity 18-2: *Growing Up Overnight*

Carefully read the following story. The figures of speech are identified for you. You will be asked to select the intended meanings of some of the figures of speech from a list of possible choices.

### Growing Up Overnight
by Barbara C. Palmer

It was a hot day in the summer of 1889. The weather was so hot that most folks talked of nothing but the *awful dog days*. But I knew that no amount of talk could change the weather. Besides, it wouldn't be long before we'd see nothing but *a blanket of snow*. And winter in Wyoming always seemed to *last a lifetime*.

I guess I was just a kid, although I kept *growing like a weed*. In six months I had grown more than I had during the past two years. Before *passing on to the happy hunting ground* last winter, Grandpa had teased me about being *wet behind the ears*. Of course, we all seemed young to Grandpa, who had lived to be 96. How I'd missed him since his death! He could *spin a yarn in no time flat*. It seemed impossible that anyone could think of such interesting stories so quickly. Those stories *brought my ears to attention* and *made my hair stand on end*. And those stories of his were the kind you wanted to hear over and over, even though I'd heard them a dozen times. One thing I learned from his stories was that *every barrel must sit on its own bottom*.

Knowing that I'd have to think for myself paid off later. It helped me *face the music* the day the outlaws rode into our valley. They came *like thieves in the night*, and I knew I would have to think for myself.

They rode in easily. You would have thought they were as *peaceful as doves* from the way they sat calmly in their saddles. The three men were well-dressed—*looking like pleasant statues* as they stopped to eye the corral of horses. In a second, I remembered their pictures on a wanted poster. They were wanted for horse stealing. I tried *to swallow the lump in my throat* as I realized how alone I was. As usual, Papa had refused to let me go along to search for wild horses. How many times had I heard him say, "Girl, you know you should stay at home where it's safe." Of course, he knew I could ride and rope as well as any of the hands he'd hired to do the job. Little did he know that I'd have *to hold down the fort*. And from the interest these three were showing in the corral, I knew I had my *work cut out for me.* There would be lots of hard work ahead if the horses were to be saved. I knew I'd have to think quickly to *save the day.*

I *felt a chill up my spine* as they rode even closer. I had been afraid before; I had even been *scared to death* a few times during the trip Grandpa, Pa, and I made from the East. As their eyes spotted the water pump, I could feel words *falling from my mouth.* "Help yourselves to some water," I said. "And take plenty for those horses of yours. You must feel *as if you've been eating dust.*" They said they were pretty thirsty after a long day in the saddle. Soon they had drunk their fill. Then, their interest returned to the horses *like miners finding gold.* Unless I could stop them, the horses would be theirs.

Just then a gust of wind *slapped my face.* The air felt a little more crisp now that the sun had started to set. Suddenly, *you could hear a pin drop.* Everything became too quiet. I chuckled to myself when I remembered that someone had said *silence is golden.* The silence was broken by the tall one. "We're interested in those horses," he said. You don't have to tell me that, I thought. Of course they were interested in the horses. In this part of the country, horses were *better than new money.* I refused to allow them to force me into *deep water.* I planned to *keep my head* and get to my rifle if there was to be a showdown. But getting to my rifle was not going to be easy. The rifle was inside the barn door. Finally, I answered, "They're not for sale, Mister. But you might be interested in taking a look at a real prize in the barn."

Well, you know the rest of the story. I walked to the barn at *a snail's pace.* I knew any quicker movement might have given away my plan. Then, I imagined that their eyes were *burning a hole through me* as I found my rifle. When I invited them to *hit the trail,* I hardly sounded *as gentle as a lamb.* To this day, I don't know what became of those outlaws. I do know that I felt different afterward. I was able to make a decision that caused me to *grow up overnight!*

### Possible Choices

The following are the figures of speech used in the story "Growing Up Overnight." Try the literal meanings for each one. Then, select the intended meaning from a list of possible choices. Don't forget to follow the steps outlined in "Here's How to Do It."

**Example:** *Last a lifetime* means
    **a.** lasts about 75 years
    **(b.)** seems as if it will never end
    **c.** is made very well

1.   *Wet behind the ears* means
    **a.** being too young to know very much
    **b.** getting your hair washed
    **c.** swimming with your head under water

2. *In no time flat* means
   **a.** quickly
   **b.** softly
   **c.** easily

3. *Spin a yarn* means
   **a.** wind thread around something
   **b.** tell a story very well
   **c.** turn around very fast

4. *Hair stand on end* means
   **a.** feel very frightened
   **b.** use a very stiff brush
   **c.** pull someone's hair very hard

5. *Face the music* means
   **a.** stand up so you can see the band
   **b.** meet trouble bravely
   **c.** try to read some musical notes

6. *To hold down the fort* means
   **a.** use a heavy stone for weight
   **b.** keep something pressed against the floor
   **c.** stay behind and take care of things

7. *Felt a chill up my spine* means
   **a.** being very scared
   **b.** feeling very cold
   **c.** having a backache

8. *You could hear a pin drop* means
   **a.** something fell
   **b.** things happened very fast
   **c.** it was very quiet

9. *Keep my head* means
   **a.** remain calm
   **b.** stay alive
   **c.** act slowly

10. *Snail's pace* means
    **a.** being very small
    **b.** moving very slowly
    **c.** keeping very calm

# Activity 18-3:  Time Enough to Win

Carefully read the following story about a football game. Notice the figures of speech. They are identified for you. After reading the selection, answer the questions that follow.

**Time Enough to Win**
by Stan M. Tullos

Once the referee placed the ball on the forty-yard stripe, the clock began ticking down the seconds. The fourth and final quarter had begun. My team, the Florida Sharks, had moved within one touchdown of our biggest rivals—the Houston Stars. We faced a tough Houston offense led by arrogant quarterback Damon Arrow whose precision passing had frustrated the Sharks every time we seemed near to realizing our dream of beating the Stars.

Damon Arrow led the Stars' offense as they broke their huddle. Coolly, Arrow looked over our defense as he *barked* signals. John Simpson, Houston's dreaded speedster, stood up and trotted to the outside. I moved from my linebacker position closer to the slot between center and guard. *Digging in my cleats* I charged to stop Arrow before he could release his pass to Simpson. Instead, fullback Bull Thompson took a fast pitchout and rumbled past me through the gaping hole I had left in the line. Strong safety Carl Cruise and cornerback Willie Sutton finally wrestled Thompson to the turf. Arrow had *faked me out of my shoes*. Houston's unruly fans roared; as I joined the defensive huddle, I could *feel the jeering Stars' laughter* on my back.

On the second play Arrow faked a handoff to Bull Thompson and dropped back, looking for an open receiver. Arrow's pass protection broke down as two Shark linemen shoved past Houston blockers. Arrow sprinted to the outside. I followed Arrow as he slid along the line, searching desperately for a receiver. I moved in, accelerated, and then speared him at full speed. When I stood up Houston's quarterback lay still. An injury time-out let the team physician run onto the field. Houston's players surrounded their leader as the doctor bent over him. Shaken, Arrow was helped to the sideline as the second string quarterback came on the field. This could be the break we needed; Houston's offense without Damon Arrow would be *like a ship without a rudder.*

As predicted, Houston could not mount a sustained drive without Arrow. Needing fifteen yards for a first down, the new quarterback ran Simpson on an end sweep. He came twelve yards short and the Stars booted the ball away. Our supporters cheered wildly as we trotted toward the sideline to be mobbed by our jubilant teammates. Victory lay just around the corner.

Our offense, however, met a new Houston defensive team on our next series. *Furious Stars swarmed through our defensive line.* Determined to make up for the loss of their quarterback, *they stung the Sharks on play after play.* Both offenses stalled as the seconds and minutes fell from the scoreboard clock which read Florida Sharks 21—Houston Stars 28.

Late in the fourth quarter J.C. Petersen, our quarterback, faced third down with nine yards remaining. Gambling, he lofted a bomb that came down in tight-end Alex Washington's outstretched arms. Alex stumbled into the end zone with the ball. Touchdown! Now was our opportunity to even the score; but Coach Dalton sent Petersen, not the kicker, back into the game. We were going for two points to win the game, not for a tie.

A roar of approval came from the stands when our fans saw Petersen dash back on the field. Then a hush fell over the stadium as all eyes focused on the Shark quarterback leaning over center. The crowd gasped as Petersen plunged behind our line surge into a tangle of players. All eyes watched the referee, waiting for his rising arms to answer their silent question. When the answer came, a moan of disappointment rose from the stands. Petersen had fallen inches short of the goal, and the scoreboard still read Florida 27—Houston 28.

After our kickoff into the end zone, Houston lined up on their twenty. A sick feeling rose in my stomach; Arrow was back marshaling the Stars' attack. Behind by one point with little more than two minutes remaining, our chances of winning seemed to fade away.

Houston had no intention of sitting on a one-point lead. On his first play, Arrow rifled the ball fifteen yards to his tight end. Gone was the Damon Arrow who had been led to the bench on wobbly knees. Vengeance was in his eyes, for he had a score to settle with me. The referee restarted the clock and precious seconds began ticking away. Arrow took the full time alotted before the center snapped the ball. He pivoted and handed the ball to a piston-driving Bull Thompson who muscled through the arm tackle of our left guard. I dove at his ankles from my linebacker position, and the outside linebacker hit him high. Pain shot through my arm as Thompson hammered for four more yards.

During the timeout we called, I tried to massage the numbness from my torn arm muscles. My arm felt *like stretched clay.* Slowly, feeling returned and with it a bone-deep throbbing. The referee's whistle signaled the end of our timeout. As he approached the line of scrimmage, Arrow gave my arm a look that clearly showed his pleasure. Using an agonizingly slow count, Arrow called signals and sent Thompson driving at me again like a runaway truck. Head down, I hit him squarely. I hung on with my good arm as Carl Cruise hustled up to knock Thompson's legs out from under him. Rising and shaking the dizziness from my head, I anxiously eyed the scoreboard as we burned our last timeout. Forty seconds remained on the clock, and Houston had two plays left. Arrow had to run only one more play, and then let the seconds tick off the clock. All our aches and bruises would have been for nothing if we couldn't regain possession of the ball and score.

The whistle sounded, and Arrow slowly and deliberately called signals. We hovered over the ball praying that somehow we could steal it. I was *as tight as a guitar string* until one of the Houston guards moved. The string snapped and I powered through, burying both the Houston center and Arrow before the whistle could stop me. But had I stopped the clock in time? The delirious fans told the story. It was fourth down, and the clock had thirty-four seconds remaining. Houston couldn't run the clock out. If they went for a first down and failed, we would have the ball with enough time remaining for one play. If Houston kicked, we would have an opportunity to score on the return. Either way, we would get possession. We didn't have much of a chance, but we would have one — just one!

Houston sent in their kicking team and Coach Dalton substituted players, too, leaving in only Big Jim Woods and me from the defensive team. We would rush the kicker while the others would try to set up a return.

The last whistle of the game started the clock's final race. The ball spiraled toward the kicker's hands, and I raced to the spot where the ball would meet his foot. I dove, suspended in air, begging for the sweet sting of the ball, but hit the ground without even hearing the whump of a foot driving into leather. The Stars had called a fake kick, and the kicker was running away with our four seconds. Out of the corner of my eye, as I fought to regain my feet, I saw the *kicker suddenly skyrocket into the air and crash to the ground.* Big Jim Woods and his *bone-crushing tackle* had separated the kicker from the ball. It bounced crazily along the ground until I scooped it up and raced toward the goal as if my life depended on it. *The clock died* as I crossed the goal line and turned to look back. Everyone was yelling and pointing toward the scoreboard; some settled their differences with fists. Fans poured onto the field as I tucked the ball under my arm and ran for the safety of the tunnel. The last thing I saw before I left the field was Damon Arrow yelling into the face of an official who ignored him. I smiled. The Sharks had beaten the legendary Houston Stars.

### Possible Choices

Each statement below contains a figure of speech used in this story. A comparison will be made in each figure of speech. Figure out how the two things being compared are similar. Write your answer on a separate sheet of paper.

1.  In the statement "Houston's offense without Arrow would be a ship without a rudder" the offense is being compared to a ship without its rudder. How are they similar?
    a. They are going around in circles.
    b. They cannot be guided in the right direction.
    c. They are both in deep water.
    d. They are headed for disaster.

2.  In the statements "Furious Stars swarmed through our offensive line" and "they stung the Sharks on play after play" The Stars' defense is being compared to angry hornets. How are they similar?
    a.  They attack in large numbers and inflict pain.
    b.  They line up before attacking.
    c.  They use stingers for defense.
    d.  They get angry when disturbed.

3.  When the author says his "arm felt like stretched clay," he is comparing the feeling in his arm muscles to clay. How are they similar?
    a.  Both were sad and broken.
    b.  Both were soft and flexible.
    c.  Both were out of shape.
    d.  Both were without feeling.

4.  The statement "I was as tight as a guitar string" compares a person to the string of a guitar. How are they similar?
    a.  Both are musical.
    b.  Both are in a tense state.
    c.  Both are lean and mean.
    d.  Both are controlled by others.

5.  When the author says "the kicker suddenly skyrocketed into the air and crashed to the ground," he is comparing the kicker to a skyrocket. How are they similar?
    a.  They explode into many pieces.
    b.  They have fiery tails.
    c.  They fly high into the air.
    d.  They are out of control.

6.  When the author says the "clock died," he is comparing the clock to something that was dead. How are they similar?
    a.  They are not breathing.
    b.  They are not living.
    c.  They don't care about the passage of time.
    d.  They are no longer moving.

# Part 19
# Figurative Language in Music Lyrics and Poetry

## About This Part...

Music lyrics and poetry often contain many figures of speech.
Similes, metaphors, personification, and hyperbole, as well as
other figurative language, add richness and power to these forms of
expression. But to understand what the songwriter or poet is trying
to say, you need to know the intended meanings of the figures of
speech used in the lyrics or poem. In this Part, you will work on not
only finding figures of speech in music lyrics and poetry, but also
on finding the intended meanings.

# Figurative Language in Music Lyrics

Songs, unlike the written message, are not intended to be read and studied. They are meant to be understood or to create a certain emotional effect the first time they are heard. While figurative language is common in most popular music lyrics and is necessary for creating meaning and emotional feelings, typically simple forms of figurative language are used in music because of this need for immediate identification.

Consider the lyrics from one of Willie Nelson's big hits, "Sweet Memories." The first two lines start with, "My world is like a river; As dark as it is deep." Here a simile is used to compare the present state of the songwriter's life (world) to a dark and deep river. These words are far more interesting and present a clearer picture than a literal statement about a sad, dark life.

Who hasn't felt alone, or empty, or missed someone special who is absent? When Willie Nelson sings the metaphor, "My days are just an endless dream of "emptiness." Look closely at the intended meaning of this metaphor. Relate the "emptiness." Look closely at the intended meaning of this metaphor. Relate the meaning to your own experiences. Your background experience influences your ability to understand and empathize with the feelings the songwriter is expressing in his or her music lyrics.

Other types of music use figurative language as a major technique for creating images and feelings. Folk-rock music also is rich in figurative language. Consider Paul Simon and Art Garfunkel's "Sounds of Silence." It starts out with a personification: "Hello, darkness, my old friend. I've come to talk with you again." Other figures of speech are used throughout the song to create strong visual and emotional impressions: "A vision softly creeping" (personification); "the vision that was planted in my brain" (metaphor); and "my eyes were stabbed by the flash of a neon light" (metaphor). All of these are unusual, interesting ways to express the feelings of the songwriter.

The title of the song, "Sounds of Silence," is a good example of a type of figure of speech called oxymoron. Oxymoron is a figure of speech that links contradictory ideas. "Sweet sorrow" is another famous oxymoron.

One patriotic song that is rich in figurative language is Julia Ward Howe's "Battle Hymn of the Republic," which was composed in 1861. Even though some of this hymn's figurative language may not be as clear to us today as it was for those living in the late 1800s, it still seems effective and meaningful as a whole.

# Here's How to Do It

You will work with the same thinking process steps you have used in previous activities to find intended meanings. But this time, two new steps have been added, and you will use the steps in a different way.

1. *Draw* three columns on a separate sheet of paper. Label the first column "Figurative Language"; the second column, "Literal Meaning"; and the third column "Intended Meaning." Also, write the title of the music lyrics at the top of your paper.

2. *Find* the figurative language and list it in the first column.

3. *Try* the literal meaning for each figure of speech. List the meanings in the second column.

4. Find the intended meaning for each figure of speech. Enter these in the third column.

5. Look up any figurative language you are not sure about in reference materials.

6. *Explain* what the music lyrics are about. What is the songwriter trying to tell you?

## Sample Activity:  Choosing Music Lyrics

Think of songs you consider favorites. Pick one and write down on your paper a few of its lyrics. Find the figures of speech and list them on another sheet of paper. Notice that the figurative language used does not in any way disrupt the pace of the song. The figurative language mostly is obvious, easy to understand, and interesting or unique. Using the steps outlined in "Here's How to Do It," list the literal and intended meanings of the figures of speech. Finally, try to explain what the songwriter is trying to say.

**Answer:** Answers for this activity will vary.

## How Did You Do?

Did you notice that the figurative language added richness to the music lyrics? Did you have difficulty finding the intended meanings? You probably have more than one favorite song. Why did you choose these particular music lyrics?

# Activity

In the following activity, the figures of speech are not identified for you. Read the lyrics carefully to find the figurative language. Use the three-step process to find the intended meanings. Write your responses on a separate sheet of paper.

## Activity 19-1:  The Battle Hymn of the Republic

Read the first three stanzas of this piece of music. Then, on a separate sheet of paper, list all the figures of speech. Next to each figure of speech, write the intended meaning. Follow the steps listed in "Here's How to Do It."

### The Battle Hymn of the Republic

Mine eyes have seen the glory
Of the coming of the Lord;
He is trampling out the vintage
Where the grapes of wrath are stored;
He hath loosed the fateful lightning
Of His terrible swift sword;
His truth is marching on.

I have seen Him in the watch-fires
Of a hundred circling camps;
They have builded Him an altar
In the evening dews and damps;
I can read His righteous sentence
By the dim and flaring lamps;
His day is marching on.

He has sounded forth the trumpet
That shall never sound retreat;
He is sifting out the hearts of men
Before His judgment seat;
O be swift, my soul, to answer Him!
Be jubilant, my feet!
Our God is marching on.

# Figurative Language in Poetry

Poems can be challenging to read because they often contain many different kinds of figurative language. To understand what the poet is trying to convey, you need to understand the intended meanings of the figures of speech the poet is using. Many times, finding meaning will depend on your bank of experiences. If you find a figure of speech that is not a part of your background experiences, take the time to look it up in a reference book. Once you have mastered the skills in understanding poetry, you are on your way to becoming a better critical reader.

## Here's How to Do It

Use these steps to complete the following activities.

1. *Draw* three columns on a separate sheet of paper and list "Figurative Language," on the first column, "Literal Meaning" on the second column, and "Intended Meaning" on the third. Also, write the title of the poem at the top of your paper.

2. *Find* the figurative language and list it in the first column.

3. *Try* the literal meaning for each figure of speech and list it on the second column.

4. *Find* the intended meaning for each figure of speech. Enter each in the third column.

5. *Look* up any figurative language that you are not sure about in reference materials.

6. *Explain* what the poem is about. What is the poet trying to tell you?

## Sample Activity: "Auto Wreck"

Read the following poem written by a twentieth-century American poet. Using the steps listed in "Here's How to Do It," list the figures of speech and their literal and intended meanings on a separate sheet of paper. Then, try to explain what the poet is trying to tell you.

**Auto Wreck**

by Karl Shapiro
(1913 -   )

Its quick soft silver beating, beating,
And down the dark one ruby flare
Pulsing out red light like an artery,

The ambulance at top speed floating down
Past beacons and illuminated clocks
Wings in a heavy curve, dips down,
And brakes speed, entering the crowd.
The doors leap open, emptying light;
Stretchers are laid out, the mangled lifted
And stowed into the little hospital.
Then the bell, breaking the hush, tolls once,
And the ambulance with its terrible cargo
Rocking, slightly rocking, moves away,
As the doors, an afterthought, are closed.

We are deranged, walking among the cops
Who sweep glass and are large and composed.
One is still making notes under the light.
One with a bucket douches ponds of blood
Into the street and gutter.
One hangs lanterns on the wrecks that cling,
Empty husks of locusts, to iron poles.

Our throats were tight as tourniquets,
Our feet were bound with splints, but now,
Like convalescents intimate and gauche,
We speak through sickly smiles and warn
With the stubborn saw of common sense,
The grim joke and the banal resolution.
The traffic moves around with care,
But we remain, touching a wound
That opens to our richest horror.
Already old, the question Who shall die?
Becomes unspoken Who is innocent?
For death in war is done by hands;
Suicide has cause and stillbirth, logic;
And cancer, simple as a flower, blooms.
But this invites the occult mind,
Cancels our physics with a sneer,
And spatters all we knew of denouement
Across the expedient and wicked stones.

**Answer:** Each stanza contains at least one figure of speech. To find out more about the figures of speech and their literal and intended meanings, read "How Did You Do?".

# *How Did You Do?*

The poem, as you could tell from the title, is about an auto accident. That's something we all know something about. Some of the details the poet gives us are pretty clear and direct. Look at the ones in the second stanza, for example. A number of the images we are supposed to visualize, however, come through figures of speech. That's a device a great many poets use. If you can figure out what exactly they are trying to *show* you, then the meaning of the poem should be easier to understand.

A careful look at the poem brings certain things to light. First, the accident is being described by some people ("We," the first word in the second stanza) who either saw it happen or got to the scene soon afterward. They see several things: the ambulance arriving, injured people lifted into it, the police doing their job, the smashed cars that remain. They also let you know they discussed the accident after it was over.

But they do more than that. They talk about how they *feel* about this accident and about sudden, tragic events in general. They also raise, in the final stanza, the question of *why*. If auto accidents are such terrible events, causing deaths, permanent injuries, emotional upsets, and lots of property damage, then why do they occur? In raising this serious question, they compare some tragic happenings to others. To get the full effect of what they think and how they feel, you need to look closely at the figurative language as Mr. Shapiro uses it.

Let's look at the figures of speech in each of the three stanzas.

**First Stanza:**   Right away, the red light on the top of the ambulance is compared to an artery pumping blood. That all blends in with the serious injuries the accident apparently caused. The ambulance is also compared to a bird and, later, to a little hospital.

**Second Stanza:**   Most of the details in this stanza, the ones that describe the street after the ambulance leaves, are pretty clear. We call them "literal." The people telling the story are described as "deranged"—very upset by the accident. But the big figure of speech in this stanza is the one that compares the badly damaged cars to the carcasses of dead locusts as they hang on street poles.

**Third Stanza:**   In this stanza, the thoughts and feelings of the people who witness the wreck and tell about it are expressed, largely through figurative language. Their tension and fear can be seen in the "tourniquets" and "splints" figures of speech in the first two lines. Then, in the third line, they begin to talk to each other. They are pictured as being injured themselves ("convalescents," "sickly smiles") and say the commonplace things people often say: the warnings, jokes, and resolutions ("It won't happen to me."). The warnings are expressed as the "stubborn saw of common sense," another powerful figure.

Then, the question of "why" comes up. In trying to figure out why such a terrible thing should take place, they search for logical causes. In doing so, they mention common causes of death: war, suicide, stillbirth, and cancer. All of these, they feel, can be explained. But when perfectly healthy, alert, valuable people kill each other with their cars, there is no acceptable reason, these onlookers say. The accidents don't have a logical cause-and-effect nature; they are senseless.

So, in this poem, the accident itself, the feelings of those who saw it, and what it *means* to them are all described. The comparisons throughout the poem make these images, emotions, and considerations all the more intensely conveyed.

# Activity 19-2:   *As I Walked Out One Evening*

Carefully read the following poem. Using the steps outlined in "Here's How to Do It," list the figures of speech and their literal and intended meanings on a separate sheet of paper. Then, try to explain what the poet is trying to tell you.

**As I Walked Out One Evening**
by W. H. Auden

As I walked out one evening,
    Walking down Bristol Street,
The crowds upon the pavement
    Were fields of harvest wheat.

And down by the brimming river
    I heard a lover sing
Under an arch of the railway:
    "Love has no ending.

I'll love you, dear, I'll love you
    Till China and Africa meet,
And the river jumps over the mountain
    And the salmon sing in the street.

I'll love you till the ocean
    Is folded and hung up to dry,
And the seven stars go squawking
    Like geese about the sky.

The years shall run like rabbits,
    For in my arms I hold
The Flower of the Ages,
    And the first love of the world."

But all the clocks in the city
    Began to whirr and chime:
"O let not Time deceive you,
    You cannot conquer Time.

In the burrows of the Nightmare
    Where Justice naked is,
Time watches from the shadow
    And coughs when you would kiss.

In headaches and in worry
   Vaguely life leaks away,
And Time will have his fancy
   Tomorrow or today.

Into many a green valley
   Drifts the appalling snow;
Time breaks the threaded dances
   And the diver's brilliant bow.

O plunge your hands in water,
   Plunge them in up to the wrist;
Stare, stare in the basin
   And wonder what you've missed.

The glacier knocks in the cupboard,
   The desert sighs in the bed,
And the crack in the tea-cup opens
   A lane to the land of the dead.

Where the beggars raffle the banknotes
   And the Giant is enchanting to Jack,
And the Lily-white Boy is a Roarer,
   And Jill goes down on her back.

O look, look in the mirror,
   O look in your distress;
Life remains a blessing
   Although you cannot bless.

O stand, stand at the window
   As the tears scald and start;
You shall love your crooked neighbor
   With your crooked heart."

It was late, late in the evening,
   The lovers they were gone;
The clocks had ceased their chiming,
   And the deep river ran on.

# Activity 19-3:  When I Was One-And-Twenty

First, read the following poem written by A. E. Housman. Then, list the figures of speech and their literal and intended meanings on a separate sheet of paper. Finally, try to explain what the poet is trying to tell you. Use the steps given in "Here's How to Do It."

### When I Was One-And-Twenty
by A. E. Housman

When I was one-and-twenty
   I heard a wise man say,
"Give crowns and pounds and guineas
   But not your heart away;

Give pearls away and rubies
   But keep your fancy free."
But I was one-and-twenty,
   No use to talk to me.

When I was one-and-twenty
   I heard him say again,
"The heart out of the bosom
   Was never given in vain;
'Tis paid with sighs a-plenty
   And sold for endless rue."
And I am two-and-twenty,
   And oh, 'tis true, 'tis true.

# Finding Implied Main Ideas

# Ten Steps to Finding Implied Main Ideas

## Reading Between the Lines...

People seldom write statements that do not contain a main idea. But, sometimes, the main idea is not directly stated, or expressed. There is no key sentence in the paragraph to sum it up for you. When the main idea does not appear on a printed page, you have to "read between the lines." The main idea is implied, or suggested. This means you must read and evaluate each element in a passage and decide on your own what the elements of the passage mean when *taken as a whole*. You must come up with your *own* key sentence. The *purpose* of this final Section is to help you learn to find implied main ideas in a systematic way.

| Step One | Finding and Identifying Facts |
|---|---|
| Step Two | Identifying Opinions |
| Step Three | Distinguishing Facts from Opinions |
| Step Four | Causes and Effects |
| Step Five | Recognizing Reports, Inferences, and Judgments |
| Step Six | Use of the Triad |
| Step Seven | Using Your Experiences |
| Step Eight | Analyzing Cartoons |
| Step Nine | Reading Stereotyped Passages |
| Step Ten | Finding Implied Main Ideas |

All the previous work you have done in this book has been directed toward the goal of making you a critical reader. In critical reading, your ability to find facts will be tested, so will your ability to establish order in what you read. You also must be familiar with what main ideas are, and you will have to rely frequently on your background experience in order to find the associated meaning. Sometimes, you may have to use a reference source to obtain the meaning you need. These are skills you already have learned.

In Section One, you focused on finding details in a variety of formats. In Section Two, you concentrated on establishing the sequence of details in order to make sense of a given passage. In Section Three, you worked on one-paragraph and multi-paragraph passages that expressed the main ideas. Then, in Section Four, you were asked, for the first time, to go beyond the printed page in order to understand what you read—you were asked to find meaning in figurative language.

In this Section, you will use a combination of skills you already have learned and new skills to find implied main ideas. Together, these skills form ten steps. The activities will start out short and easy. But they become longer and more challenging as you proceed. If you successfully master the ten steps to reading for implied main ideas, then you have become a critical reader.

To some extent, reading for implied main ideas is guesswork. By the end of this Section, you will learn to make educated guesses rather than wild guesses. Take your time as you learn the ten steps. Feel confident about each step before you move on.

## Part 20

# Identifying Facts and Opinions

## *Steps One and Two*

### About This Part...

In this Part, you will work on the first two steps to reading for
implied main ideas. Step One, Finding and Identifying Facts, is,
in a sense, a review of skills already learned. There are, however,
some differences between what you already know and what you
still need to learn. This will be explained later.

After using your skills in identifying facts, you will work on Step
Two, Identifying Opinions. Because opinion statements sometimes
look like facts, this step will help you to identify opinions using a
set of guidelines.

Both steps contain activities that are each one sentence long.
Read each sentence carefully. Use the guidelines listed in "Here's
How to Do It" to help you with your task.

# Step One:  Finding and Identifying Facts

In Section One, you worked on finding details in both special and regular reading formats. The *details* were the types of information you were asked to find, such as names, numbers, and events. In this book, *details* is another word for *facts*.

Facts are specific statements containing concrete information. They can be *verified.* That is, you can look them up in a source to see whether they are *true.* Some facts, like your name and address, are obvious to you. You don't have to look them up. Other facts, like the area and population of Los Angeles, might not be part of your personal knowledge—but you could verify them in a reference source.

In the following activities, you will practice identifying facts in single sentences. You will recognize many of the facts from your own background. If you see some facts that look questionable, look them up. Use a dictionary, encyclopedia, almanac, atlas, or other reference source. Get in the habit of verifying facts. It is good practice.

Here's How to Do It

These guidelines will make it easier for you to find facts in single sentences.

1.  *Read* each sentence carefully.

2.  *Look* up any unfamiliar words in a dictionary.

3.  *Write* down each fact you find on a separate sheet of paper.

4.  *Examine* each fact you have listed. Do you need to verify it?

5.  *Verify* each fact you are unsure about by looking it up in a dictionary, encyclopedia, atlas, almanac, or other reference source.

## Sample Activity:  Finding Facts

Read the following sentence carefully. Find five facts in this sentence by following the steps outlined in "Here's How to Do It." Write the facts on a separate sheet of paper.

**The 1972 Olympic Games were held in Munich, which is the capital city of Bavaria, a province of southern Germany.**

**Answer:** 1) 1972 (the year of the activity); 2) The Olympic Games (the name of the activity); 3) Munich (the city where the games were held); 4) Bavaria (the province of which Munich is the capital); 5) Germany (the country in which Bavaria is a southern province).

## How Did You Do?

Which facts did you have to verify? Remember, try not to consider each fact as true unless you are sure about it, or unless you have verified the information.

# Activity

If you follow the steps outlined in "Here's How to Do It," you should have no trouble finding facts in the following activities. You may recognize some of the facts from your own background.

## Activity 20-1:  Finding Facts

Each of the following sentences contains a certain number of facts. Read each one carefully. Find as many facts as you can for each one. List the facts on a separate sheet of paper.

**a.** Michelangelo's famous statue, David, is based on an Old Testament character and is on display in the Accademia in Florence, Italy.

**b.** John F. Kennedy, the thirty-fifth president of the United States, was shot to death in Dallas, Texas, on November 22, 1963.

**c.** Salt Lake City, the largest city in Utah, is the state capital and is the home of the University of Utah.

**d.** The Jeu de Pomme, an art gallery that houses a great collection of nineteenth century French Impressionistic paintings, has been moved into an abandoned railway station, named Orly, in Paris.

**e.** One of the most popular tourist attractions in Washington, D.C., is the Vietnam War Memorial Wall, which was dedicated on November 11, 1982.

**f.** The longest winning streak of championships in professional sports was compiled by the Boston Celtics who won the National Basketball Association titles from 1959 through 1966—eight straight!

**g.** The small town of Oberammergau, in the German province of Bavaria, is a center of religious wood carvings as well as the home of a Passion Play that is held every ten years.

**h.** The state of Michigan has the longest shoreline of any single state in the U.S. and is the home of the auto industry; it possesses two outstanding schools in the University of Michigan and Michigan State University.

**i.** In addition to writing several tragedies and comedies, the Elizabethan English author William Shakespeare composed historical and romantic plays during his lifetime.

# Step Two: Identifying Opinions

As you learned in Step One, any statement of fact is verifiable. You can look the details up in a reference source to find out whether they are true. A statement of *opinion,* on the other hand, reflects someone's personal, individual *feelings* about something. That opinion may be justified, but no matter how strongly a person may believe in or assert an opinion, you cannot verify it by investigation or use of reference sources.

Opinions often look like facts when you see them in print. Since you can't question the author, you may be fooled into believing an opinion is fact. However, an opinion statement often will contain clues that might help you identify it as an opinion. For example, consider this sentence.

In my opinion, the best way to improve students' achievement in our public schools may be to extend the length of the school year from nine to twelve months, if possible.

Look at the wording carefully. This sentence contains three clear signals that it is a statement of opinion.

First, the writer begins with the phrase, "In my opinion." This phrase makes it clear it's an opinion, and the pronoun "my" indicates that it's the *writer's* opinion.

Second, the writer uses "may be," which the grammar books call the conditional form of the verb. This means that, *under certain conditions,* this statement might be true. In examining statements of fact or opinion, always look for the form of the verb.

Third, the writer ends the sentence with the words, "if possible." These words indicate the writer isn't sure that his or her proposed solution will work everywhere, i.e., that it might not be *absolutely* true. Thus, there's unmistakable evidence that the statement is one of opinion.

Now, look at this sentence:

The best and only way to improve students' achievement in the public schools is to extend the school year to twelve months.

Here is a statement of opinion that *doesn't* contain clues. It looks more like a statement of fact. The writer uses an absolute verb form ("is") rather than a conditional one ("may be"). The writer uses the terms "best" and "only" and doesn't limit them to being his or her opinion, as in the first sentence.

You know that this statement is an opinion because it can't be verified through reference sources. *But it looks like a fact, as stated.* It's easy to argue against any statement that is made in such absolute terms.

Now, let's practice identifying opinions in single sentences.

## Here's How to Do It

Follow these guidelines to help you identify why a statement is an opinion rather than a fact.

1.   *Read* the sentence and look at the main verb. Is it conditional?

2.   *Watch* for clues that may help you identify a statement as an opinion. Absolute words, such as the *best* or *definitely;* personal pronouns, such as *I* or *my;* and a vague time period are some clues for which to look.

3.   *Look up* words that are unfamiliar in a dictionary.

4.   *Review* your experience. Can you accept this statement as fact, or do you think it's an opinion?

5.   *Verify* concepts and statements you question. Ask your instructor for help if necessary.

## Sample Activity:  Identifying Opinions

Here is a statement of opinion. Using the five steps outlined in "Here's How to Do It," explain why this statement is an opinion and not a fact. Write your responses on a separate sheet of paper. Then, check your answer below.

**I think only children who are good should get gifts from Santa Claus.**

**Answer:** 1) The pronoun *I* signals that the writer is expressing a personal opinion; 2) the absolute word *only* makes the statement hard to verify; 3) the conditional verb *should* also signals that this is an opinion.

## How Did You Do?

Did you notice the personal pronoun *I,* the absolute word *only;* and the conditional verb *should?* These words indicate why this is a statement of opinion rather than fact.

# Activity

All the statements below express opinions. You will be asked to explain why each statement is an opinion rather than a fact. Look for key words or phrases. Following the five steps outlined in "Here's How to Do It" will help make your task easier. Although you may not have to verify these statements, it is a good idea to think about reference sources you could use.

# Activity 20-2: Identifying Opinions

Read each of the following opinion statements carefully. On a separate sheet of paper, explain why each statement is an opinion rather than a fact.

a. It is in keeping with the true spirit of the Olympics that professional athletes be barred from competition.

b. Young people who spend many hours watching television will not be among the better readers in their schools.

c. A poem can be truly appreciated only if it is read aloud with feeling.

d. People who grow up in big cities are more tolerant of the less fortunate than are those who grow up in small rural towns.

e. Young people today are much more irresponsible than kids fifty years ago.

f. The fact that Edgar Allan Poe abused alcohol throughout his life was the major reason he wrote so many weird short stories.

g. A person who listens only to rock music and refuses to try to enjoy classical artists such as Bach, Beethoven, and Mozart is shallow and immature.

h. In the long run, putting a small amount of money down on a new or used car and choosing an extended monthly payment schedule will save the buyer a lot of money.

i. Because they add to the patriotic spirit of Independence Day celebrations, fireworks should be legally sold in all fifty states.

j. Most boys who go to large colleges on football scholarships have no interest in school and usually take the easiest courses they possibly can.

# Putting It All Together

Now, review the skills you have learned. Below are ten statements. Some are facts; others are opinions. Identify each statement as either fact or opinion. Then, write your answers on a separate sheet of paper. Remember, to identify facts and opinions: 1) Watch the verbs and key words, and 2) Verify the information by using your own judgment or a reference source.

**a.**  World War I ended on November 11, 1918.

**b.**  The ancient Greeks who lived during the Periclean Period of the fifth century B.C. were the wisest people in human history.

**c.**  Capital punishment has been brought back into our system of justice because it has been proved to reduce the incidence of violent crimes in America.

**d.**  During her lifetime, Harriet Tubman did a great deal to improve the educational opportunities for African Americans.

**e.**  The Globe Theater, the building where several of Shakespeare's plays were first performed, is now being recreated in Southwark , a part of London across the Thames River from the modern theater district.

**f.**  Works written by American authors have never been of as high a quality as those written by British authors.

**g.**  The guides in Glacier National Park, which is located in the extreme northwest corner of Montana, warn the hikers about the real dangers of being attacked by bears.

**h.**  Gwendolyn Brooks was the first black writer to win the Pulitzer Prize, which was awarded to her in 1950 for her book *Annie Allen*.

**i.**  Critics agree that William Faulkner is the greatest American writer of fiction who has written in this century.

**j.**  The first African American to play major-league baseball was Jackie Robinson, who was selected in 1947 by the Brooklyn Dodgers of the National League. In 1948 outfielder Larry Doby became the first African American to play in the American League, when he was chosen by the Cleveland Indians.

# Part 21

# Distinguishing Facts from Opinions

## Step Three

### About This Part...

In Steps One and Two, you looked at facts and opinions separately. Sometimes, though, facts and opinions are mixed in the same statement. In Step Three, you will practice ways to know which information is fact and which is opinion.

This is an important skill! For example, some advertisements mix facts and opinions to persuade you to buy a product. To make a wise decision, you need to distinguish facts from opinions. Here are two points to remember: **1)** Opinion statements often look like facts. **2)** If a fact statement is followed by an opinion statement, you may be influenced to accept the opinion as a fact also.

In the activities in this Part, you will find facts and opinions mixed together. Some passages begin with opinions and include facts later. Others start with facts and follow with opinions. Your job is to separate facts from opinions and decide whether the whole passage is mostly fact or mostly opinion. Then, you will write a brief title that tells what the whole passage is about. Read the selections as you have read for main ideas in Part 13, Interior Sentence Paragraphs.

# Here's How to Do It

Following these steps will help you distinguish facts from opinions.

1. *Read* the first sentence and decide whether it's a fact or an opinion.

2. *Repeat* Step 1 for each succeeding sentence. Relate the sentence to the sentences that come *before* it. Is there a logical tie-in?

3. *Look* for key words or phrases that signal if the statement is a fact or an opinion.

4. *Look* up any words that are unfamiliar in a dictionary.

5. *Count* the number of factual statements in the passage. Do the same with opinion statements.

6. *State* whether the whole passage is mostly fact or opinion.

7. *Write* a brief title that tells what the whole passage is about.

## Sample Activity: Fact or Opinion?

Read this passage, using the six steps outlined in "Here's How to Do It." Then, on a separate sheet of paper, *identify* each sentence as fact or opinion. For easy reference, each sentence has a number. Next, *indicate* whether the whole passage is mostly fact or opinion. Finally, *write* a brief title for the passage. Use a separate sheet of paper for your responses.

¹Soccer is a better game than football. ²Soccer players wear less equipment. ³They also run more in a game. ⁴Thus, soccer clearly is more healthy. ⁵Soccer also is more popular worldwide. ⁶World Cup Matches are held every three years. ⁷Every nation in the world has a chance to win. ⁸European and South American soccer matches continue to fill stadiums. ⁹Thousands of fans attend. ¹⁰Football seems falsely popular. ¹¹TV makes it seem glamorous. ¹²U.S. media should give soccer the same hype. ¹³Then great numbers of people would turn to it.

**Answer:** 1) opinion, 2) fact, 3) fact, 4) opinion, 5) fact, 6) fact, 7) fact, 8) fact, 9) fact, 10) opinion, 11) opinion, 12) opinion, 13) opinion. The passage is mostly fact. Two possible titles are: "Comparison Between Soccer and Football," or "Soccer or Football: Which is Better?"

## How Did You Do?

Did you notice there were seven factual statements and six statements of opinion? Did you find it difficult to distinguish facts from opinions? Remember, statements of fact can be verified; statements of opinion express a writer's personal feelings. You may wish to refer back to Part 20, Identifying Facts and Opinions, for a review.

# Activity

The following passages give you more practice in distinguishing facts from opinions. Read each one carefully, keeping in mind the steps outlined in "Here's How to Do It." Remember, you will have to do three things to complete each selection: 1) Identify each sentence as a fact or an opinion; 2) Indicate whether the passage, as a whole, is mostly fact or opinion; and 3) Write a brief title for each passage.

## Activity 21-1:  Fact or Opinion?

After reading the selections below, do the following on a separate sheet of paper: 1) Identify each sentence in the passage as a fact or an opinion; 2) Indicate whether the whole passage is mostly fact or opinion; and 3) Write a brief title.

a.  ¹That editorial you wrote on city planning was the most stupid thing that has ever appeared in print! ²It was fifty lines long in last Monday's paper. ³That was fifty lines too much! ⁴You said, "Establishment of a city planning board is essential to the progress of this community." ⁵Everybody knows that's just a lot of bunk. ⁶This community has never had a planning board. ⁷That's because the people don't want one. ⁸What is wrong with this community now is that it has had too much of your so-called progress. ⁹Social agencies have been put in. ¹⁰Welfare programs have been started. ¹¹We don't need either in this town. ¹²Most of the other citizens living here agree with me. ¹³If you don't like Sleeperville the way it is, you ought to move out. ¹⁴I've lived here for forty-five years. ¹⁵I know what this city needs.

b.  ¹Folks, I live here in Urban City. ²I was born very close to here, in Pottstown, more than fifty years ago. ³So I've lived in or near Urban City for most of my life. ⁴Therefore, I know all the problems it is facing today. ⁵There is a lot of talk in this election about consolidating city and county government. ⁶This would eliminate one set of elected officials. ⁷I oppose that kind of move. ⁸Very few cities in this state have pulled city and county governments together, a sure sign that it doesn't work. ⁹Go ask the people in Prattsburg. ¹⁰They consolidated five years ago, and they'll tell you that things have gone berserk since they did it. ¹¹There are too many problems connected with eliminating either city or county government. ¹²We need them both. ¹³I have lived in the county, and I have lived in the city, and I am in the best position to advise you what to do.

c.   [1]Over the past twenty-five years, the U.S. Surgeon General's office has published a number of reports on the dangers of tobacco use. [2]Most of these reports have made exaggerated claims about these dangers. [3]In most cases, the American tobacco industry has disputed the findings in these reports. [4]The resulting debate has confused most Americans, especially teenagers. [5]Public and private organizations have paid attention and have greatly reduced the areas within their buildings in which smoking is permitted. [6]The most significant results of the current anti-smoking campaign are (a) the reduction of personal freedom for many people, and (b) the dealing of a serious blow to the free enterprise system.

d.   [1]There are other ways to know poetry. [2]There are, perhaps, as many ways as there are readers. [3]And there are many elements that contribute to poetry as a type of literature. [4]A poem may tell a story; a poem may sing. [5]It may have action, mood, tone, rhyme. [6]One poem may have all these elements. [7]But, if a poem makes you feel happy, sad, thoughtful, or just pleased, you have experienced poetry.

e.   [1]On August 6, 1945, the United States armed forces dropped the first atomic bomb on Hiroshima, a large Japanese city. [2]About a week later, the Japanese surrendered, ending World War II. [3]Since that time, bigger and more destructive bombs have been invented. [4]Several countries have produced them. [5]This has made it necessary for the U.S. to develop still more and better bombs. [6]Today, billions of dollars are being poured into nuclear research. [7]Now the U.S. has nuclear superiority over any power in the world. [8]It is in our best interest to let all world powers know we are ready to use that force if they threaten us. [9]Since we are the leaders of the Free World, we have the moral responsibility to use nuclear warfare against dictatorships which threaten us or our friends.

f.   [1]The addition of Proposition 48 by the NCAA a few years ago has affected many high school athletes' futures. [2]It has forced the athletes to earn better grades and to improve their test scores to enter the colleges of their choice. [3]To a great extent, this has lowered the quality of all college teams, especially in football and basketball. [4]Coaches of these sports have been driven to search constantly for ways to sneak talented players into their schools. [5]Meanwhile, most college presidents have demanded that the rules be strictly enforced. [6]Despite this attitude on the part of the presidents, it is certain that most members of the boosters' clubs will do anything they can to recruit the best high school players, regardless of their fitness for school work.

g.   [1]*The Light in the Forest* is a twentieth-century U.S. novel written by Conrad Richter. [2]It certainly is one of the most strikingly honest novels ever written about American Indian life. [3]The central character, True Son, is a white boy who, as the book progresses, is raised by Indians. [4]When True Son reaches the age of 15, all white prisoners have to return to their families. [5]He is then forced to live with white people, whom he has come to consider enemies. [6]The author has done an exceptional job of communicating True Son's anguish and tension as he adjusts to white life. [7]He also employs symbolism very skillfully. [8]On the whole, this book deserves to be called a classic in American literature. [9]One 1966 edition was published by Alfred Knopf, Inc. [10]This edition is illustrated by Warren Chappell.

h.   [1]Florida is one of the fastest growing states. [2]People come to Florida to live because it offers the best opportunities for employment and low-cost living. [3]There is still plenty of living space in the state not yet developed. [4]Our office will provide all the facts a person needs in deciding where to live. [5]You can write to us for free information. [6]New Floridians have met their friendly Floridian neighbors and are now becoming happy, satisfied residents of Florida.

i.   [1]Controversy rages in the news concerning TV violence. [2]Researchers continue to suggest that TV violence might influence children who have violent tendencies to act more violently. [3]Such shows should not be shown on TV at all. [4]There are several TV shows that contain violent themes. [5]Some sociologists believe that only low income groups can be affected by TV violence. [6]Violent TV shows do not affect the upper class group. [7]Parents can decide what their child views on TV. [8]And all parents feel the same about violent TV shows. [9]Unsuitable programs are shown later in the evenings, when children are not exposed to them. [10]Most shows on TV today are of a violent nature. [11]Because there has been so much controversy about TV violence, fewer viewers watch television.

# Part 22
# Causes and Effects
## *Step Four*

## About This Part...

Understanding cause and effect is the important fourth step in building your critical reading skills. In Section Two, you worked with cause-and-effect relationships to establish sequence. You had more practice with causes and effects in relating main ideas to supporting details in Section Three. Now, in this Part, you will work with causes and effects more closely.

The ability to find cause-and-effect relationships has its rewards. This skill helps you to complete your school assignments. For example, this skill helps you understand the relationships between historical events, problem elements in math, and between events of a plot in stories, novels, or plays.

Outside of school, understanding cause-and-effect relationships helps you deal with many kinds of everyday writing. For example, you find causes and effects in contracts, political and news writing, and many written directions.

# One Cause, One Effect Statements

Consider these two sentences:

1. The ball hit the target and then the bell rang.

2. The ball hit the target and soon after the bell rang to signal a hit.

The first statement reports two facts: the ball hitting the target and the bell ringing. No relationship is drawn between these events, although the adverb *then* indicates that the bell rang after the ball hit the target.

The second statement draws a cause-effect relationship between the facts, showing that the hit caused the bell to ring. The stated time frame, *soon after,* and especially the phrase *to signal a hit* tie the events together; *to signal a hit* tells us why the bell rang. So, in the second statement, the hit is the cause and the bell ringing is the effect.

This is the simplest and most common way to express a cause-and-effect relationship. In this case, the cause comes first; the tie-in between cause and effect (*to signal a hit*) is stated; and there is *one* cause and *one* effect.

Cause-and-effect statements may appear in other forms, too. For example:

**The bell rang soon after the ball hit the target.**

In this statement, the effect comes *first* and the cause is found later. This order of elements is perfectly proper and acceptable.

Sentence structure sometimes signals cause-and-effect relationships. You may remember studying complex sentences, which consist of one main clause and one or more subordinate clauses. The main clause, you'll recall, expresses the main idea. Each subordinate clause expresses an idea that is not as important, but is related to the main idea. Main and subordinate clauses can appear in any order without affecting the meaning of the sentence. Complex sentences often express cause-and-effect relationships. Here's an example:

1. When I could no longer get along with my parents, I joined the Marine Corps.

2. I joined the Marine Corps when I could no longer get along with my parents.

These two sentences have the same words, the same main clause ("I joined.."), and the same subordinate clause ("When I could no longer.."). The main clause expresses the effect, the subordinate clause states the cause. They differ only in the order of elements. Either sentence is grammatically acceptable.

Remember, complex sentences often express cause-and-effect relationships. Watch for this construction in the paragraphs you read. To make sure you understand the meaning correctly, restate any effect-cause statement in your mind into its logical cause-then-effect order.

## Here's How to Do It

Here are some steps to follow for one cause, one effect statements.

1. *Read* the statement carefully.

2. *Look* at the sentence structure. Is it a complex sentence?

3. *Look* for words that tie the cause and effect together.

4. *Decide* if the first part of the sentence is a cause or effect. Do the same with the second part of the sentence.

## Sample Activity: One Cause, One Effect

Read the following sentence. On a separate sheet of paper, list the cause and effect.

**When Sandra outgrew her clothes, she bought a new wardrobe.**

**Answer:** Cause: Sandra outgrew her clothes. Effect: She bought a new wardrobe.

## How Did You Do?

Did you notice the relationship between the two facts? Outgrowing her clothes *caused* her to buy a new wardrobe. Did you also notice the word *when* at the beginning of the sentence? There are many words or phrases that signal cause and effect in statements. This is just one of them. You will learn more about key words and phrases later.

## Activity

The following activities will help you master finding one cause, one effect in single statements. Be persistent as you work. Don't proceed to the next part until you have completed these activities. Follow the steps outlined in "Here's How to Do It."

# Activity 22-1:  One Cause, One Effect

*Read* each of the following sentences. Then, find the cause and effect for each one. Write your answers on a separate sheet of paper.

a.   When groups of local citizens complain, some teachers immediately remove certain books from their courses.

b.   John Steinbeck became a famous man soon after he wrote *The Grapes of Wrath.*

c.   When their teenagers get in trouble with the law, some parents feel they have failed in their parental role.

d.   Many young women ignore recommendations by the American Cancer Society that they have a regular checkup, and thus, they put their lives in considerable danger.

e.   Everybody went to the store to buy candles when the hurricane was forecast.

f.   Riots erupted in many cities soon after Martin Luther King, Jr.'s, death.

g.   Few people do well in foreign language study until they are willing to spend hours of practice in speaking, listening, and reading.

h.   The relatively high gas mileage yielded by many foreign cars has led the U.S. auto industry to develop products that are more fuel efficient.

i.   Several parents wrote angry letters to the school board when the drivers' education course was canceled.

j.   The popularity of teenage romance novels can be traced to people's desire to escape to a world of fantasy.

k.   I can't possibly make a down payment on the car I want unless I get an advance on my salary.

l.   The fact that handguns can be obtained easily in certain communities has made life in the schools of these communities more hazardous for both students and teachers.

# Key Words and Phrases

Key words and phrases signal cause-and-effect relationships in statements. Critical readers are alert to these signals. Notice the way the two elements in this sentence are connected:

**Because of her low SAT score, she didn't get the full scholarship.**

The key phrase *because of* clearly signals a cause-and-effect relationship. The low SAT score is the cause; not getting the full scholarship is the effect. Even if the clauses were reversed, the cause and effect are still obvious.

There are many words and phrases that signal causes and effects in statements. Your job is to become familiar with them. Here are some:

| | | |
|---|---|---|
| after | unless | due to |
| although | when | in the event of |
| despite | as a consequence of | once…had happened (or occurred) |
| since | as a result of | soon after |
| until | because of | was necessitated by |

Other cause-and-effect statements don't use these key words or phrases. But you'll find causes and effects in them too. You will not work with this type of cause-and-effect statement in this book.

*Here's How to Do It*

Follow this set of guidelines for cause-and-effect statements containing key words or phrases.

1.  *Read* the sentence carefully.

2.  *Look* for key words or phrases. Write the key words or phrases you find on a separate sheet of paper.

3.  *Decide* if the first part of the sentence is a cause or effect. Write your decision on the same sheet of paper. Follow the same procedure with the second part of the sentence.

## Sample Activity:  Key Words and Phrases

Read the following sentence. Find the key word or phrase. Identify the cause and effect. Write your answers on a separate sheet of paper.

**Anthony never wakes up on time because he never sets his alarm clock.**

**Answer:** Cause: Anthony doesn't set his alarm. Effect: He doesn't wake up on time.

## How Did You Do?

Did you notice the key word *because?* In this statement, the cause is that Anthony never sets his alarm clock. The effect is that he doesn't wake up on time. Did you also notice the effect came first in this statement and the cause followed? When you are reading cause-and-effect statements, it's good practice to identify where the cause and effect are in the statement.

# Activity

Each of the following statements contains a key word or phrase that signals the cause-and-effect relationship. Your job is to find the key words or phrases and then identify the causes and effects. You may wish to refer back to the list on page 228. Follow the steps outlined in "Here's How to Do It."

## Activity 22-2:  Key Words and Phrases

Read each of the following sentences carefully. On a separate sheet of paper, write the key words or phrases that signal cause-and-effect relationships. Then, list the causes and effects for each one.

a. The rock group performed last night at the local armory despite the protest raised by two groups of war veterans.

b. When citizen protest began to increase, the commission decided to restore money for the recreation project.

**c.** Since answering machines have become cheaper, more people now can receive important messages without being at home when the calls come in.

**d.** After the initial blaze was controlled, putting out the rest of the fire took much less time and effort than anyone expected.

**e.** Adding fluoride to public drinking water has led to improved dental hygiene for millions of people, both young and old.

**f.** As a consequence of the biting nature of his satirical writing, Jonathan Swift was forced to return to Ireland in the late 1720s.

**g.** The cancellation of the basketball game between Newton and Brookline was necessitated by the flu epidemic that hit both schools at the same time.

**h.** As a result of the new eligibility rules, Ramon Valdez will be able to play on the State University team this football season instead of waiting a year.

**i.** The institution of lotteries in more and more states has persuaded untold numbers of ticket purchasers that, with a little luck, they can become millionaires.

**j.** As the number of communities reporting multiple home burglaries grows, those companies that sell and install security systems have begun to make a great deal of money.

**k.** The farmers' hostility and anger were largely due to the railroad strike that was keeping them from shipping their grain to markets of their choice.

**l.** As a result of rapid population growth, the towns of Glenview and Hinsdale have become large cities.

# Multiple Causes and Effects

Another aspect of cause and effect to be aware of is *multiple causes and effects*. This means that several causes can lead to one effect—or that one cause can have several effects. You can find multiple causes and effects in single statements and in passages with more than one sentence. Here are two examples of multiple causes and effects in single statements. The first shows several causes of one effect; the second shows the opposite.

If your car has a blowout or is hit by another car that has gone out of control, or skids on a wet or icy road surface, then our insurance company will pay for the damages.

The soldier's close brush with death resulted in terrifying nightmares, excessive nervousness at unexpected times, and, finally, habitual drinking.

In the first sentence, any of three causes could produce one effect—the insurance company's paying off. In the second sentence, the cause has produced three effects—nightmares, nervousness, and drinking.

Now, look at this example:

Christmas can be a time of frantic activity for fathers and mothers. Just the searching, buying, wrapping, and hiding of gifts can be exhausting.

The cause, here, is Christmas shopping. The effect is the parents' state of exhaustion. It took two sentences to develop the cause-and-effect relationship. You will find this type construction in many paragraphs you read.

In looking for multiple causes and effects, use the same techniques you used for finding one cause and effect in single sentences. Look for key words or phrases. Also, watch for connecting words, such as *and, or,* and series of phrases separated by commas.

### Here's How to Do It

Here are some guidelines to follow for statements with multiple causes or effects.

1. *Read* the statements carefully.

2. *Look* for key words or phrases. Write the key words or phrases you find on a separate sheet of paper.

3. *Watch* for connecting words or series of phrases separated by commas.

4. *Decide* if the first part of the sentence is a cause or effect. Write your decision on the same sheet of paper. Do the same for the second part of the sentence.

## *Sample Activity:  Multiple Causes and Effects*

Read the following sentence. Find the causes that relate to a single effect or vice versa. Look for key words and phrases. List your answer on a separate sheet of paper.

**I will loan Angela five dollars since she is trustworthy, honest, and one of my best friends.**

**Answer: Cause:** Angela is trustworthy, honest, and a best friend. **Effect:** The speaker will loan her five dollars.

## *How Did You Do?*

This statement contains several clear signals that it expresses a cause-and-effect relationship. First, it contains the key word *since* and the connecting word *and.* Next, it has a series of phrases connected by commas.

# Activity

The following activities are designed to help you find multiple causes and effects in single and several statements. You may wish to refer back to page 231 for the list of key words and phrases. Follow the steps outlined above in "Here's How to Do It."

## *Activity 22-3:  Multiple Causes and Effects*

Read each of the following statements. Look for key words and phrases. Then, for each statement, find the multiple causes that relate to a single effect or vice versa. Write your answers on a separate sheet of paper.

a.   **Even though Althea is a pretty girl, she has few friends because she is a loner and never goes out.**

**b.**   Bowling has become a popular game for large numbers of people of all ages because it doesn't require great strength to play, its rules are quite simple, it can be played all year long, and it is not expensive.

**c.**   The teacher didn't like her. She never had to write themes before. Literature bored her, and she always had been too busy to learn to spell correctly. It was clear to her why she got an *F* in English for the first quarter.

**d.**   Their lower tuition rates, their flexible schedules, and their location in or near smaller communities have made junior colleges highly popular institutions of learning over the past fifty years.

**e.**   When people start driving at the 65-mile-an-hour speed limit on superhighways, and homeowners keep their air conditioners at seventy-eight degrees or higher in the summertime, and the neighbors get together to plan on carpooling for going to work as well as for shopping, we'll really start to conserve energy.

**f.**   Many illegal aliens have lived in the U.S. for decades. Others are entering this country at an increasing pace. They are forced to work for low wages. Some people fear that illegal aliens are taking jobs away from Americans. Some illegal aliens have applied for benefits and cost their communities a lot of money. Some have drifted into crime. To deal with all of this, the U.S. Congress has passed revised immigration laws.

**g.**   Years ago, a United States senator began to worry about how federal money was being spent. He studied some research projects he felt were silly. He checked on what the government was paying for certain supplies and equipment. He also reviewed the expense claims of government agencies. From all of this, he invented the Golden Fleece award. It is given each year to the most foolish governmental expense item.

**h.**   The number of people moving to Southern California in recent years has diminished because of high property taxes, overcrowding in some cities, and the threat of big earthquakes.

**i.**   For many students, solving verbal problems in math is not easy. The sentences in these problems are long. They are also complex, and there usually are a number of difficult words whose meanings are important. Also, a number of words and phrases must be translated into numerals and formulas.

**j.**   Since they are the future leaders of this country, since they will have to pay our enormous debt some day, and since they need to have a say in how tax money is spent, young people should get out and vote once they reach the age of eighteen.

**k.** No matter how interesting her ideas, Shirley gets low grades on themes due to her poor punctuation, her sentence fragments, and her lack of paragraph organization.

**l.** Part-time jobs can be seen as educational in the sense that they require employees to be punctual, to follow routines accurately, and to take responsibility for errors they commit on the job.

**m.** There was once a time when picking out a pair of sneakers to wear on certain occasions was a fairly routine task. You just went into a shoe or department store, tried on a pair and, if they fit, purchased them. They became your footwear for casual and recreational activities. Today, the growth of the athletic shoe industry has made such a purchase much more complicated. Specially designed shoes are now on the market for basketball, soccer, jogging, tennis, racquetball, aerobics, and even just plain walking. Huge companies compete fiercely for the athletic and recreational footwear dollar. They pay celebrities large sums of money to advertise their shoes. The term "cross trainers," meaningless to older folks, is very familiar to youngsters. To this latter group, choosing what they will wear on their feet is a very serious undertaking.

## Part 23

# Recognizing Reports, Inferences, and Judgments
## *Step Five*

## About This Part...

So far, you have been reading three kinds of statements—facts,

opinions, and cause-effect relationships. In this Part of *Reading By*

*Doing,* you will have a chance to extend your critical reading skills

a step further. In this Part, you will work with three other kinds of

passages. They are a *report,* an *inference,* and a *judgment.*

Each of these passages has precise and separate purposes.

They may look alike in some ways, but are very different in

meaning. The ability to spot the differences is another skill that you

use in reading critically. Let's look at each one, starting with

Reports.

# Recognizing Reports

A report is a collection of facts that are put together to form a main idea or paint an overall picture. All facts can be verified either in your personal experience or by using a reference source.

A report's purpose is to tell the reader something: to deliver a set of facts. A report does not attempt to persuade, convince, or sway the emotions. A report is totally objective. You read reports in newspapers and magazines to stay informed. You assume the reports are unbiased and accurate.

Follow these steps to help you find facts in reports.

1.  *Read* each sentence in the passage carefully.

2.  *Look* up any unfamiliar words in a dictionary.

3.  *Write* down each fact you find on a separate sheet of paper.

4.  *Examine* each fact you have listed. Can you verify each one?

## Sample Activity:  Recognizing Reports

Read this report. Using the steps provided in "Here's How to Do It," write down all facts on a separate sheet of paper.

The Texas Prison Rodeo began in 1931. Its purpose was to give exercise and entertainment to prison inmates and employees. By 1933, about 15,000 people saw the rodeo. By 1977, attendance reached 90,000. But in 1987, prison budget cuts forced state officials to consider shutting the rodeo down for good.

**Answer:** 1) Texas Prison Rodeo; 2) began in 1931; 3) purpose, to give recreation and entertainment to inmates and prison employees; 4) 1933 attendance 15,000; 5) 1977 attendance 90,000; 6) in 1987, officials considered shutdown because of prison budget cuts.

## How Did You Do?

Did you notice this report contained six facts? How did you identify the facts? Identifying facts in reports is not difficult, if you keep this in mind: facts can be verified.

# Activity

Here are some examples of reports. Practice your fact-finding skills as you read them. Follow the steps given in "Here's How to Do It."

## Activity 23-1:  Recognizing Reports

Read each of the following reports carefully. Using the guidelines given in "Here"s How to Do It," find all the facts included in each report. Write your answers on a separate sheet of paper.

**a.** In the hills of east-central Kentucky stands a small, private school named Berea College. It was opened after the Civil War for the main purpose of educating freed slaves living in Appalachia. It always has been as it is today, run largely by low-income students who are on work-study programs. The best-known feature of the college is the Boone Tavern, which has a memorable restaurant. The waiters and waitresses are students dressed in colonial outfits, serving delicious, old-fashioned food such as "spoon bread." Boone Tavern also has a gift shop with many items handcrafted by students. Berea continues to exemplify the principle of students' willingness and ability to contribute to the cost of their college education.

**b.** Just outside Columbus, in west-central Georgia, is Fort Benning. It is the site of the Infantry School for beginning Army officers, who learn the techniques of leadership in combat there. It also houses an Airborne Training Center, where soldiers learn to become paratroopers. The Advanced Officers' Training Program, located on the main post, provides captains, majors, and lieutentant colonels with an update of military strategy. Farther from the main post is the Officers' Candidate School.

c.    Following the Civil War, two large high schools, named Male High School and Manual High School, were opened in Louisville, Kentucky. As its name shows, Male High admitted only males for a long period, but in the 1950s, girls were allowed to enroll. In 1884, Male and Manual played their first football game, and, in 1984, they played their 100th game, in the longest continuous high school football rivalry in the U.S. In that historic game, Male High dominated, 42-7.

d.    Early in the 1800s, two English poets, William Wordsworth and Samuel Taylor Coleridge, wrote an essay entitled "Lyrical Ballads," which described the ways in which they thought poetry should be written. Soon after that, these two authors were writing poems that demonstrated their ideas. These were called Romantic poems. After Wordsworth and Coleridge, three other famous Romantics imitated their ideas: Lord Byron, Percy Bysshe Shelley, and John Keats.

e.    On May 25, 1979, a thirty-year-old man named John Spenkelink was put to death in the electric chair in Raiford Prison of Starke, Florida. This marked the first execution of a person against his will in this country since 1964. In 1977, a convict named Gary Gilmore was voluntarily executed by a firing squad in Utah.

# Recognizing Inferences

Another type of statement is an *inference*. It is an educated guess about something based on facts. An inference is not a wild guess or an opinion, because a wild guess disregards facts, and an opinion can be based on whim, prejudice, or emotion. An inference is considered carefully. When you make an inference, you examine a set of facts and then decide that, *taken as a whole,* they mean something.

As you know, a fact can be verified. An inference cannot be verified in the same way. But a good inference does pull together the facts and draw a conclusion from them, based on the data provided.

Although inferences are often stated orally, drawing inferences is a vital part of critical reading. As a reader, you use your own reasoning power to pull the data together and draw a conclusion.

The following activities will help you get started in recognizing inferences. Some of the passages contain a statement of inference. Others do not. Your job will be to *find* a statement of inference. If one does not exist, you will write your own.

## Here's How to Do It

Follow these steps to help you find the statements of inference in the passages you read *or* to draw your own inferences.

1.  *Read* each sentence in the passage carefully.

2.  *Look* up words that are unfamiliar in a dictionary.

3.  List each fact you find on a separate sheet of paper.

4.  Relate the facts to each other. This means you must look at all the facts together and see if there is a connection.

5.  Write down any statement of inference you find. If no inference is stated, draw your own and write it down.

6.  *Check* the facts in the statement of inference. Can they be verified?

7.  *Relate* the statement of inference to the facts in the passage.

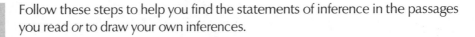

## Sample Activity:  Recognizing Inferences

Read the passage on page 240 carefully. Find the statement of inference or draw your own. Use the list of steps provided in "Here's How to Do It." Write your answer on a separate sheet of paper.

The American Physical Society called a meeting to review the new research in superconductors. It was held in the New York Hilton on March 19, 1987. Despite short notice, physicists flew in from all over the world. Within three minutes of the doors' opening, all 1,200 conference room seats were filled. Nearly 1,000 more scientists crowded into the aisles. Hundreds more followed the reports on TV monitors in the halls. Shouts and cheers rang out as reports were given. Most participants stayed until 6:00 A.M. This meeting created extraordinary excitement among scientists.

**Answer:** This meeting created extraordinary excitement among scientists.

## How Did You Do?

Did you find the inference? In this Sample Activity, the statement of inference is the last sentence of the passage. The statement expresses a conclusion using the facts given in the passage.

# Activity

The following will challenge your reasoning power. Read each sentence carefully and pull out the facts in each one. Then, decide whether a passage contains a statement of inference. If the inference is not stated, draw one from the facts given. Don't forget to follow the guidelines listed in "Here's How to Do It."

## Activity 23-2: Recognizing Inferences

Read each of the following passages carefully. Find the statement of inference or draw one of your own for each selection. Use a separate sheet of paper for your answers.

a.   Barbara easily won the 100 yard-dash early in this meet. Then, with only 30 minutes rest, she dominated the field in the 220. She has had one forty-five-minute break since then, and she looks fresh and enthusiastic. She's a good bet to win the 440, which comes up shortly.

b.   Coach Hawkins has two undefeated seasons in a row at school so he has had three excellent job offers from larger and wealthier schools. However, he has just built a large home close to the school and his wife, who grew up in this town, has told friends that she wants to stay here.

**c.**    The pulling down of the Berlin Wall in 1989 set in motion the collapse of Communist governments in most countries in Central Europe, as well as Russia. Today, such formerly staunch Communist states as Czechoslovakia, Romania, Bulgaria, and Albania are converting from Communist dictatorships to democratic forms of government with free-enterprise economic systems. This change seems to be worldwide in scope, raising the possibility that Castro's Cuba, only ninety miles from our shores, will someday adopt a democratic form of government.

**d.**    Many of the best teams in the National Football League are in cities of the Northeast and northern Midwest. The games scheduled in those cities during November, December, and January are often played in snow and biting cold. To create more comfortable conditions for both players and fans, Minneapolis and Detroit, homes to the Vikings and Lions, respectively, have built domed stadia, complete with climate-control equipment. Other cities with similar climates, like Chicago (the Bears) and Buffalo (the Bills), will probably construct similar facilities before the end of the twentieth century.

e.   When Franklin D. Roosevelt died in 1945, Vice President Harry S Truman became president. In 1963, Vice President Lyndon B. Johnson became president, hours after the assassination of John F. Kennedy. When President Richard M. Nixon resigned in 1974, Vice President Gerald R. Ford took the job. Presidents tend to be extremely careful in choosing the best qualified individual to serve as their running mate.

# Recognizing Judgments

Like inferences, *judgments* are statements based on facts. Unlike inferences, however, *judgments* express a feeling or bias about the facts. Judgments are personal and subjective; they express the writer's personal ideas about the value of a subject. Not all people will agree on a judgment.

Judgments are difficult to verify. Some judgments seem more reasonable than others, but all can be disputed by another intelligent reader with the same facts.

Writers express judgments directly and indirectly. When a judgment is directly stated, you may see verbs such as *like* and *dislike,* and adjectives such as *better* or *worse, worthwhile* or *worthless, reasonable* or *unreasonable,* and *valid* or *phony.* But some judgment statements omit such words and evaluate in a more indirect way. These statements must be studied carefully.

Sometimes the differences between inferences and judgments are very small. Don't worry about that. What's important is that you understand that both are derived from a report or a set of facts. In both cases, the writer pulls the facts together and makes a statement. Remember that an inference is a conclusion based closely on the facts, while a judgment contains some valuing, some personal acceptance or rejection of the facts.

Now let's work with some statements that express judgments.

# Here's How to Do It

Follow the guidelines below to help you find statements of judgment in the passages you read.

1.  *Read* each sentence carefully.

2.  *Look* up unfamiliar words in a dictionary.

3.  *List* each fact you find on a separate sheet of paper.

4.  *Relate* the facts to each other. That is, review and consider all the facts together. How might people feel about them?

5.  *List* words or phrases that express or seem to express judgment.

6.  *Write* down any statement of judgment you find. Or, determine what judgment the author wants you to make and write it down.

7.  *Look* at the statement you wrote down and *decide* whether your judgment of the facts is the same as the one presented in the passage.

## Sample Activity:  Recognizing Judgments

The following passage contains a statement of judgment. Read the whole passage carefully. Find the statement of judgment and write it on a separate sheet of paper. Use the list of steps provided in "Here's How to Do It."

The two giant pandas Yong Yong and Ling Ling were flown from Beijing, China, to New York. Their three-month visit to Bronx Zoo had taken seven years to arrange. Zookeepers planted bamboo trees for them to eat and tried to prepare for expected crowds of 2,000 people per hour. The preparation is worthwhile because the risk to the animals is too great. There are only 1,000 giant pandas left in the world right now.

**Answer:** The preparation is worthwhile because the risk to the animals is too great.

# How Did You Do?

Did you find the statement of judgment? It is the fourth sentence in the passage. In this statement, the key word *worthwhile* indicates that the judgment is stated directly.

# Activity

Some of the following passages contain statements of judgment; some do not. As you work through the following passages, pay special attention to words which seem to indicate a personal, subjective feeling. These key words often will lead you to the author's judgment. You may wish to write down the key words as you see them. Read the passages carefully, keeping in mind the steps outlined in "Here's How to Do It."

## Activity 23-3:  Recognizing Judgments

Read the following passages carefully. For each selection, find the statement of judgment, if there is one. If there is no statement of judgment, decide what judgment the author wants you to make. Use a separate sheet of paper for your answers.

a.   Studies done during the past twenty years have shown that American children and teenagers spend a great deal of time each day watching television, sometimes eight to ten hours a day. Several of these studies also indicate that these same groups either don't like to read or are bored by reading. These feelings about reading include newspapers and magazines, not just school materials. If our civic leaders don't begin to work with parents and teachers to change this situation, the U.S.A. will become illiterate, like third-world countries, before the twenty-first century begins.

b.  Many Americans consider the British dialect of the English language better than the American dialect. To some, clothes made by British tailors have more class than U.S. clothes, and they enjoy flashing their British clothing labels. Some Americans also think it's a great accomplishment to win a Rhodes scholarship, which allows a student to attend Oxford University in England. In these and other matters of style and culture, Americans feel inferior to Britons, and well they should.

c.  The U.S. Marines have enjoyed a long, proud history, based upon their engagement in all American wars fought since 1798 and their participation and achievements in some major historical battles. They boast striking uniforms and a stirring fighting song, which help make Marine tradition seem more glamorous than those of the Army, Navy, or Air Force. The Marines invest a lot of money in publicity. It is no wonder that so many young men want to join the Marines after high school or college graduation.

**d.**   Throughout this century, the United States has maintained a large military. And, for most of this period, those who served in the armed services were mostly males. Women were seldom found as service personnel except for the nursing corps of each branch (Army, Navy, etc.). Since World War II, small groups of women have served mostly in clerical jobs. In the past twenty-five years, however, increasing numbers of women have joined all branches. They have also been accepted into the major service academies: West Point, Annapolis, and the Air Force Academy. Still, progress for women in our military has been slow. Furthermore, there have been numerous reports in recent years of female members of the various branches being abused and harassed by their male counterparts. Until we have more female government leaders, women will continue to have a hard time gaining the recognition and rewards they deserve in the U.S. armed forces.

**e.**   Major TV networks show comedies about home life each night during prime time. These shows present whites, blacks, Hispanics, and other ethnic groups as stereotypes. Some shows feature families in comic situations and make humorous, taunting remarks about parent-child relations. The shows often portray single men and women in various romantic situations. The tone of these shows is insulting and mindless, which reflects the nonintellectual tastes of most viewers.

# Part 24
# Use of the Triad
## *Step Six*

### About This Part...

In Part 23, you practiced recognizing reports, inferences, and judgments in separate passages. The next step is to combine these types of statements.

A triad is a set of three statements. Each set covers a theme or topic. For example:

1. This painting, which is called "A Bowl of Fruit," is black, white, and pink.

2. The artist doesn't know how to paint.

3. The painting is called "abstract."

In a triad, the first sentence always will be a "report," i.e., a collection of facts. Here, the facts are the name of the painting and its colors. The second and third sentence in a triad are based on facts pulled from the first sentence. The second sentence will *sometimes* be an inference. The third will sometimes be a judgment. Here, the second sentence is a judgment and the third sentence is an inference.

Your job will be to identify which statement (second or third) makes an inference and which statement makes a judgment.

## Here's How to Do It

In working on the triad activities follow these steps:

1. *Read* the first sentence. Study the sentence and look at each fact in that sentence.

2. *Read* the second sentence and study each detail in that sentence.

3. *Read* the third sentence and study each detail in that sentence.

4. *Relate* both the second and third statements to the first. Which one makes an educated guess (inference)? Which one expresses a feeling or a bias about the facts (judgment)?

## Sample Activity:   The Triad

Read the three sentences below. Identify which statement makes an inference and which makes a judgment. Relate the second and third statements to the first. Use a separate sheet of paper for your answer.

### The Triad

1. This man has gray, thinning hair, is five feet tall, and weighs 240 pounds.
2. This man would have real trouble making the mile relay on the Olympic track team.
3. This man would look rather silly in a brief, leopard skin swimsuit.

**Answer:** The second sentence makes an inference. The third sentence makes a judgment.

# How Did You Do?

Is your analysis of the triad similar to the following? There are three facts in the first sentence. They are 1) the color and condition of the man's hair, 2) his height, and 3) his weight. Try to picture this man in your mind.

The second sentence begins with the words *This man.* These words signal you to recall the facts in the first sentence. No one knows how fast he can run. The facts about him, however, lead you to make an *educated guess* that he is not very fast. Also note the conditional word *would* indicates this statement is not a fact. It is an inference.

Like the second statement, the third sentence uses the words *This man* to signal you to recall the facts. This statement also contains a key phrase. The phrase *would look rather silly* expresses the writer's personal and arbitrary point of view. Finally, the words *to me* are presumed to exist after the phrase *would look rather silly.* These words always imply a judgment. Look for them in such statements.

# Activities

Because recognizing a statement of inference or judgment sometimes can be difficult, read the sentences in the triads carefully. Remember that the first sentence always will be a collection of facts. In the next two sentences, look for key words or phrases which express an inference or a judgment. Following the steps listed in "Here's How to Do It" will make your task easier.

## Activity 24-1:  The Church

First, read the sentences in the following triad. Then, using the guidelines in "Here's How to Do It," identify which statement makes an inference and which makes a judgment. Finally, relate the second and third statements to the first. Use a separate sheet of paper.

1.  This church has a tall, conical-shaped roof, two large abstract paintings for front windows, and a tall, bare cross placed to one side.

2.  This church was designed by a modern architect.

3.  People can't really feel close to God while worshiping in that church.

## Activity 24-2:  *The Comic Strip*

Read the sentences in the following triad. Follow the guidelines in "Here's How to Do It." On a separate sheet of paper, identify which statement makes an inference and which makes a judgment. Relate the second and third statements to the first.

1. That comic strip places churches, schools, social clubs, political parties, and civic organizations in several humorous situations.

2. Reading that comic strip will lead young people to have less respect for their communities.

3. The designer of that comic strip can be identified by the term *satirist*.

## Activity 24-3:  *The Strict Teacher*

Follow the guidelines in "Here's How to Do It." After reading the triad below, identify which statement makes an inference and which makes a judgment. Relate the second and third statements to the first. Use a separate sheet of paper for your answer.

1. This teacher enforces strict rules of conduct, assigns lots of homework, and gives a limited number of high grades.

2. This teacher believes firmly that academic success will improve the quality of students' adult lives.

3. This teacher has no patience with students who aren't hard workers and high achievers.

## Activity 24-4: *Hemingway's Themes and Characters*

First, read the triad below. Then, using the steps in "Here's How to Do It," identify which statement makes an inference and which makes a judgment. Finally, relate the second and third statements to the first. Use a separate sheet of paper for your answer.

1. Most of Ernest Hemingway's stories deal with bull fighters, combat personnel, big-game hunters, and male adventurers.

2. Hemingway was deeply concerned with the macho aspects of men's lives.

3. It would be hard for female readers to get very interested in Hemingway's stories.

# Activity 24-5:  Greek Myths

Read the following sentences about Greek myths. Follow the guidelines in "Here's How to Do It." On a separate sheet of paper, identify which statement makes an inference and which makes a judgment. Relate the second and third statements to the first.

1. Many myths were of Greek origin and were later adopted by the Romans.

2. The Romans weren't talented enough to come up with their own ideas about gods and goddesses.

3. The Greeks probably influenced the Roman notion of deities.

# Activity 24-6: The Term Paper

Read the sentences in the following triad. Follow the guidelines in "Here's How to Do It." On a separate sheet of paper, identify which statement makes an inference and which makes a judgment. Relate the second and third statements to the first.

1. The term paper submitted by this student has been written in pencil on notebook paper and displays several erasures, crossed-out words, and sentences without capital letters or periods.

2. This term paper was written at the very last minute, just before it was due.

3. The student who wrote this term paper doesn't care at all about success in school.

## *Activity 24-7: The House*

Carefully read the following statements about a house. Using the guidelines in "Here's How to Do It," identify which statement makes an inference and which makes a judgment. Relate the second and third statements to the first. Use a separate sheet of paper for your responses.

1. The house on the weedy lot had peeled paint, loose shutters, and three cracked windowpanes.

2. The owner of that house was a lazy, shiftless individual.

3. The house hasn't been occupied for a long while.

# Activity 24-8:  Socrates

Follow the guidelines in "Here's How to Do It." After reading the triad below, identify which statement makes an inference and which makes a judgment. Relate the second and third statements to the first. Use a separate sheet of paper for your answers.

1. One of the classical philosophers was an Athenian named Socrates who wrote no books and kept no schools.

2. Socrates lived before the days of printing.

3. Other philosophers who were able to write printed books are of more value to us than Socrates.

# Activity 24-9:  The Painting

First, read the triad below. Then, using the guidelines in "Here's How to Do It," identify which statement makes an inference and which makes a judgment. Finally, relate the second and third statements to the first. Use a separate sheet of paper for your answer.

1. The painting had many colors, several unusual features, and no familiar elements such as trees, people, or houses.

2. The painting was done by a modern artist.

3. People who think they are sophisticated would be the ones to enjoy that painting.

# Activity 24-10:  The Car

Read the following sentences about a car. Follow the guidelines in "Here's How to Do It." On a separate sheet of paper, identify which statement makes an inference and which makes a judgment. Relate the second and third statements to the first.

1. The car has long, sleek lines, extra-large tires, dual carburetors, and a very large, loud muffler system.

2. Due to the need to conserve gasoline these days, cars like that should not be allowed to operate on the highways.

3. That car was designed for racetrack driving.

## Part 25

# Using Your Experiences

*Step Seven*

## About This Part...

In developing reading skills the most important ingredient is your personal experience. From the time you were born, you've been gathering and storing experience. It becomes part of your background. The more experiences you store, the better you understand what you read.

Throughout this Section, you've been learning about the importance your experiences play in understanding what you read. The next step is to learn to *use* your experience to increase your reading skills. In this Part, you'll work on an activity called the Herber Exercise. It will help you to relate your experience to the task of understanding what you read in a systematic way. It's better to do this exercise in groups. But you can do it on your own as well. Do one step at a time. For this Part, there is no "Here's How to Do It." You'll use the steps outlined in the Sample Activity.

# Sample Activity:  Nation and Responsibilities

## Step One

1.  *Take* a blank piece of paper and draw a line down the middle.

2.  *Write* the word *Nation* at the upper left on the paper.

3.  *Think* about the word. Then, list any word that pops into your head such as, *country, flag, U.S., Canada, government.*

4.  *Give* yourself three minutes to write down as many words as you can.

5.  *Stop* when the three minutes are up. Be sure all the words are on the left side of the paper.

6.  *Count* the words.

## Step Two

1.  *Write* the word *Responsibilities* at the upper right on the paper.

2.  *Think* about this word. List any word you can think of which relates to it, such as *family, job, earning, taxes.*

3.  *Give* yourself exactly three minutes to write down as many words as you can. Use the whole time. Keep thinking.

4.  *Count* the words.

## Step Three

1.  *Choose* a word from the column under *Nation* and match it up with one under *Responsibilities.*

2.  *Choose* words that match up in *meaning,* such as *government* (from under *Nation*) with *taxes* (from under *Responsibilities*).

3.  *Match* five words under *Nation* with five words under *Responsibilities.*
    Write your match ups on a separate sheet of paper.

4.  *Take* your time doing these match ups. There is no time limit.

5.  *Study* your match ups. You only need five. Be sure they are your best.

### Step Four

1.  *Read* the six "predictive statements" below. Think about each of them.

2.  *Use* a separate sheet of paper to answer the predictive statements. Indicate
    whether you agree, disagree, or are undecided. It's all right to discuss them
    with others, but the answers should reflect your own opinion.

3.  *Think* hard before making each decision.

4.  *Keep* your answers. You will need them later.

---

## Predictive Statements

After each predictive statement, indicate whether you *agree, disagree,* or are
*undecided* about it.

1.  When democratic societies are established, they should not support the
    freedom of other societies.

2.  Wealthy nations often feel a moral responsibility to help poorer ones.

3.  Neighboring countries usually ignore the invasion of powerful outsiders.

4.  It makes good sense for two powerful opponents to try to negotiate
    before attacking each other.

5.  Tyranny, poverty, disease, and war can be considered enemies
    of people.

6.  Promises made in public addresses are almost always ones which can be
    met quickly and easily.

---

### Step Five

*Read* the selection that follows. It is the well-known inaugural address of the late
president, John F. Kennedy. The address was delivered in January 1961. As you read
it, think of the things you did in the first four steps—the word lists, the match ups,
and the choices in the predictive statements.

## John F. Kennedy's Inaugural Address

We observe today not a victory of party but a celebration of freedom—symbolizing an end as well as a beginning—signifying renewal as well as change. For I have sworn before you and Almighty God the same solemn oath our forebears prescribed nearly a century and three-quarters ago.

The world is very different now. For man holds in his mortal hands the power to abolish all forms of human poverty and all forms of human life. And yet the same revolutionary beliefs for which our forebears fought are still at issue around the globe—the belief that the rights of man come not from the generosity of the state but from the hand of God.

We dare not forget today that we are the heirs of that first revolution. Let the word go forth from this time and place, to friend and foe alike, that the torch has been passed to a new generation of Americans—born in this century—tempered by war, disciplined by a hard and bitter peace, proud of our ancient heritage—and unwilling to witness or permit the slow undoing of those human rights to which this nation has always been committed, and to which we are committed today at home and around the world.

Let every nation know, whether it wishes us well or ill, that we shall pay any price, bear any burden, meet any hardship, support any friend, oppose any foe to assure the survival and the success of liberty.

This much we pledge—and more.

To those old allies whose cultural and spiritual origins we share, we pledge the loyalty of faithful friends. United, there is little we cannot do in a host of new cooperative ventures. Divided, there is little we can do—for we dare not meet a powerful challenge at odds and split asunder.

To those new states whom we welcome to the ranks of the free, we pledge our word that one form of colonial control shall not have passed away merely to be replaced by a far more iron tyranny. We shall not always expect to find them supporting our view. But we shall always hope to find them strongly supporting their own freedom—and to remember that, in the past, those who foolishly sought power by riding the back of the tiger ended up inside.

To those people in the huts and villages across the globe struggling to break the bonds of mass misery, we pledge our best efforts to help them help themselves, for whatever period is required—not because the Communists may be doing it, not because we seek their votes, but because it is right. If a free society cannot help the many who are poor, it cannot save the few who are rich.

To our sister republics south of our border, we offer a special pledge—to convert our good words into good deeds—in a new alliance for progress—to assist free men and free governments in casting off the chains of poverty. But this peaceful revolution of hope cannot become the prey of hostile powers. Let all our neighbors know that we shall join with them to oppose aggression or subversion anywhere in the Americas. And let every other power know that this hemisphere intends to remain the master of its own house.

To that world assembly of sovereign states, the United Nations, our last best hope in an age where the instruments of war have far outpaced the instruments of peace, we renew our pledge of support—to prevent it from becoming merely a forum for invective—to strengthen its shield of the new and the weak—and to enlarge the area in which its writ may run.

Finally, to those nations who would make themselves our adversary, we offer not a pledge but a request: that both sides begin anew the quest for peace, before the dark powers of destruction unleashed by science engulf all humanity in planned or accidental self-destruction.

We dare not tempt them with weakness. For only when our arms are sufficient beyond doubt can we be certain beyond doubt that they will never be employed.

But neither can two great and powerful groups of nations take comfort from our present course—both sides overburdened by the cost of modern weapons, both rightly alarmed by the steady spread of the deadly atom, yet both racing to alter that uncertain balance of terror that stays the hand of mankind's final war.

So let us begin anew—remembering on both sides that civility is not a sign of weakness, and sincerity is always subject to proof. Let us never negotiate out of fear. But let us never fear to negotiate.

Let both sides explore what problems unite us instead of belaboring those problems which divide us.

Let both sides, for the first time, formulate serious and precise proposals for the inspection and control of arms—and bring the absolute power to destroy other nations under the absolute control of all nations.

Let both sides seek to invoke the wonders of science instead of its terrors. Together let us explore the stars, conquer the deserts, eradicate disease, tap the ocean depths and encourage the arts and commerce.

Let both sides unite to heed in all corners of the earth the command of Isaiah—to "undo the heavy burdens...and let the oppressed go free."

And if a beachhead of cooperation may push back the jungles of suspicion, let both sides join in creating a new endeavor—not a new balance of power, but a new world of law, where the strong are just and the weak secure and the peace preserved.

All this will not be finished in the first 100 days. Nor will it be finished in the first 1,000 days, nor in the life of this Administration, nor even perhaps in our lifetime on this planet. But let us begin.

In your hands, my fellow citizens, more than mine, will rest the final success or failure of our course. Since this country was founded, each generation of Americans has been summoned to give testimony to its national loyalty. The graves of young Americans who answered the call to service are found around the globe.

Now the trumpet summons us again—not as a call to bear arms, though arms we need—not as a call to battle, though embattled we are—but a call to bear the burden of a long twilight struggle, year in and year out, "rejoicing in hope, patient in tribulation"—a struggle against the common enemies of man: tyranny, poverty, disease and war itself.

Can we forge against these enemies a grand and global alliance, north and south, east and west, that can assure a more fruitful life for all mankind? Will you join in that historic effort?

In the long history of the world, only a few generations have been granted the role of defending freedom in its hour of maximum danger. I do not shrink from this responsibility—I welcome it. I do not believe that any of us would exchange places with any other people or any other generation. The energy, the faith, the devotion which we bring to this endeavor will light our country and all who serve it—and the glow from that fire can truly light the world.

And so, my fellow Americans: ask not what your country can do for you—ask what you can do for your country.

My fellow citizens of the world: ask not what America will do for you, but what together we can do for the freedom of man.

Finally, whether you are citizens of America or citizens of the world, ask of us the same high standards of strength and sacrifice which we ask of you. With a good conscience our only sure reward, with history the final judge of our deeds, let us go forth to lead the land we love, asking His blessing and His help, but knowing that here on earth God's work must truly be our own.

**Answer:** Responses will depend on students' background experiences.

# *How Did You Do?*

Did you notice, after reading the speech, that there were some things you already knew about the topic? Here's what the exercise accomplished.

1.  In Steps One and Two, you gathered information. You thought about what you knew about *Nation* and *Responsibilities*. You pulled those things out of your head (that is, your experiences), and you recorded them.

2.  In Step Three, you analyzed your lists. From a long list of words, you selected a few; they were the ones best suited to be matched. When you matched them, you were perceiving relationships. You were putting one concept with another concept to form the basis of a *main idea*. That is, you thought about a nation *in relation to* responsibilities (which is basically what the Kennedy address is about).

3.  In Step Four, you evaluated some aspects of a nation and its responsibilities. Those six statements all had to do with that main idea. *They were also topics in the Kennedy speech.* Thus, they predicted for you what to think about and judge in the speech before you read it.

4.  Having gathered, analyzed, related, and evaluated your experiences of a topic, you were then asked to read about it in Step Five. The whole process helped you to check what you already knew about the topic.

# Activity

In the activity that follows, you will have a chance to apply the steps you followed in the Sample Activity.

## Activity 25-1:  *Loved Ones and Challenges*

Do the activity below on a separate sheet of paper. Follow the step-by-step method you used in the Sample Activity.

### Step One

The first words are *Loved Ones.* Write them at the top left on your sheet. In this column, begin writing down as many words as you can think of that relate to these words. Give yourself three full minutes. Count the words.

### Step Two

The second word is *Challenges.* Write this word at the upper right on the paper. Write any word you think of which relates to it in any way. Again, allow yourself exactly three minutes to list the words. Then, count the words.

### Step Three

Now match up five words from the *Loved Ones* column with five words from the *Challenges* column. Work at your own speed. Write them down on a separate sheet of paper.

### Step Four

Read the predictive statements on the next page and indicate whether you agree, disagree, or are undecided. Think carefully about each one before you answer.

## Predictive Statements

1. Wrestling can be a show of affection between two people.

2. Young people grow up fast.

3. Youngsters seldom keep trying even when they don't succeed right away.

4. Few mothers worry when roughhousing goes on at home.

5. Adults often get embarrassed when they lose a contest to their children.

6. It is puzzling to some youngsters when they find out that their father is losing his power.

### Step Five

Now, read the essay that follows. As you do so, think about the information you gathered, analyzed, related, and evaluated in Steps One through Four.

## The Cub

by Lois Dykeman Kleihauer

One of his first memories was of his father bending down from his great height to sweep him into the air. Up he went, gasping and laughing with delight. He could look down on his mother's upturned face as she watched, laughing with them, and at the thick shock of his father's brown hair and at his white teeth.

Then he would come down, shrieking happily, but he was never afraid, not with his father's hands holding him. No one in the world was as strong, or as wise, as his father.

He remembered a time when his father moved the piano across the room for his mother. He watched while she guided it into its new position, and he saw the difference in their hands as they rested, side by side, upon the gleaming walnut. His mother's hands were white and slim and delicate; his father's, large and square and strong.

As he grew, he learned to play bear. When it was time for his father to come home at night, he would lurk behind the kitchen door. When he heard the closing of the garage doors, he would hold his breath and squeeze himself into the crack behind the door. Then he would be quiet.

It was always the same. His father would open the door and stand there, the backs of his long legs beguilingly close. "Where's the boy?"

He would glance at the conspiratorial smile on his mother's face, and then he would leap and grab his father about the knees, and his father would look down and shout, "Hey, what's this? A bear—a young cub!"

Then, no matter how tightly he tried to cling, he was lifted up and perched upon his father's shoulder, and they would march past his mother, and together they would duck their heads beneath the doors.

And then he went to school. And on the playground he learned how to wrestle and shout, how to hold back tears, how to get a half nelson on the boy who tried to take his football away from him. He came home at night and practiced his new wisdom on his father. Straining and puffing, he tried to pull his father off the lounge chair while his father kept on reading the paper, only glancing up now and then to ask in mild wonderment, "What are you trying to do, boy?"

He would stand and look at his father. "Gee whiz, Dad!" And then he would realize that his father was teasing him, and he would crawl up on his father's lap and pummel him in affectionate frustration.

And still he grew—taller, slimmer, stronger. He was like a young buck, with tiny new horns. He wanted to lock them with any other young buck's, to test them in combat. He measured his biceps with his mother's tape measure. Exultantly, he thrust his arm in front of his father. "Feel that! How's that for muscle?"

His father put his great thumb into the flexed muscle and pressed, and the boy pulled back, protesting, laughing. "Ouch!"

Sometimes they wrestled on the floor together, and his mother moved the chairs back. "Be careful, Charles—don't hurt him."

After a while his father would push him aside and sit in his chair, his long legs thrust out before him, and the boy would scramble to his feet, half resentful, half mirthful over the ease with which his father mastered him.

"Doggone it, Dad, someday—" he would say.

He went out for football and track in high school. He surprised even himself now, there was so much more of him. And he could look down on his mother. "Little one," he called her, or "Small fry."

Sometimes he took her wrists and backed her into a chair, while he laughed and she scolded. "I'll—I'll take you across my knee."

"Who will?" he demanded.

"Well—your father still can," she said.

His father—well, that was different.

They still wrestled occasionally, but it distressed his mother. She hovered about them, worrying, unable to comprehend the need for their struggling. It always ended the same way, with the boy upon his back, prostrate, and his father grinning down at him. "Give?"

"Give." And he got up, shaking his head.

"I wish you wouldn't," his mother would say, fretting. "There's no point in it. You'll hurt yourselves; don't do it any more."

So for nearly a year they had not wrestled, but he thought about it one night at dinner. He looked at his father closely. It was queer, but his father didn't look nearly as tall or broad-shouldered as he used to. He could even look his father straight in the eyes.

"How much do you weigh, Dad?" he asked.

His father threw him a mild glance. "About the same; about a hundred and ninety. Why?"

The boy grinned. "Just wondering."

But after a while he went over to his father where he sat reading the paper and took it out of his hands. His father glanced up, his eyes at first questioning and then narrowing to meet the challenge in his son's. "So," he said softly.

"Come on, Dad."

His father took off his coat and began to unbutton his shirt. "You asked for it," he said.

His mother came in from the kitchen, alarmed. "Oh, Charles! Bill! Don't—you'll hurt yourselves!" But they paid no attention to her. They were standing now, their shirts off. They watched each other, intent and purposeful. The boy's teeth gleamed again. They circled for a moment, and then their hands closed upon each other's arms.

They strained against each other, and then the boy went down, taking his father with him. They moved and writhed and turned, in silence seeking an advantage, in silence pressing it to its conclusion. There was the sound of the thumps of their bodies upon the rug and of the quick, hard intake of breath. The boy showed his teeth occasionally in a grimace of pain. His mother stood at one side, both hands pressed against her ears. Occasionally her lips moved, but she did not make a sound.

After a while the boy pinned his father on his back. "Give!" he demanded.

His father said, "Heck, no!" And with a great effort he pushed the boy off, and the struggle began again.

But at the end his father lay prostrate, and a look of bewilderment came into his eyes. He struggled desperately against his son's merciless, restraining hands. Finally he lay quiet, only his chest heaving, his breath coming loudly.

The boy said, "Give!"

The man frowned, shaking his head.

Still the boy knelt on him, pinning him down.

"Give!" he said, and tightened his grip. "Give!"

All at once his father began to laugh, silently, his shoulders shaking.

The boy felt his mother's fingers tugging fiercely at his shoulder. "Let him up," she said. "Let him up!"

The boy looked down at his father. "Give up?"

His father stopped laughing. But his eyes were still wet. "Okay," he said. "I give."

The boy stood up and reached a hand to his father to help him up, but his mother was before him, putting an arm about his father's shoulders, helping him to rise. They stood together and looked at him, his father grinning gamely, his mother with muffled pain in her eyes.

The boy started to laugh. "I guess I—" He stopped. "Gosh, Dad, I didn't hurt you, did I?"

"Heck, no, I'm all right. Next time…"

"Yeah, maybe next time…"

And his mother did not contradict what they said, for she knew as well as they that there would never be a next time.

For a moment the three of them stood looking at one another, and then, suddenly, blindly, the boy turned. He ran through the door under which he had ducked so many times when he had ridden on his father's shoulders. He went out the kitchen door, behind which he had hidden, waiting to leap out and pounce upon his father's legs.

It was dark outside. He stood on the steps, feeling the air cool against his sweaty body. He stood with lifted head, looking at the stars, and then he could not see them because of the tears that burned his eyes and ran down his cheeks.

# Part 26
# **Analyzing Cartoons**
## *Step Eight*

## **About This Part...**

In this Part you'll take the next step in building your skill in reading for implied main ideas. You will work with cartoons. All cartoons tell a story through pictures. Many include captions, which are short statements that comment on the picture.

The cartoon and its caption are about something. What they mean to you depends on your background. You have to know something in advance about the topic. Since cartoons do not state their meaning directly, you have to infer the meaning using facts that you know to be true from your background experience.

To understand what a cartoon has to say, you need to relate it to your own experiences. In this Part, a short paragraph follows each cartoon. It gives you a brief background about the subject. You will recognize some of this information from your own experience. Then, from a list of possible choices, you are to select the statement that best expresses the implied main idea.

## Here's How to Do It

Carefully read the six steps listed below. They can help you find the implied main ideas in cartoons.

1.  List on a separate sheet of paper the physical details you see in the cartoon.

2.  *Describe* the placement of the details in the cartoon.

3.  *Read* the caption and relate it to the cartoon.

4.  *Read* "The Background." It tells you what you should know about the subject. Then, *consider* and *discuss* it with other students and your teacher.

5.  *Choose* the statement from "The Possible Choices" list which best expresses the implied main idea.

6.  *Think* about your answer. Then, discuss it with others.

## Sample Activity:  Talking Trees

Carefully study the cartoon on page 267. Following the steps outlined in "Here's How to Do It," choose the statement that best expresses the implied main idea. Write your response on a separate sheet of paper.

I NEVER THOUGHT THEY WERE WORTH PROVIDING OXYGEN FOR, ANYHOW.

### The Background

To understand this cartoon, you need to know that trees, like other plants, convert water, carbon dioxide, and minerals into the oxygen that we breathe. You also need to understand that the people shown are building houses and a shopping center.

### The Possible Choices

**a.** Talking trees can say some rather funny things.

**b.** People enjoy watching work being done on construction sites.

**c.** The human desire to increase personal comfort and profits can destroy the environment.

**d.** Progress must continue even if it means a few trees must be destroyed.

**Answer:** Statement c best expresses the implied main idea.

## How Did You Do?

Did you follow each of the six steps listed in "Here's How to Do It"? Compare your work to the following. You should have written down similar facts.

1.  *List the physical details in the cartoon.*
    a.  Billboard that advertises a new shopping-living area
    b.  Bulldozer
    c.  Some uprooted trees
    d.  Two trees talking
    e.  People by the billboard

2.  *Describe the placement of details.*
    a.  The people are watching the work.
    b.  The bulldozer is knocking down the trees.
    c.  The trees (in the foreground) are talking to each other.

3.  *Relate the caption to the cartoon.*
    a.  The caption is in quotation marks, which signals that the trees are talking to each other.
    b.  The tree, which is speaking, refers to "they," who are the people.
    c.  Trees provide oxygen for people to breathe. (People need oxygen.)
    d.  People are destroying trees and other plant life in order to build Mar-Vue.

4.  *Read "The Background." Consider and, if possible, discuss what you already know about the subject.*

    The trees are talking to each other (seeing this takes close observation in Step One) just before they are knocked over by the bulldozer that is being used in building the development.

    People need oxygen. Trees provide oxygen, but people destroy trees.

5.  *Choose the statement that best expresses the implied main idea.*
    Sentence C

6.  *Discuss your answer.*
    a.  The first statement has nothing to do with the topic of destruction of the environment. It is very far from what is implied.
    b.  The second answer only reflects a detail in the cartoon. There are no inferences or judgments expressed in this statement.
    c.  The third statement reflects the destruction of the environment in building things for our convenience.
    d.  The fourth statement is contrary to the details, their relationship, and the caption. The kind of progress pictured in the cartoon is viewed negatively.

# Activities

The following cartoons contain points of view on important issues. Study each carefully. Below each cartoon is a short paragraph about its background. You may recognize some of them from your own experiences. Choose the statement you think best expresses the implied main idea. Carefully follow each of the steps provided in "Here's How to Do It."

# Activity 26-1:  Superman

Study the Superman cartoon carefully. Using the guidelines in "Here's How to Do It," choose the sentence that best expresses the implied main idea. Write your responses on a separate sheet of paper.

" HOW DO YOU <u>KNOW</u> HE'S SUPERMAN?"

## The Background

This cartoon requires background in two areas. First, you have to know about the comic strip "Superman." Mild-mannered Clark Kent becomes Superman by removing his everyday street clothing and revealing his Superman outfit. This wardrobe change always occurs in some out-of-the-way place, usually a telephone booth. Second, you must be aware of the concern people have regarding peculiar behavior, such as changing clothing in public.

## Possible Choices

**a.**  Superman is coming to the rescue.

**b.**  Decent people are shocked by unusual public behavior.

**c.**  What we already know from comic strips can help us deal humorously with strange behavior.

**d.**  Tougher measures are needed by the law to deal with those who undress in public.

# *Activity 26-2: Red Riding Hood*

Carefully study the cartoon below. Following the guidelines in "Here's How to Do It," select the statement which best expresses the implied main idea. Write your responses on a separate sheet of paper.

"LITTLE GIRL, TELL HIM I'M AN ENDANGERED SPECIES!"

## The Background

Again, you need two kinds of knowledge in order to see the humor in this cartoon. You need to know the tale of Little Red Riding Hood and the big bad wolf. You also need to know about the concern of today's people for conservation of the environment. The wolf is considered an endangered species—a fact that the wolf is begging the girl to support.

## Possible Choices

**a.** Some hunters shoot first and think afterward.

**b.** The morals in some fairy tales don't agree with facts of modern life.

**c.** Sportsmen are gradually destroying our environment.

**d.** Readers love stories that feature a rescue that occurs just at the critical moment.

# Activity 26-3:  Smokers' Graveyards

First, study the following cartoon. Then, choose the sentence that best expresses the implied main idea. Use the guidelines in "Here's How to Do It." Write your responses on a separate sheet of paper.

## The Background

The topic here is the current campaign to eliminate, or at least reduce, the smoking habits of people worldwide. A new slant on this problem arose when medical researchers discovered that people who are close to smokers can come down with cancer and other diseases, as well as the smokers themselves. Since there is no caption here, you must get it all from the picture.

## Possible Choices

a.  Some graveyards are now being reserved for certain kinds of people.

b.  Those who happen to be near smokers can be harmed by that smoke.

c.  There is a great deal of confusion among experts as to who truly is affected by people's smoking.

d.  All people who smoke or find themselves next to smokers will die before their time.

## *Activity 26-4:  Studying the Stars*

Study the following cartoon. Follow the guidelines given in "Here's How to Do It." Choose the sentence that best expresses the implied main idea. Write your response on a separate sheet of paper.

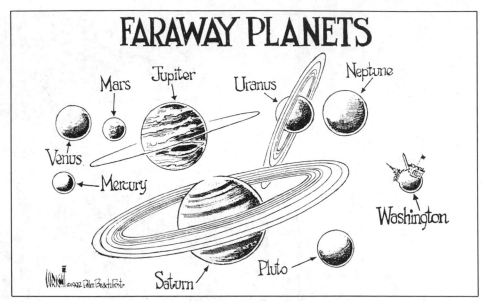

Reprinted by permission of Don Wright, *The Palm Beach Post.*

### The Background

There are two background factors present in this cartoon. One is the ongoing study of outer space. The National Aeronautics and Space Administration (NASA) has been analyzing the planets of the universe for years. The second is the attitude of many U.S. citizens that the lawmakers and political leaders who serve in the nation's capital are really out of touch with the rest of the country.

## Possible Choices

a. Knowledge of the planets in the universe has grown a great deal in recent years.

b. Our national security depends heavily on our knowledge of outer space.

c. Studies being done by the National Aeronautics and Space Administration are chiefly financed by the federal government.

d. The American people understand what's going on in Washington, D.C., about as well as they understand what's going on in outer space.

## *Activity 26-5:* *Classroom Hazards*

Study the cartoon below. Follow the guidelines in "Here's How to Do It." Find the statement that best states the implied main idea. Write your response on a separate sheet of paper.

Reprinted by permission of Don Wright, *The Palm Beach Post.*

### The Background

A major concern of many school administrators and teachers is the number of students who are carrying weapons into school buildings—and using them. Classroom teachers fear for their own safety, as well as that of their students.

### Possible Choices

**a.** Teachers today are not giving enough homework to most of their students and should do so.

**b.** Teachers are pretty much out of touch with the way today's students think and behave.

**c.** The issue of students carrying weapons into our schools has become a crisis of great magnitude.

**d.** Today's students are more likely to demand negotiation with teachers over homework rather than just accepting it.

# *Activity 26-6: "We are the world..."*

Study the political cartoon below. Follow the guidelines in "Here's How to Do It." Find the statement that best expresses the implied main idea. Write your response on a separate sheet of paper.

"WE ARE THE WORLD, WE ARE THE CHILDREN..."

Hy Rosen
Courtesy *Albany Time-Union*, Albany, N.Y.

## The Background

Massive famine in Africa, brought on by drought and worsened by civil war, grabbed and held the attention of the world in 1985. By midyear nearly half a million people had died of malnutrition. Images of starving children begging for food stirred the conscience of the world.

One response to this disaster was a sixteen-hour, nonstop rock concert organized in London and in Philadelphia by the Irish singer and songwriter Bob Geldof. The theme of the concert, which raised over $70 million in relief, was "We are the world, we are the children . . ."

## Possible Choices

**a.** Africa is a troubled part of the world.

**b.** Africa suffers from famine.

**c.** Africans like to sing.

**d.** Everyone has a duty to help victims of a disaster.

# Part 27
# **Reading Stereotyped Passages**
*Step Nine*

## About This Part...

We all accumulate experiences that make strong, distinct impressions on us. Thes impressions, at least some of them, develop into attitudes, which are deep-seated, long-lasting interests.

In this next step to becoming a better critical reader, you will be thinking about some of the attitudes people commonly develop. The passages you read will offer examples of attitudes based on familiar experiences. These are known as *stereotypes.*

Stereotypes aren't necessarily bad attitudes. They simply reflect the attitudes some people develop about common experiences they've had. For example, if every studious, hard-working, very intelligent student you come across in school wore glasses, you might develop the stereotype that *all* intelligent students wear glasses. The activities in this Part provide examples of attitudes that grow out of inferences drawn and judgments made during reading.

## Here's How to Do It

When you read a stereotyped passage, follow these steps:

1. *Read* the passage slowly and carefully.

2. *Try* to get the total picture conveyed by the passage. Close your eyes and try to gain a visual impression.

3. The last statement, you will notice, is incomplete. *Complete* it on your own; that is, make a complete sentence using your own idea. (There are no wrong answers!)

4. *Write* at least two more sentences to complete the impression you have gained from the passage.

5. You have written three sentences: the one you completed and two of your own. This should expand the one-paragraph passage. Now, if you wish, add more sentences to your paragraph.

Whatever sentences you have written are part of the original passage. Do not number them one, two, three. They relate to each other and are, in fact, part of the one-paragraph passage.

## Sample Activity: Stereotyped Passages

Read the following stereotyped passage. Complete the paragraph by writing at least three sentences of your own. Write your statements on a separate sheet of paper. Be ready to read your statements to the rest of the class. Remember, there are *no* wrong answers. You will find that other students' sentences will be different from yours. That's to be expected. Just compare them with yours.

A young woman is hitchhiking along a busy highway. She has long, uncombed hair. She wears a sweatshirt with a picture of Mickey Mouse. Her jeans are faded and torn. Her feet are bare. She carries a knapsack on her back. **This young woman is...**

**Answer:** Here are some answers that were received from students who have read and completed this same passage. 1. "This young woman is a bum. She is going wherever her next ride will take her. She has no real goals in life. She may get in trouble." 2. "This young woman is a college student trying to get home for the weekend. She has no money and had no means of earning any to pay for a bus ticket. She loves her parents a great deal and wants to be with them for a few days." 3. "This young woman is running away from home. Her parents do not understand her, and she feels trapped by her present life. She will try to get a job, make new friends, and take care of herself as best she can."

## *How Did You Do?*

Did you notice that your answer differed from your classmates? Reread *your* statements one more time silently. Think about these facts:

1.  The reading assignment was clear. In it, you found short, easy sentences. There were few hard words.

2.  The reading assignment was a *report*. The sentences contained facts. You didn't have to draw any inferences or make any judgments while reading them.

3.  All the students had the same task. That is,
    they read the same passage;
    they had the same amount of time to do the work; and
    they had the same assignment.

4.  Despite the sameness of the task, many students came out with different reactions. That's because common experiences affect people in different ways.

5.  The fact that we are all different made the complete statements come out the way they did. It was your experience, not the passage, that made the difference.

The important thing to remember here is that some reading tasks lead to answers that differ from each other. On your standardized tests, you look for one right answer. In most *critical* reading, there is no one right answer. You combine *your* experience with the text you read. Since people have different experiences, their answers will be different.

# Activity

Read the passages below. Follow the steps listed in "Here's How to Do It." Complete each paragraph with at least three sentences of your own. If you wish to add additional sentences to each paragraph, feel free to do so. Write your sentences on a separate sheet of paper. Don't show them to others until everyone has completed each assignment. Remember, there are no wrong answers.

# Activity 27-1:  Stereotyped Passages

Read the selections below carefully. Then, complete each of the paragraphs with
at least three sentences of your own. Write the sentences on a separate sheet
of paper.

a.  You spot this man on a narrow dirt road, driving an old pickup
    truck with a dented fender. He's unshaven and wearing a visored hat
    and a woolen shirt with sleeves rolled up to the elbows. Behind him,
    a shotgun and a carbine are mounted in the truck. **This man is...**

b.  This high school senior has long, straight, and uncombed hair and
    thick, shell-rimmed glasses; she wears a white blouse, dark skirt,
    brown loafers, and little makeup. She carries a large pile of books
    under her arm as she moves silently from class to class. **This girl is...**

c.  This woman can be seen walking along the street of a large city. Her hair
    is neat and closely trimmed. She wears a dark, two-piece suit with a
    subtle, contrasting blouse revealed at the neck. Her eyeglasses have
    plain, dark rims and her shoes are plain, low-heeled pumps. In her hand,
    she carries a leather, designer briefcase with silver initials attached.
    **This woman is...**

d.  At a racetrack, you notice a man in a bright plaid, wide-lapeled suit
    and gleaming, black, pointed-toe shoes, smoking a black cigar. Before
    each race, he moves rapidly between people, taking their money and
    writing hurriedly in his notebook. **This man is...**

e.  On a Saturday afternoon in early October, a tall, muscular man
    saunters from a large college football stadium, wearing an expensive,
    tweed jacket and pants and a V-neck crimson sweater and striped
    tie. He wears a triumphant grin on his sun-reddened face and carries
    a large, crimson pennant saying "Go Big Red!" **This man is...**

# Part 28
# Finding Implied Main Ideas
*Step Ten*

## About This Part...

Everything you have done in this Section so far has been in preparation for this final step. You have dealt with facts and opinions; causes and effects; reports, inferences, and judgments; and used your experiences—all for the purpose of drawing a conclusion about what a writer wishes to express.

Step Ten is organized in two ways. In Choosing Statements, you will *select* the implied main idea from a list of possible choices. Then, in Writing Statements, you will *write* your own key sentence—one that expresses the implied main idea.

# Choosing Statements

This first set of activities is arranged like Part 26, Analyzing Cartoons. You will be given a selection to read and a list of possible choices. From this list, you will select the statement that best expresses the implied main idea of the passage. This time, however, you will work with paragraphs rather than cartoons. In Part 26, each cartoon was followed by a paragraph that said something about the subject. In this Part, rely on your own experiences and review in your mind what you know about the subjects. If you are unsure about something, check the information in a reference source.

*Here's How to Do It*

The following steps can help you select the implied main idea from a list of possible choices.

1. *Read* the passage slowly and carefully.

2. *Look* at each statement for the details it contains. Write them down on a separate sheet of paper.

3. *Relate* the details to each other. That is, look at all of the details together. Do you see a connection?

4. *Review* what you know about the passage. This time, there is no background information on the topic. If you are not sure about something, use a reference source to verify the information.

5. *Choose* the statement, from the list of possible choices, that best expresses the implied main idea.

6. *Discuss* the answers with others.

## Sample Activity:  The School Office

Carefully read the following passage. To choose the statement that expresses the implied main idea, follow the steps outlined in "Here's How to Do It." Write your answer on a separate sheet of paper.

### The School Office

The boy sat rigidly in a chair in the main office. Secretaries bustled about, moving from desk to desk and answering telephones. Student assistants typed, delivered messages, and shot occasional, questioning glances at him. In a corner of the office, two people were whispering together. He was sure he heard them use his name. The principal's door opened, and a serious-faced boy, a classmate of his, was ushered out. A drop of sweat trickled down. The principal's door closed. No one told him what would happen.

**Possible Choices**

a.   Whipped cream is seldom used on sausage pizza.

b.   Students working in a school office often gossip about other students.

c.   Some people stay cool and unconcerned when in trouble.

d.   Life in classrooms can be difficult.

e.   Waiting in a school office to face a principal can make a person nervous.

**Answer:** The statement in letter e best expresses the implied main idea.

# How Did You Do?

Is your analysis of each possible choice similar to the following?

a.   The first statement has nothing to do with any aspect of the passage.

b.   The second statement is related to one supporting detail in the passage. To find an implied main idea, the reader must look at all details. Generally, one detail by itself isn't enough.

c.   The third statement is in direct contradiction to the details in the passage, all of which indicate, to a greater or lesser degree, the boy's nervousness.

d.   The fourth statement is not much closer to the main idea. The passage is about a school, but its entire focus is on the main office of that school. Classrooms are never mentioned.

e.   The fifth statement is the most accurate indication of the main idea. It includes the activity, the place, and the emotions that can be found throughout the passage.

# Activities

Read each of the following passages. After each selection is a list of possible choices. Choose the statement that best expresses the implied main idea. Remember, first you must find the details, relate them to each other, and review your experiences before making a choice. Don't forget to discuss your answers with others. Carefully follow the guidelines given in "Here's How to Do It."

## Activity 28-1:  Jack's Goals

Read the following passage. Using the guidelines given in "Here's How to Do It," choose the statement that best expresses the implied main idea. Write your answer on a separate sheet of paper.

## Jack's Goals

Jack had read somewhere that he should write down his goals in life, but he considered this a waste of time. He knew in a general way what he wanted: money enough to live well, recognition, a chance to express his talents. But when he tried to narrow it down to what he wanted most, it was harder to decide. Would he be willing to take a high-paying job that would cost him his self-respect? Would he want prestige at the price of pushing other people around? Would he express his talents if it meant giving up his ideals? What about security?

### Possible Choices

**a.** Jack should write down his goals in life.

**b.** Jack should be willing to take a high-paying job.

**c.** Jack already knew specifically what he wanted out of life.

**d.** Jack should push other people around.

# Activity 28-2:  *Your Skin*

Read the passage below. Follow the guidelines in "Here's How to Do It." Find the statement that best expresses the implied main idea. Write your answer on a separate sheet of paper.

## Your Skin

Your snug-fitting, elastic skin can stand heat or cold, wetness or dryness. It repairs itself, grows with you, cannot be outgrown, and lasts for a lifetime.

It clothes every inch of you. No piece of clothing can compare with your airtight, watertight skin.

### Possible Choices

**a.** Skin is necessary for life.

**b.** Skin can be easily replaced.

**c.** Some people have no skin.

**d.** Skin is made of elastic.

# *Activity 28-3:  Going On Trial*

Read the passage. Then select the sentence that best expresses the implied main idea. Don't forget to follow the guidelines in "Here's How to Do It."

There are thousands of accused citizens waiting to be tried today. Court dockets are running far behind in all states, but especially those states with the most people, such as New York, California, Texas, and Florida. Those awaiting trial who are poor must be represented, for the most part, by public defenders. These lawyers are almost all overworked. They also are paid fairly low wages. People with money, however, are able to hire the best attorneys from high-priced law firms. Such lawyers usually have small case loads and can really concentrate on the trials of the people they represent. Those accused persons, the ones who are well-off financially, have a much better chance of being acquitted, thereby avoiding jail or heavy fines.

## Possible Choices

a.  Our current system of justice, to a great degree, favors the rich over the poor.

b.  Overworked public defenders are usually unable to provide an adequate defense for their clients.

c.  The entire judicial system in the U.S. is in serious need of an immediate, radical overhaul.

d.  Slick lawyers often are able to get clients off who should really go to jail.

# Activity 28-4:  Overcoming Bad Decisions

Carefully read the passage below. Then choose the statement that expresses best the implied main idea. Don't forget to review the steps in "Here's How to Do It."

## The Mayor and Others

*The Mayor of Casterbridge* is a novel published in 1886 by the British Victorian writer, Thomas Hardy. Its main character, Henchard, gets drunk one day and sells his wife and small child to a sailor. When this happens, Henchard is a young man. He achieves respect and financial success as the years go on, but he spends the rest of his life trying to make up for his early mistakes. This kind of youthful bad decision is reflected in the lives of many young people today. Involvement with street gangs, abuse of drugs and alcohol, unwanted pregnancy, and total indifference to schoolwork puts thousands of them behind the eight ball during their teenage years. Some of them do as Henchard did; others never make a comeback. Too often, the adult leaders of their communities are judgmental and self-righteous in their refusal to give young people who have made bad decisions a *real* chance to get back on their feet.

### Possible Choices

**a.** Most teenagers who mess up don't make an honest effort to succeed in later life.

**b.** If Henchard could make a comeback, so should every young person who makes a big mistake.

**c.** Young people who make mistakes early on have a chance to recoup, but they must battle tough odds.

**d.** The temptations of life today are overwhelming to most teenagers in this country.

# Activity 28-5:  Henry James

Carefully read the passage below about Henry James. Then choose the statement that best expresses the implied main idea. Write your answer on a separate sheet of paper. Don't forget to follow the guidelines in "Here's How to Do It."

## Henry James

Many of Henry James's novels can be hard to read. This well-known American author wrote short stories and novels that are rather long and seldom have a lot of action. His sentences and paragraphs can be very complicated so that his plots are hard to follow. He uses a great deal of extended description with piled-up details. However, James's work provides some important insights into American life at the turn of the century. It shows readers interesting differences between the British and American peoples. He develops insights into his characters' thoughts and feelings with the greatest care.

## Possible Choices

**a.** Henry James covered most of this century in his writing.

**b.** Although hard to read, there is much to be gained from reading James's work.

**c.** James usually wrote on the most thrilling and sensational issues of his time.

**d.** Many of James's most memorable characters were Englishmen.

# Activity 28-6:  Martin Luther King, Jr.

Read the following passage carefully. Use the guidelines in "Here's How to Do It" to find the statement that best expresses the implied main idea. Write your answer on a separate sheet of paper.

## Martin Luther King, Jr.

Martin Luther King, Jr., went to jail several times for protesting injustice, beginning with his first civil rights crusade in Montgomery, Alabama, in 1955— until his assassination in Memphis in 1968. While in jail, he was pushed around, knocked down, and intimidated. Many times, during protest marches King led, he was the target of fruit, bricks, and bottles thrown by crowds. He was always the target of spying and rumor because of his motives in the civil rights movement and his personal life. He often saw his followers beaten, clubbed, stoned, and spat on. There was frequent verbal abuse, sometimes intensely obscene in nature. During this entire period, he was able to convince and train his followers in the principles of nonviolence that made his movement very successful. King advanced the cause of civil rights for minority groups during the years of his direction of the Southern Christian Leadership Conference. His tactics gave way to those of younger, more militant groups later on, but his achievements have been lasting ones.

### Possible Choices

**a.** King restricted his work to within his church.

**b.** King's tactics worked for a while, but now they are no longer effective.

**c.** The tactics of nonviolence, developed and practiced by King, were highly effective in promoting the cause of civil rights.

**d.** There was general public acceptance for King's civil rights movement.

# Activity 28-7:  Rudyard Kipling

First, read the passage below. Then, choose the sentence that best expresses the implied main idea. Write your answer on a separate sheet of paper. Don't forget to use the guidelines provided in "Here's How to Do It."

## Rudyard Kipling

The English novelist and poet Rudyard Kipling was born in 1865; during his years of productive writing, the British Empire spread all over the world, until British flags flew over lands in Africa, Asia, many islands of the Pacific, and the Middle East. British soldiers and sailors conquered these countries, and British governors ruled them; Kipling wrote about these conquests in his novels, poems, and plays about wars in African countries, in Egypt, and in India; his great hero was the British soldier who might be well educated or cultured but was tough and heroic. Today, more than fifty years after Kipling's death, Britons both young and old continue to read his works with joy.

### Possible Choices

**a.** Stories about war can be found everywhere.

**b.** Kipling lived during the American Revolution.

**c.** No one reads the works of Kipling anymore.

**d.** British people still enjoy reading about glories of the past.

# Activity 28-8:  Wiretapping

Read the selection below. Follow the guidelines in "Here's How to Do It." Choose the sentence that best expresses the implied main idea. Write your answer on a separate sheet of paper.

## Wiretapping

Those in favor of wiretapping say it is the best way to intercept and record conversations that lead to the arrest of criminals. They claim that, if used fairly and wisely by police officers and detectives, the lives and property of countless law-abiding people can be saved and protected. As they see it, wiretapping will reduce error in dealing with crime and allow the police to collect undeniable evidence on the wrongdoers. Their opponents claim, however, that past records show that much wiretapping has not been done wisely or carefully; it has been done almost at the whim of law officers. Thus, anyone who is under the vaguest suspicion can be subject to this eavesdropping if wiretapping goes unchecked. However, there is even a more serious claim being made. The possibility exists for anyone whom the authorities don't like to have his or her phone tapped. If free speech is to be preserved, they believe, wiretapping must be carefully controlled or eliminated.

### Possible Choices

**a.** Wiretapping is the best means of controlling criminal activities.

**b.** There are two sides to the question of whether wiretapping is a valid means of controlling criminal activities.

**c.** Freedom of speech is the right of every individual.

**d.** Wiretapping should be completely eliminated in a country that supports freedom of speech.

# Activity 28-9: E-Z Terms

Read the following passage carefully. Then choose the statement that best expresses the implied main idea. Don't forget to review the steps in "Here's How to Do It."

### E-Z Terms

Walking down streets in cities both large and small, we often see signs in commercial outfits that read, "Buy Now, Pay Later." People who want to own things often are drawn to such opportunities. They see things they like: new cars, beautiful clothes, attractive furniture, great sporting goods, exciting vacation deals. Almost all these are offered on "E-Z Terms." And, too often, people commit themselves to long payment schedules of large sums at high interest rates. Those who finally own what they bought have sometimes paid four or five times its real value. Others can't keep up the payments and lose the possession. Still others, suckered by slick advertisements of wonderful luxuries being enjoyed by beautiful people, break the law to pay for what they possess. They embezzle money where they work, they borrow from friends or family and leave town, they write worthless checks, and they even commit robbery. Such slaves to possessions of "E-Z Terms" can be found everywhere.

## Possible Choices

**a.** The credit policies of the business community have made the chance to own things better for all.

**b.** People who wish to own things should analyze the terms of any payment contract they are asked to sign.

**c.** No one can trust an agency or business that offers long-term payment opportunities to customers.

**d.** People who don't want to go broke should ignore advertisements of all goods and services to be procured on terms.

# Activity 28-10:  TV and the Olympics

Read the following selection. Use the guidelines in "Here's How to Do It" to find the statement that best expresses the implied main idea. Write your answer on a separate sheet of paper.

### TV and the Olympics

In the early part of the twentieth century, the Olympic Games were described first in the newspapers and later on radio. Since 1960, however, they have been on TV. As TV techniques have improved, more people have had better views of more events. Americans who usually have been very interested in watching TV football, basketball, and baseball have seen more sports with the expansion of Olympics coverage. Today, bobsledding, volleyball, gymnastics, and cycling are providing lots of popular TV viewing. As more world games are featured on TV, we will see more kinds of sports and games.

### Possible Choices

**a.** TV is becoming more and more important in American life.

**b.** It is important that we, as Americans, retain our loyalty to football, basketball, and baseball.

**c.** The Olympics are here to stay.

**d.** Olympic broadcasts have increased American interest in more sports.

# Writing Statements

In this next set of activities, you will have the opportunity to write your own key sentence—a statement that expresses the *implied main idea*. Read the passages carefully. You will notice that, as you work through the activities, the passages become more challenging. Take your time and be persistent in your work.

## Here's How to Do It

As you read the passages, follow these steps.

1. *Read* the entire passage slowly and carefully.

2. *Write* the key details as you find them on a separate sheet of paper.

3. *Review* the details. Then, relate them to each other. Do you see the connection?

4. *Review* your experiences related to the subject.

5. *Write* down one sentence you think expresses the main idea. Do it quickly and don't worry about its appearance. Write this sentence on scrap paper.

6. *Compare* your statement with others. Discuss them.

7. *Revise* your sentence, if you feel it is necessary, after you have discussed it with others.

8. *Write* the final form on the same sheet of paper where the details are listed.

## Sample Activity: Writing Statements

Carefully read the following passage. Be certain you identify the key details as you see them. Follow the steps outlined in "Here's How to Do It." After you have read the paragraph, write a statement you think expresses the implied main idea. Write the details and statement on a separate sheet of paper.

Some people do not mind when they do not collect a debt on time. They usually are satisfied with a promise. Others get very angry at those who don't pay on the exact date. They say and sometimes do things that can cause trouble for the person who owes them money. It is best to talk to these people in advance when payments cannot be made on time. Still other people do not say or do anything when debts are not paid; but they remember. These people usually need convincing reasons why money is not paid when due. Keeping their trust can be very important later on for any borrower.

**Answer:** It is important to know how to deal with people to whom we owe money.

# *How Did You Do?*

Have you written the key sentence on scrap paper? Don't worry about its appearance. It's important that you get the idea down while the passage is still fresh in your mind. Later, you can go back and insert the proper punctuation, correct spelling, and so on. Discuss your sentence with others. Revise it, if necessary, so that it represents the key sentence for the passage. Write down the revised key sentence—the sentence you believe best expresses the main idea of the paragraph.

# Activities

Below are passages that range from short to long and from easy to difficult. Carefully read each selection. Then, after following the steps listed in "Here's How to Do It," write a sentence that best expresses the selection's implied main idea. Remember to *share your ideas!*

## *Activity 28-11:  Image vs. Intellect*

Read the passage below. Then, following the steps given in "Here's How to Do It," write a statement you feel expresses the implied main idea. Write your statement on a separate sheet of paper.

### Image vs. Intellect

Whether it's on a local channel or on one of the three major networks, when you watch the evening news on TV, you notice how handsome or beautiful the anchorpersons usually are. They are almost never overweight. The males all have a full head of hair, and the females are perfectly coiffed. For both, their clothing is always very expensive looking. Their facial features are always regular: no long noses, bushy eyebrows, or protruding ears. Their teeth are pearly white, showing no evidence of dental surgery. They sit in an erect but comfortable posture at the anchor desk and glance only occasionally at the papers on the desk before them. Their accents mostly sound the same, showing no hint of New England, Middle Atlantic, or Deep South pronunciation. There's a good chance these anchors spend more time with their hair driers than with their research.

# *Activity 28-12: All Quiet*

Read the following passage from Erich Maria Remarque's novel *All Quiet on the Western Front*. Using the steps in "Here's How to Do It," write a statement you think expresses the implied main idea. Write your response on a separate sheet of paper.

## All Quiet

I am operated on and vomit for two days, my bones will not grow together, so the surgeon's secretary says. Another fellow's have grown crooked; his arm had to be broken again. It is disgusting.

Among our new arrivals are two young soldiers with flat feet. The chief surgeon discovers them on his rounds and is overjoyed. "We'll

*All Quiet on the Western Front* is set during World War I and is told from the viewpoint of a young German soldier, much like the ones shown in this photo taken of German soldiers as they marched off to war in 1914. *Photo: Bettmann Archives*

soon put that right," he tells them. "We will just do a small operation, and then you will have perfectly sound feet. Enter them in our list, sister."

As soon as he is gone, Josef, who knows everything, warns them: "Don't you let him operate on you! That is a special scientific stunt of the old boy's. He goes absolutely crazy whenever he can get hold of anyone to do it on. He operates on you for flat feet, and there's no mistake, you don't have them anymore; you have club feet instead, and have to walk all the rest of your life on sticks."

"What should we do, then?" asks one of them.

"Say no. You're here to be treated for your wound, not your flat feet. Did you have any trouble with them in the field? No, well, there you are! You still can walk, but once the old boy gets you under the knife you'll be crippled. What he wants is little dogs to experiment with, so the war is a glorious time for him, as it is for all the surgeons. You take a look down below at the staff; there are a dozen fellows hobbling around that he has operated on. A lot of them have been here since 'fourteen' and 'fifteen.' Not a single one of them can walk better than he could before, almost all of them worse, and most only with plaster legs. Every six months he catches them again and breaks their bones afresh, and every time he promises it to be the successful one. You take my word, he won't dare do it if you say no."

"Ach, man," says one of the two unfortunates, "better your feet than your brain-box. There's no telling what you'll get if you go back out there again. They can do with me just as they please, so long as I get back home. Better to have a club foot than be dead."

The other, a young fellow like ourselves, won't have it done. One morning the old man has the two hauled up and lectures and jaws at them so long that, in the end, they consent. What else could they do? They are mere privates, and he is a big bug. They are brought back chloroformed and plastered.

It is going badly with Albert. They have taken him and amputated his leg. The whole leg had been taken off from the thigh. Now he hardly speaks anymore. Once he says he will shoot himself the first time he can get hold of his revolver again.

A new convoy arrives. Our room gets two blind men. One of them is a very youthful musician. The sisters never have a knife with them when they feed him; he has already snatched one from a sister. But in spite of this caution there is an incident. In the evening, while he is being fed, the sister is called away, and leaves the plate with the fork on his table. He gropes for the fork, seizes it and drives it with all his force against his heart, then he snatches up a shoe and strikes with it against the handle as hard as he can. We call for help and three men are necessary to take the fork away from him. The blunt prongs had already penetrated deep. He abuses us all night so that no one can go to sleep. In the morning he has lockjaw.

Again the beds become empty. Day after day goes by with pain and fear, groans and death gurgles. Even the Death Room is no use anymore, it is too small; fellows die during the night in our room. They go even faster than the sisters can cope with them.

But one day the door flies open, the flat trolley rolls in, and there on a stretcher, pale, thin, upright, and triumphant, with his shaggy head of curls, sits Peter. Sister Libertine with beaming looks pushes him over to his former bed. He is back from the Death Room. We have long supposed him to be dead.

He looks around: "What do you say now?"

And even Josef has to admit it is the first time he has ever known of such a thing.

Gradually a few of us venture to stand up. And I am given crutches to hobble around on. But I do not make much use of them; I cannot bear Albert's gaze as I move about the room. His eyes always follow me with such a strange look. So I sometimes escape to the corridor—there I can move about more freely.

On the next floor below are the abdominal and spinal cases, head wounds, and double amputations. On the right side of the wing are the jaw wounds, gas cases, nose, ear, and neck wounds. On the left, the lung wounds, pelvis wounds, joint wounds, and intestinal wounds. Here a man realizes for the first time how many places a man can get hit.

And there is only one hospital, one single station; there are hundreds of thousands in Germany, hundreds of thousands in France, hundreds of thousands in Russia. How senseless is everything that can ever be written, done, or thought, when such things are possible. It must all be lies and of no account when the culture of a thousand years could not prevent this stream of blood being poured out. These torture chambers in their hundreds of thousands. A hospital alone shows what war is.

I am young, I am twenty years old; yet I know nothing of life but despair, death, fear, and fatuous superficiality cast over an abyss of sorrow. I see how people are set against one another, and in silence, unknowingly, foolishly, obediently, innocently slay one another. I see that the keenest brains of the world invent weapons and words to make it yet more refined and enduring. And all soldiers of my age, here and over there, throughout the whole world, see these things; all my generation is experiencing these things with me. What would our fathers do if we suddenly stood up and came before them and proffered our account? What do they expect of us if a time ever comes when the war is over? Through the years our business has been killing—it was our first calling in life. Our knowledge of life is limited to death. What will happen afterward? And what shall come of us?

# *Activity 28-13: Our Cultural Heritage*

Carefully read the following passage. Then, following the guidelines in "Here's How to Do It," write a statement that expresses your own concept of its implied main idea.

## Our Cultural Heritage

Since the mid-1980s, much has been said about the need to improve the "cultural literacy" of America's young people. Claims were made by critics that schools were not teaching students enough about their literature, history, geography, art, and music. When asked to define and illustrate their terms, these critics used examples that were almost entirely Caucasian contributions. More recently, this definition has been challenged by many critics and educators who believe the contributions of minority writers and artists need to be included. Are not the novels of Toni Morrison, which describe the African American experience, part of American culture? And what about the poetry of writers such as Luis Omar Salinas, a Mexican American who was born in Texas and now lives in California? Native and Asian Americans also need to be included.

## *Activity 28-14:  Water Supply*

Carefully read the following passage. Follow the guidelines in "Here's How to Do It." Then, write a statement you think expresses the implied main idea. Write your response on a separate sheet of paper.

### Water Supply

There is only so much water on earth, and it seems people are trying to spoil as much of it as possible. True, oceans may be a source of water supply in the future, but right now people must rely on fresh water. Rivers and lakes must be kept free from pollution by careful management of factories and cities.

## *Activity 28-15:   Paying for College*

First, read the passage. Then, write a statement that expresses its implied main idea. Follow the steps in "Here's How to Do It" in writing that statement.

### Paying for College

There was a time when talented high school students with limited financial resources could find ways to pay their way through college. Today's outlook is not as bright. As state after state goes broke, the tuition being charged to public colleges is being raised. Not so with scholarship and loan programs; they are being cut. The end of the Cold War means that few R.O.T.C. scholarships are available. As the college athletic programs feel the budget pinch, there aren't as many grants-in-aid for promising athletes. The current tighter job market for college graduates doesn't help either.

# Activity 28-16:  Baby Talk

Read the short passage below. Then, using the steps in "Here's How to Do It," write a statement you think expresses the implied main idea. Write your response on a separate sheet of paper.

### Baby Talk

TV language can be called baby talk, since some TV commercials use toddlers to do the selling. Consider, for example, the advertisement showing little girls laundering their dolls' clothes in Sudsy Dudsy. Or consider the advertisement featuring a little boy who holds up a roll of paper and cries, "Boopsy tissues tear so nice!"

# Activity 28-17:  Styles of Architecture

Read the passage below. Follow the guidelines provided in "Here's How to Do It." On a separate sheet of paper, write a statement you think expresses the implied main idea.

### Styles of Architecture

The Romans lived under stately porticoes amid the pomp of great temples. They found an ever-present dignity that must have followed them even into the poverty and confusions of the crowded, many-storied *insulae.* The wide forums and the glittering *thermae* were songs in which the Roman soul made itself known above the cries of the circus and the clash of civil swords. The Gothic cathedrals were, in part, prayers of thanks for the revival of cities. The *piazze* into which Venice poured her splendor rejoiced with that new enfranchisement. These are not merely ornaments but summations of a city's spirit to which houses and streets, walls, canals, and the domes of public buildings are the harmonious counterparts. Florence, Padua, Cordoba, the Paris of Richelieu, and the Philadelphia of Franklin might have been the work of a single architect, so consistent is the expression of their streets and structures.

# *Activity 28-18:  Sports Reporter*

Read this long selection carefully. Then, using the guidelines in "Here's How to Do It," write a statement you think expresses the implied main idea. Write your response on a separate sheet of paper.

### Sports Reporter

When I decided to become a candidate for sports reporter on our high school newspaper, I thought I knew why I was doing it. I enjoy writing, and I've been writing for pleasure as much as for assignments since I was in grade school. Writing is effortless for me; I frequently write to relax, for example, entries in my diary, letters to relatives, and poems that just spring into my mind so that, by the time I reached tenth grade, writing had become a way of life with me.

Then there was my interest in sports. I have an older brother who played three sports in our school and who, when he graduated last year, was awarded a full athletic scholarship at State University. My younger brother, now in junior high, is already six feet tall and 175 pounds and still growing; he could well break all his older brother's records as super jock of Hyacinth Street. I play tennis, field hockey, and softball, and I have been a swimmer on our AAU team for the past six years, so, we are an athletic family and, you might say, I consider myself "one of the boys."

But there's something deeper here, and I consider it often. Our school has never had a female sports reporter, so I've said to myself (about 1,000 times by now) why not me? I really believe I *know* more about our school athletic program than about 90 percent of the boys here, and I can write better than the other 10 percent. If you want it straight, I think that *I'm* the woman to break the sports reporting sound barrier at this school. These fast-talking, well-groomed women on TV do their thing in the press box and on the sidelines, and I get all psyched up. So once, when I was feeling really confident, I put in my name for the reporter job. There was a lot of talk and some grumbling among the not-so-macho guys who wanted the job; but when the smoke cleared, I was there in the winner's circle—the Barbara Walters of the Midville High Weekly Flash sports page.

My first set of problems occurred when I began working closely with our senior editor of the paper. It was bad enough that he was one of the not-so-macho guys who opposed my appointment; worse yet, he found out I had called him that, so his greetings are lukewarm. He is always bugging me about getting my column in on time—and he never does that to his male coworkers; he lets me know he doesn't think I can do the job. He doesn't think I can get "close enough" to the action (I haven't tried to go the locker room route yet, and he says he is afraid the sports page is losing its punch. It's frustrating to work with him, but the girls on the staff encourage me and so do many of the female students. It's interesting that my female teachers haven't said a word yet, not one of them; I feel deep down they are looking the other way and wishing that I'd turn to fashion news. No way, ladies; I'm into cleats and shoulder pads right now.

When I interview the boys on the team, I get one of two responses: the first is the "you're kidding" routine. That group of clowns won't take a question, asked in seriousness, seriously, and they joke and exaggerate and digress. When I accuse them of doing those things, most of them get mad; and they reply by asking, "How can *you* understand? *You've* never played." I sometimes retort what I learned in English class: that although Stephen Crane had never been to war, he wrote a great war novel, *The Red Badge of Courage*. Most of them clam up on that one; I have concluded they do this because they can't read.

The other response I get from the youthful Midville gladiators (a direct quote from our local daily) is one of embarrassment. This type tries to be nice or at least put on a good act, as he stutters, clears his throat, and mostly won't look me in the eye. He is a halting master of trite phrases, and talks of "the will to win" and "getting our game plan together" and other such overused phrases. Some of *these* guys even wonder why I don't use quotes. *I'm* embarrassed to put what they say in my story for fear my readers may think I'm making it up.

But my real problem is the coach. It has been a tradition in the school for years to get a statement from the coach about (a) last week's game and (b) the outlook for next Friday night. That is as traditional at Midville on Mondays as corn dogs, french fries, and escalloped corn is on the lunch menu, so when my first Monday came, I was, as they say in football, mentally ready. My problem was the coach wasn't: He paused, he repeated himself, he digressed, and in general acted like he really wished he were somewhere else—far away. Then, after twenty minutes of nothing, he asked, "Well, young lady, does that wrap it up?" Astonished, I made the fatal mistake of saying, "Wrap *what* up?" and at the same time, flashed my blank notepad. Grumbling that he wished we'd get somebody who *understood* football, he retreated to his sanctuary in the boys' locker room. To make a long story short, that was my first interview with our beloved coach and my best one; our meetings have deteriorated into a ten-minute session of grunts, groans, and an occasional burp. The second burp usually indicates the "interview" is over. To translate it all into a story, I have become a creative writer.

My public has shown mixed reactions over my debut as a sports journalist. The girls divide along party lines. There are the loyalists, the junior libbers, who rally to my cause (whatever that is) and say, "hang in there;" we'll show these male chauvinists. I'm not really sure they ever read my stuff; the fact that I'm in there fighting is enough for them, and, in all honesty, their conversations make me uneasy. But I like them better than my female opponents who want to see me quit, who don't feel I "have any place" writing that column, and who really want me in junior miss fashion reporting. They like the boy-girl setup at Midville the way it was: with the boys in the action and the girls screaming and flourishing their pompons. Not exactly my sentiments, but they do get to me. Sometimes I'm not sure whose side anybody is on.

The boys don't say much. I don't have a boyfriend right now (I can wait), but I've always had lots of sort-of-buddies to rap with. We mostly talked about sports—*before* I started *writing* about them, that is; now they don't come near. They greet me in an offhand manner, and I've yet to get the first compliment, or *sarcastic remark* even, about my sports column. My theory is they think that if they ignore me, I might go away. It's terrible to feel you have to be a malignancy to succeed in life.

I'm writing all this in retrospect, in a way: the football season has just ended (we went four and six this year; I somehow vaguely feel that's my fault), and basketball is about to begin, and, I must admit, I'm really uptight about it all. You see, football was one thing—all boys participating—but three years ago, our enlightened administration put in a girls' basketball team so there are two teams for the sports editor to cover this winter. I'm really not sure how I'm going to handle it: how much ink do I give each team? Which coach can I really talk with? Will I lean toward one group or the other? What if one team does much better than the other? And the thing that's really getting to me is that now I can go into a locker room. Should I ask for a male assistant, and if I do, is that a sign of weakness on my part? I'm still thinking it all over; "all" being the past season, my present dilemma, and my future happiness. Making a breakthrough has some things to say for it: I could write a book.

# Activity 28-19:  Green Plants

First, read this selection. Then, using the guidelines in "Here's How to Do It," write a statement you think expresses the implied main idea. Write your response on a separate sheet of paper.

### Green Plants

Green plants create food from simple substances in water and air; every other living creature—plant and animal—must consume plants, animals, or their remains. Food manufactured by green plants supports every kind of forest life as it is broken into elements that are reused; therefore, plants are considered the starting point in a food cycle.

Green plant food stores the sun's energy, and many creatures depend directly on green plants for food—smaller beings such as insects and larger beings such as deer, moose, tapirs, and elephants. Whether they consume leaves, bark, roots, fruits, or seeds, the plant eaters convert food made by green plants into the tissues of their own bodies.

At the cycle's next stage are animals that consume plant eaters, including many small animals—insects, shrews, and lizards—along with reptiles, birds, and mammals like wolves and the great cats. Whenever one of these consumes a plant eater, it assimilates the energy that was stored first in the green plants and then in the plant eater; some predators also obtain energy third-hand by preying on another meat eater, for example, when a hawk eats a snake. Some animals, such as bears, prey on both plants and animals.

The cycle always returns to the air and the soil: Plants and animals die and decay, releasing minerals to the soil and gases to the air so these minerals and gases are ready for use again by growing green plants.

Food is vital to keeping forest life in balance: Because only so much food is available for each kind of animal, when the population of a species grows too large, food is insufficient and some die; and when a population shrinks too much, food is abundant and more animals survive, bringing the population to normal levels.

Sometimes, however, a particular species of animal can increase greatly, threatening the entire way of forest life, as happened about twenty-five years ago in a spruce forest high in the Rocky Mountains.

In this forest lived a beetle the size of a housefly, whose larvae fed on spruces and occasionally killed an old or diseased tree. Healthy trees protected themselves by producing resin that killed many of these beetle larvae; woodpeckers and other insects ate them.

Then a severe windstorm blew over many spruces; these stayed alive for a time but were too weak to produce much resin; consequently, beetle larvae could feed safely in these trees and began to multiply. Within three years, the beetles were so numerous they killed healthy as well as weak trees; within six years, they'd destroyed enough timber to build houses for two million people.

# Reading Selections Index

# Subject Index

# NTC ENGLISH AND COMMUNICATION ARTS BOOKS

**Business Communication**
Business Communication Today! *Thomas & Fryar*
Handbook for Business Writing, *Baugh, Fryar, & Thomas*
Meetings: Rules & Procedures, *Pohl*

**Dictionaries**
British/American Language Dictionary, *Moss*
NTC's Classical Dictionary, *Room*
NTC's Dictionary of Changes in Meaning, *Room*
NTC's Dictionary of Debate, *Hanson*
NTC's Dictionary of Literary Terms, *Morner & Rausch*
NTC's Dictionary of Theatre and Drama Terms, *Mobley*
NTC's Dictionary of Word Origins, *Room*
NTC's Spell It Right Dictionary, *Downing*
Robin Hyman's Dictionary of Quotations

**Essential Skills**
Building Real Life English Skills, *Starkey & Penn*
English Survival Series, *Maggs*
Essential Life Skills, *Starkey & Penn*
Essentials of English Grammar, *Baugh*
Essentials of Reading and Writing English Series
Grammar for Use, *Hall*
Grammar Step-by-Step, *Pratt*
Guide to Better English Spelling, *Furness*
How to be a Rapid Reader, *Redway*
How to Improve Your Study Skills, *Coman & Heavers*
NTC Skill Builders
Reading by Doing, *Simmons & Palmer*
Developing Creative & Critical Thinking, *Boostrom*
303 Dumb Spelling Mistakes, *Downing*
TIME: We the People, *ed. Schinke-Llano*
Vocabulary by Doing, *Beckert*

**Genre Literature**
The Detective Story, *Schwartz*
The Short Story & You, *Simmons & Stern*
Sports in Literature, *Emra*
You and Science Fiction, *Hollister*

**Journalism**
Getting Started in Journalism, *Harkrider*
Journalism Today! *Ferguson & Patten*
Publishing the Literary Magazine, *Klaiman*
UPI Stylebook, *United Press International*

**Language, Literature, and Composition**
An Anthology for Young Writers, *Meredith*
The Art of Composition, *Meredith*
Creative Writing, *Mueller & Reynolds*

Handbook for Practical Letter Writing, *Baugh*
How to Write Term Papers and Reports, *Baugh*
Literature by Doing, *Tchudi & Yesner*
Lively Writing, *Schrank*
Look, Think & Write, *Leavitt & Sohn*
Poetry by Doing, *Osborn*
World Literature, *Rosenberg*
Write to the Point! *Morgan*
The Writer's Handbook, *Karls & Szymanski*
Writing by Doing, *Sohn & Enger*
Writing in Action, *Meredith*

**Media Communication**
Getting Started in Mass Media, *Beckert*
Photography in Focus, *Jacobs & Kokrda*
Television Production Today! *Kirkham*
Understanding Mass Media, *Schrank*
Understanding the Film, *Bone & Johnson*

**Mythology**
The Ancient World, *Sawyer & Townsend*
Mythology and You, *Rosenberg & Baker*
Welcome to Ancient Greece, *Millard*
Welcome to Ancient Rome, *Millard*
World Mythology, *Rosenberg*

**Speech**
Activities for Effective Communication, *LiSacchi*
The Basics of Speech, *Galvin, Cooper, & Gordon*
Contemporary Speech, *HopKins & Whitaker*
Dynamics of Speech, *Myers & Herndon*
Getting Started in Public Speaking, *Prentice & Payne*
Listening by Doing, *Galvin*
Literature Alive! *Gamble & Gamble*
Person to Person, *Galvin & Book*
Public Speaking Today! *Prentice & Payne*
Speaking by Doing, *Buys, Sill, & Beck*

**Theatre**
Acting & Directing, *Grandstaff*
The Book of Cuttings for Acting & Directing, *Cassady*
The Book of Scenes for Acting Practice, *Cassady*
The Dynamics of Acting, *Snyder & Drumsta*
An Introduction to Modern One-Act Plays, *Cassady*
An Introduction to Theatre and Drama, *Cassady & Cassady*
Play Production Today! *Beck et al.*
Stagecraft, *Beck*

For a current catalog and information about our complete line
of language arts books, write:
National Textbook Company
a division of NTC Publishing Group
4255 West Touhy Avenue
Lincolnwood (Chicago), Illinois 60646-1975 U.S.A.